# SYDNEY OMARR'S®

## DAY-BY-DAY ASTROLOGICAL GUIDE FOR

# TAURUS

APRIL 20–MAY 20

# 2007

By Trish MacGregor
with Carol Tonsing

A SIGNET BOOK

SIGNET
Published by New American Library, a division of
Penguin Group (USA) Inc., 375 Hudson Street,
New York, New York 10014, USA
Penguin Group (Canada), 90 Eglinton Avenue East, Suite 700, Toronto,
Ontario M4P 2Y3, Canada (a division of Pearson Penguin Canada Inc.)
Penguin Books Ltd., 80 Strand, London WC2R 0RL, England
Penguin Ireland, 25 St. Stephen's Green, Dublin 2,
Ireland (a division of Penguin Books Ltd.)
Penguin Group (Australia), 250 Camberwell Road, Camberwell, Victoria 3124,
Australia (a division of Pearson Australia Group Pty. Ltd.)
Penguin Books India Pvt. Ltd., 11 Community Centre, Panchsheel Park,
New Delhi - 110 017, India
Penguin Group (NZ), cnr Airborne and Rosedale Roads, Albany,
Auckland 1310, New Zealand (a division of Pearson New Zealand Ltd.)
Penguin Books (South Africa) (Pty.) Ltd., 24 Sturdee Avenue,
Rosebank, Johannesburg 2196, South Africa

Penguin Books Ltd., Registered Offices:
80 Strand, London WC2R 0RL, England

First published by Signet, an imprint of New American Library,
a division of Penguin Group (USA) Inc.

First Printing, June 2006
10 9 8 7 6 5 4 3 2 1



Printed in the United States of America



PUBLISHER'S NOTE

While the author has made every effort to provide accurate telephone numbers and Internet addresses at the time of publication, neither the publisher nor the author assumes any responsibility for errors, or for changes that occur after publication. Further, publisher does not have any control over and does not assume any responsibility for author or third-party Web sites or their content.

# CONTENTS

INTRODUCTION

# Astrology to Use Every Day

Are you living your life to the fullest? Whether you want a more rewarding career, financial freedom, better relationships, or a romantic love life, astrology can help you make it happen. No matter what your goal, astrology's age-old techniques work just as well today as they did thousands of years ago. You can apply them to so many areas of your life to make the best decisions concerning your career, love, money, health, and even clothing and vacations.

In relationships, astrology can help you understand every sun-sign combination, which is very handy when you meet someone special. You'll be amazed at how knowing only the person's sun sign can help resolve a conflict or improve communication. What's more, astrology gives you a way to troubleshoot potential problems in advance and, if they crop up, find a way to turn them around.

On a deeper level, astrology can be a tool for personal growth and insight into your own special place in the cosmos. Like your genetic imprint, your astrology chart is unique. It is a map of your moment in time, which has its own code, based on the sun, moon, and planets at the time and place you were born. What is especially intriguing is that this system can offer specific, practical guidance, even when using only one of the elements of the code, your sun sign.

For those who would like to know more about astrology, this book provides user-friendly information to start you on your astrological journey. Then you can put your whole astrological portrait together by looking up the other planets in your horoscope. If you want to delve deeper, we'll show you the best astrology Web sites, where you can find sophisticated software and free education. If you're inter-

ested in connecting with other astrologers, we provide an extensive resource list of contacts and organizations, as well as computer program recommendations for fun or serious study.

As the saying goes, "Timing is everything." We'll deal in many ways with the question of timing: the difficult times (which also present positive challenges), times with potential for delays and misunderstandings, and the best times to take risks and to kick back and relax. You will learn when to use the downtime when Mercury is retrograde to reconnect with old friends, troubleshoot, and reevaluate where you're going and with whom.

This guide provides the tools you need to plan the best year ever, to enhance every aspect of your life, plus astonishingly accurate day-by-day forecasts to follow along in your own activities. Let it empower you to make 2007 a year of growth and prosperity!

CHAPTER 1

# The Big Trends of 2007

## Prepare for Changes Ahead

Astrologers judge the trends of a year by following the slow-moving planets, from Jupiter through Pluto. A change in sign indicates a new cycle, with new emphasis. The farthest planets (Uranus, Neptune, and Pluto), which stay in a sign for at least seven years, cause a very significant change in the atmosphere when they change signs. Shifts in Jupiter, which changes every year, and Saturn, every two years, are more obvious in current events and daily lives. Jupiter generally brings a fortunate, expansive emphasis to its new sign, while Saturn's two-year cycle is a reality check, bringing tests of maturity, discipline, and responsibility.

## Sagittarius Is the Sign to Watch

In the final year of Pluto's transit of Sagittarius, it will be accompanied and intensified by Jupiter, the planet of expansion. This duo is superpowerful because Sagittarius is the sign Jupiter rules, making 2007 the grand finale for many of the key trends that began in 1995, when Pluto first entered Sagittarius.

Until January 2008, slow-moving Pluto will be emphasizing everything associated with Sagittarius to prepare us philosophically and spiritually for things to come. Perhaps the most pervasive sign of Pluto in Sagittarius over the past few years has been globalization in all its forms. We are

re-forming boundaries, creating new forms of travel, interacting with exotic cultures and religions as never before.

In truth-telling Sagittarius, Pluto has shifted our emphasis away from acquiring wealth to a quest for the meaning of it all, as upward strivers discover that money and power are not enough and religious extremists assert themselves. We search the cosmos for something to believe in when many lies and scandals are brought to public view, exposing leaders in the corporate, political and religious domains. When ideals and idols are shattered, we reevaluate our goals and ask ourselves what is really important.

Sagittarius is the sign of linking everything together; therefore, the trend has been to find ways to connect on spiritual, philosophical, and intellectual levels. The spiritual emphasis of Pluto in Sagittarius has filtered down to our home lives, as religion and religious controversy have entered local communities. Vast church complexes that combine religious activities with sports centers, health clubs, malls, and theme parks are being built. Religious education and book publishing have expanded as well.

Sagittarius is known for love of animals, especially horses. It's no surprise that horse racing has become popular again and that America has never been more pet happy. Look for extremes related to animal welfare, such as vegetarianism as a lifestyle. As habitats are destroyed, the care, feeding, and control of wild animals will become a larger issue, especially when deer, bears, and coyotes invade our backyards.

The Sagittarius love of the outdoors combined with Pluto's power has already promoted extreme sports, especially those that require strong legs, like rock climbing, trekking, or snowboarding. Expect the trend toward more adventurous travel to continue, as well as fitness- or sports-oriented vacations. Exotic hiking trips to unexplored territories, mountain-climbing expeditions, spa vacations, and sports-associated resorts are part of this trend.

Publishing, which is associated with Sagittarius, has been transformed by global conglomerates and the Internet. Look for more inspirational books aimed at those who are interested in spirituality outside of traditional religions.

## What's Next? Capricorn Brings Us Down to Earth

Next year, Pluto will join Jupiter in Capricorn, which marks a major shift in emphasis to Capricorn-related themes. Capricorn is a practical, building, healing earth sign. It is an active, cardinal sign that symbolizes rising from the waters of the emotions to the top of the mountain, surmounting obstacles all the way, demanding maturity and down-to-earth common sense. Capricorn relates to structures, institutions, order, mountains and mountain countries, mineral rights, issues involving the elderly and growing older—all of which will be emphasized in the coming years.

This shift begins in December 2007, which starts activating all the cardinal signs (Aries, Cancer, Libra, Capricorn). At the end of 2007, you should feel the rumblings of change in the Capricorn area of your horoscope and in the world at large. The last time Pluto was in Capricorn was the period of the Revolutionary War. Therefore this may be an important time in U.S. politics, as well as a reflection of the aging and maturing of American society in general.

## Saturn Moves from Leo to Virgo: The Maturing of the Baby Boomers, Reforms in Care and Maintenance

Saturn, the planet of limitation, testing, and restriction, has been transiting Leo since mid-July 2005, forcing us to grow up and get serious in the Leo areas of our lives. Many of the fun things in life fall under the banner of Leo: entertainment, show business, children, play, recreation, love affairs, hobbies, performing, talent, the creative arts, and recognition by others. Since Saturn tends to put a damper on Leo's fun, expect some restrictions on the entertainment business, shows with more serious themes and actors. Leo is associated with children, and with Saturn come the burdens and responsibilities of bringing them up.

The subject of aging in general belongs to Saturn, and

the Leo archetype in this area is the aging film star determined to hold on to youth. Love affairs and flirtations, part of Leo's sunny side, may this year involve older people. Maturing baby boomers will demand more awareness from the media. Therefore we will see more older people on television and in films, more entertainment tailored to an aging population, a harbinger of the even stronger Saturnian trends coming up in 2008. Since Leo is also associated with speculation and gambling, in fact all games, expect more stringent regulation and controversy around big-time casinos and sports.

Saturn in Leo demands hard work in creative ventures, responsibility when interacting with others. Leo types can't get away with casual love affairs, or with being high-handed, arrogant, or divalike in any way. Leo divas will have to earn their applause. This could tone down the blatant celebrity-worshipping culture that has arisen over the past few years. No longer will it be enough to be famous for being famous. The emphasis will be on true values rather than the trappings of success. Flashy lifestyles, bling bling jewelry, and showing off will be out.

Saturn moves into Virgo on September 2, 2007, which is followed soon after by a solar eclipse in Virgo on September 11. This is a time when Virgo issues—health care and maintenance and moral standards and controls—will come to the fore. We will adjust the structures of our lives, making changes so that we can function at an efficient level. We'll be challenged with a reality check in areas where we have been too optimistic or expansive.

## Jupiter in Sagittarius

During the year that Jupiter remains in a sign, the fields associated with that sign—comedy, fun, travel, laughter—will be the ones that arouse excitement and enthusiasm, usually providing excellent opportunities for expansion, fame, and fortune. Jupiter remains in fun-loving Sagittarius, the sign it rules, until December 18.

One place we will notice the Jupiter influence is in fashion, which should have a cheerful, colorful look. Sagittarius

has great fashion flair, which should show up in ethnic influences and exciting new sportswear.

Those born under Sagittarius should have many opportunities during the year. However, keep your feet on the ground. The flip side of Jupiter is that there are no limits. You can expand off the planet under a Jupiter transit, which is why the planet is often called the Gateway to Heaven. If something is going to burst (such as an artery) or overextend or go over the top in some way, it could happen under a supposedly lucky Jupiter transit. So be aware.

Those born under Gemini may find their best opportunities working with partners this year, as Jupiter will be transiting their seventh house of relationships.

## Continuing Trends

Uranus and Neptune continue to do a kind of astrological dance called a mutual reception. This is a supportive relationship where Uranus is in Pisces, the sign ruled by Neptune, while Neptune is in Aquarius, the sign ruled by Uranus. When this dance is over in 2011, it is likely that we will be living under very different political and social circumstances.

## Uranus in Pisces

Uranus, known as the Great Awakener, tends to cause both upheaval and innovation in the sign it transits. During previous episodes of Uranus in Pisces, great religions and spiritual movements have come into being, most recently Mormonism and Christian Fundamentalism. In its most positive mode, Pisces promotes imagination and creativity, the art of illusion in theater and film, the inspiration of great artists. A water sign, Pisces is naturally associated with all things liquid—oceans, oil, alcohol—and with those creatures that live in the water—fish, the fishing industry, fish habitats, and fish farming. Currently there is a great

debate going on about overfishing, contamination of fish, and fish farming. The underdog, the enslaved, and the disenfranchised should also benefit from Uranus in Pisces.

Since Uranus is a disruptive influence that aims to challenge the status quo, the forces of nature that manifest will most likely be in the Pisces area: oceans, seas, and rivers. We have seen unprecedented rainy seasons, floods, mud slides, and disastrous hurricanes. Note that 2005's devastating Hurricane Katrina hit an area known for both the oil and fishing industries.

Pisces is associated with the prenatal phase of life, which is related to regenerative medicine. The controversy over embryonic stem cell research should continue to be debated. Petroleum issues, both in the oil-producing countries and offshore oil drilling, will come to a head. Uranus in Pisces suggests that development of new hydroelectric sources may provide the power we need to continue our current power-thirsty lifestyle.

As in previous eras, there should continue to be a flourishing of the arts. We are seeing many new artistic forms developing now, such as computer-created actors and special effects. The sky's the limit on this influence.

Those who have problems with Uranus are those who resist change, so the key is to embrace the future.

## Neptune in Aquarius

Neptune is a planet of imagination and creativity, but also of deception and illusion. Neptune is associated with hospitals, which have been the subject of much controversy. On the positive side, hospitals are acquiring cutting-edge technology. The atmosphere of many hospitals is already changing from the intimidating and sterile environment of the past to that of a health-promoting spa. Alternative therapies, such as massage, diet counseling, and aromatherapy, are becoming commonplace, which expresses this Neptune trend. New procedures in plastic surgery, also a Neptune glamour field, and anti-aging therapies are restoring the illusion of youth.

However, issues involving the expense and quality of

health care and the evolving relationship between doctors, drug companies, and HMOs reflect a darker side of this trend.

## What About the New Planets?

Our solar system is becoming more complex; astronomers continue to discover new objects circling the sun. In addition to the familiar planets, there are comets, cometoids, asteroids, and strange icy bodies in the Kuiper Belt beyond Neptune. The newest object at this writing is a planetlike orb that has a tiny moon. It is tentatively nicknamed Xena, after the TV heroine. Once Xena's orbit is established, astrologers will observe what effect this planet has on our horoscopes. Astrologers have long hypothesized about distant planets on the outer reaches of the solar system, but most astrologers stop with Pluto, which itself is quite controversial. Some scientists insist that tiny Pluto, only one-fifth the size of Earth, is not a full-fledged planet. However, anyone experiencing a zap to the horoscope from this little object knows that it is a force to be reckoned with! Time will tell about Xena and her yet to be discovered siblings!

CHAPTER 2

# Your Best Times This Year

Have you ever felt that success is a matter of timing, that you could set your schedule on a successful course if you coordinated your activities with times when the planets give you the green light? On the other hand, it's useful to know when not to act, when it would be better to kick back and review where you're going.

For instance, when mischievous Mercury creates havoc with communications and you can't seem to make progress with projects, you'll use the time to best advantage by backing up your vital computer files, clearing out your files and closets and reading between the lines of contracts. That's the time to be extra patient with coworkers and double-check all messages. Mark your social calendar when Venus passes through your sign—that's when you're the flavor of the month. You've got extra sex appeal, so it's time to get a knockout new outfit or hairstyle. Then ask someone you'd like to know better to dinner. Venus timing can also help you charm clients with a stunning sales pitch or make an offer they won't refuse.

In this chapter, you will learn how to find your best times as well as which times to avoid. You will also learn how to read the moods of the moon and make them work for you. Use the information and tables in this chapter and the planet tables in this book, and also use the moon sign listings in your daily forecasts.

Here are the happenings to note on your agenda:

- Dates of your sun sign (high-energy period)
- The month previous to your sun sign (low-energy period)
- Dates of planets in your sign this year

- Full and new moons (pay special attention when these fall in your sun sign!)
- Eclipses
- Moon in your sun sign every month, as well as moon in the opposite sign (listed in daily forecast)
- Mercury retrogrades
- Other retrograde periods

## Your High-Power Time

Every birthday starts off a new cycle of solar energy for you. You should feel a new surge of vitality as the powerful sun enters your sign. This is the time when predominant energies are most favorable to you. So go for it! Start new projects, make your big moves (especially when the new moon is in your sign, doubling your charisma). You'll get the recognition you deserve now, when everyone is attuned to your sun sign. Look in the tables in this book to see if other planets will also be passing through your sun sign at this time. Venus (love, beauty), Mars (energy, drive), and Mercury (communication, mental sharpness) reinforce the sun and give an extra boost to your life in the areas they affect. Venus will rev up your social and love life, making you seem especially attractive. Mars amplifies your energy and drive. Mercury fuels your brainpower and helps you communicate. Jupiter signals an especially lucky period of expansion.

There are two downtimes related to the sun. During the month before your birthday period, when you are winding up your annual cycle, you could be feeling especially vulnerable and depleted. So at that time get extra rest, watch your diet, and take it easy. Don't overstress yourself. Use this time to gear up for a big "push" when the sun enters your sign.

Another downtime is when the sun is in a sign opposite your sun sign (six months from your birthday). That's when the prevailing energies are very different from yours. You may feel at odds with the world. You'll have to work harder for recognition because people are not on your wavelength.

However, this could be a good time to work on a team, in cooperation with others, or behind the scenes.

## Plan Your Day with the Moon

The moon is a powerful tool to divine the mood of the moment. You can work with the moon in two ways. Plan by the *sign* the moon is in; plan by the *phase* of the moon. The sign will tell you the kind of activities that suit the moon's mood. The phase will tell you the best time to start or finish a certain activity.

Working with the phases of the moon is as easy as looking up at the night sky. During the new moon, when both the sun and moon are in the same sign, begin new ventures—especially activities that are favored by that sign. Then you'll utilize the powerful energies pulling you in the same direction. You'll be focused outward, toward action, and in a doing mode. Postpone breaking off, terminating, deliberating, or reflecting—activities that require introspection and passive work. These are better suited to a later moon phase.

Get your project under way during the first quarter. Then go public at the full moon, a time of high intensity, when feelings come out into the open. This is your time to shine—to express yourself. Be aware, however, that because pressures are being released, other people will also be letting off steam. Since confrontations are possible, take advantage of this time either to air grievances or to avoid arguments. Traditionally, astrologers often advise against surgery at this time, which could produce heavier bleeding.

About three days after the full moon comes the disseminating phase, a time when the energy of the cycle begins to wind down. From the last quarter of the moon to the next new moon, it's a time to cut off unproductive relationships, do serious thinking, and focus on inward-directed activities.

You'll feel some new and full moons more strongly than others, especially those new moons that fall in your sun sign and full moons in your opposite sign. Because that full moon happens at your low-energy time of year, it is likely

to be an especially stressful time in a relationship, when any hidden problems or unexpressed emotions could surface.

## Full and New Moons in 2007

All dates are calculated for eastern standard time and eastern daylight time.

Full Moon—January 3 in Cancer
New Moon—January 18 in Capricorn

Full Moon—February 2 in Leo
New Moon—February 17 in Aquarius

Full Moon—March 3 in Virgo (lunar eclipse)
New Moon—March 18 in Pisces (total solar eclipse)

Full Moon—April 2 in Libra
New Moon—April 17 in Aries

Full Moon—May 2 in Scorpio
New Moon—May 16 in Taurus

Full Moon—May 31 in Sagittarius
New Moon—June 14 in Gemini

Full Moon—June 30 in Capricorn
New Moon—July 14 in Cancer

Full Moon—July 29 in Aquarius
New Moon—August 12 in Leo

Full Moon—August 28 in Pisces (lunar eclipse)
New Moon—September 11 in Virgo (solar eclipse)

Full Moon—September 26 in Aries
New Moon—October 11 in Libra

Full Moon—October 26 in Taurus
New Moon—November 9 in Scorpio

Full Moon—November 24 in Gemini
New Moon—December 9 in Sagittarius
Full Moon—December 23 in Cancer

# How to Time by the Moon Sign

To forecast the daily emotional "weather," to determine your monthly high and low days, or to synchronize your activities with the cycles of the moon, take note of the moon sign under your daily forecast at the end of the book. Here are some of the activities favored and the moods you are likely to encounter under each moon sign.

## Moon in Aries: Get Moving!

The new moon in Aries is an ideal time to start new projects. Everyone is pushy, raring to go, rather impatient, and short-tempered. Leave details and follow-up for later. Competitive sports or martial arts are great ways to let off steam. Quiet types could use some assertiveness, but it's a great day for dynamos. Be careful not to step on too many toes.

## Moon in Taurus: Lay the Foundations for Success

Do solid, methodical tasks like follow-through or backup work. Make investments, buy real estate, do appraisals, do some hard bargaining. Attend to your property. Get out in the country or spend some time in your garden. Enjoy creature comforts, music, a good dinner, sensual lovemaking. Forget starting a diet—this is a day when you'll feel self indulgent.

## Moon in Gemini: Communicate

Talk means action today. Telephone, write letters, fax! Make new contacts, stay in touch with steady customers.

You can juggle lots of tasks today. It's a great time for mental activity of any kind. Don't try to pin people down—they, too, are feeling restless. Keep it light. Flirtations and socializing are good. Watch gossip—and don't give away secrets.

## Moon in Cancer: Pay Attention to Loved Ones

This is a moody, sensitive, emotional time. People respond to personal attention, to mothering. Stay at home, have a family dinner, call your mother. Nostalgia, memories, and psychic powers are heightened. You'll want to hang on to people and things (don't clean out your closets now). You could have shrewd insights into what others really need and want. Pay attention to dreams, intuition, and gut reactions.

## Moon in Leo: Be Confident

Everybody is in a much more confident, warm, generous mood. It's a good day to ask for a raise, show what you can do, dress like a star. People will respond to flattery, enjoy a bit of drama and theater. You may be extravagant, treat yourself royally, and show off a bit—but don't break the bank! Be careful you don't promise more than you can deliver.

## Moon in Virgo: Be Practical

Do practical down-to-earth chores. Review your budget, make repairs, be an efficiency expert. Not a day to ask for a raise. Tend to personal care and maintenance. Have a health checkup, go on a diet, buy vitamins or health food. Make your home spotless. Take care of details and piled-up chores. Reorganize your work and life so they run more smoothly and efficiently. Save money. Be prepared for others to be in a critical, faultfinding mood.

## Moon in Libra: Be Diplomatic

Attend to legal matters. Negotiate contracts. Arbitrate. Do things with your favorite partner. Socialize. Be romantic. Buy a special gift, a beautiful object. Decorate yourself or your surroundings. Buy new clothes. Throw a party. Have an elegant, romantic evening. Smooth over any ruffled feathers. Avoid confrontations. Stick to civilized discussions.

## Moon in Scorpio: Solve Problems

This is a day to do things with passion. You'll have excellent concentration and focus. Try not to get too intense emotionally. Avoid sharp exchanges with loved ones. Others may tend to go to extremes, get jealous, overreact. Great for troubleshooting, problem solving, research, scientific work—and making love. Pay attention to those psychic vibes.

## Moon in Sagittarius: Sell and Motivate

A great time for travel, philosophical discussions, setting long-range career goals. Work out, do sports, buy athletic equipment. Others will be feeling upbeat, exuberant, and adventurous. Risk taking is favored. You may feel like taking a gamble, betting on the horses, visiting a local casino, buying a lottery ticket. Teaching, writing, and spiritual activities also get the green light. Relax outdoors. Take care of animals.

## Moon in Capricorn: Get Organized

You can accomplish a lot now, so get on the ball! Attend to business. Issues concerning your basic responsibilities, duties, family, and elderly parents could crop up. You'll be expected to deliver on promises. Weed out the deadwood from your life. Get a dental checkup. Not a good day for gambling or taking risks.

## Moon in Aquarius: Join the Group

A great day for doing things with groups—clubs, meetings, outings, politics, parties. Campaign for your candidate. Work for a worthy cause. Deal with larger issues that affect humanity—the environment and metaphysical questions. Buy a computer or electronic gadget. Watch TV. Wear something outrageous. Try something you've never done before. Present an original idea. Don't stick to a rigid schedule—go with the flow. Take a class in meditation, mind control. yoga.

## Moon in Pisces: Be Creative

This can be a very creative day, so let your imagination work overtime. Film, theater, music, ballet could inspire you. Spend some time alone, resting and reflecting, reading or writing poetry. Daydreams can also be profitable. Help those less fortunate. Lend a listening ear to someone who may be feeling blue. Don't overindulge in self-pity or escapism, however. People are especially vulnerable to substance abuse now. Turn your thoughts to romance and someone special.

# Retrogrades: When the Planets Seem to Backstep

All the planets, except for the sun and moon, have times when they appear to move backward—or retrograde—as it seems from our point of view on earth. At these times, planets do not work as they normally do. So it's best to "take a break" from that planet's energies in our life and to do some work on an inner level.

## Mercury Retrograde: The Key Is in "Re"

Mercury goes retrograde most often, and its effects can be especially irritating. When it reaches a short distance ahead of the sun several times a year, it seems to move backward

from our point of view. Astrologers often compare retrograde motion to the optical illusion that occurs when we ride on a train that passes another train traveling at a different speed—the second train appears to be moving in reverse.

What this means to you is that the Mercury-ruled areas of your life—analytical thought processes, communications, scheduling—are subject to all kinds of confusion. Be prepared. Communications equipment can break down. Schedules may be changed on short notice. People are late for appointments or don't show up at all. Traffic is terrible. Major purchases malfunction, don't work out, or get delivered in the wrong color. Letters don't arrive or are delivered to the wrong address. Employees will make errors that have to be corrected later. Contracts don't work out or must be renegotiated.

Since most of us can't put our lives on "hold" during Mercury retrogrades, we should learn to tame the trickster and make it work for us. The key is in the prefix *re-*. This is the time to go back over things in your life, *re*flect on what you've done during the previous months. Now you can get deeper insights, spot errors you've missed. So take time to *re*view and *re*evaluate what has happened. *Re*st and *re*ward yourself—it's a good time to take a vacation, especially if you *re*visit a favorite place. *Re*organize your work and finish up projects that are backed up. Clean out your desk and closets. Throw away what you can't *re*cycle. If you must sign contracts or agreements, do so with a contingency clause that lets you *re*evaluate the terms later.

Postpone major purchases or commitments for the time being. Don't get married (unless you're *re*marrying the same person). Try not to *re*ly on other people keeping appointments, contracts, or agreements to the letter; have several alternatives. Double-check and *re*ad between the lines. Don't buy anything connected with communications or transportation (if you must, be sure to cover yourself).

Mercury retrograding through your sun sign will intensify its effect on your life.

If Mercury was retrograde when you were born, you may be one of the lucky people who don't suffer the frustrations of this period. If so, your mind probably works in a very intuitive, insightful way.

The sign in which Mercury is retrograding can give you an idea of what's in store—as well as the sun signs that will be especially challenged.

## Mercury Retrogrades in 2007

Mercury has three retrograde periods this year.
February 14 to March 8 from Pisces back to Aquarius
June 15 to July 9 in Cancer
October 11 to November 1 from Scorpio back to Libra

### Venus Retrograde: Relationships Move Backward

Retrograding Venus can cause your relationships to take a backward step, or it can make you extravagant and impractical. Shopping till you drop and buying what you cannot afford are problems at this time. It's *not* a good time to redecorate—you'll hate the color of the walls later. Postpone getting a new hairstyle. Try not to fall in love either. But if you wish to make amends in an already troubled relationship, make peaceful overtures at this time.

## Venus Retrogrades in 2007

Venus turns retrograde in Virgo from July 27 until September 8, when it turns direct in Leo.

### Use the Go Power of Mars

Mars shows how and when to get where you want to go. Timing your moves with Mars on your side can give you a big push. On the other hand, pushing Mars the wrong way can guarantee that you'll run into frustrations in every corner. Your best times to forge ahead are during the weeks when Mars is traveling through your sun sign or your Mars sign (look these up in the tables in this book). Also con-

sider times when Mars is in a compatible sign (fire with air signs, or earth with water signs). You'll be sure to have planetary power on your side.

# Mars Retrogrades in 2007

Mars turns retrograde on November 15 until January 30, 2008, from Cancer to Gemini.

## When Other Planets Retrograde

The slower-moving planets stay retrograde for months at a time (Jupiter, Saturn, Neptune, Uranus, and Pluto).

When Saturn is retrograde, it's an uphill battle with self-discipline. You may not be in the mood for work. You may feel more like hanging out at the beach than getting things done.

Neptune retrograde promotes a dreamy escapism from reality, when you may feel you're in a fog (Pisces will feel this, especially).

Uranus retrograde may mean setbacks in areas where there have been sudden changes, when you may be forced to regroup or reevaluate the situation.

Pluto retrograde is a time to work on establishing proportion and balance in areas where there have been recent dramatic transformations.

When the planets move forward again, there's a shift in the atmosphere. Activities connected with each planet start moving ahead, plans that were stalled get rolling. Make a special note of those days on your calendar and proceed accordingly.

# Other Retrogrades in 2007

The five slower-moving planets all go retrograde in 2007.

Jupiter retrogrades four months from April 5 to August 6 in Sagittarius.

Saturn turned retrograde on December 5, 2006, until

April 19, 2007. It turns retrograde again on December 19 for the duration of the year.

Uranus retrogrades from June 23 to November 24 in Pisces.

Neptune retrogrades from May 24 to October 31 in Aquarius.

Pluto retrogrades from March 31 to September 7 in Sagittarius.

CHAPTER 3

# What Planets Could Rock Your World This Year

It's been said that knowledge is power, so why not use astrology's wisdom to ride with the tide this year and make the planets work for you?

## Eclipses Clear the Air

Eclipses can bring on milestones in your life, if they aspect a key point in your horoscope. In general, they shake up the status quo, bringing hidden areas out into the open. During this time, problems you've been avoiding or have brushed aside can surface to demand your attention. A good coping strategy is to accept whatever comes up as a challenge that could make a positive difference in your life. And don't forget the power of your sense of humor. If you can laugh at something, you'll never be afraid of it.

## What Is the Best Thing to Do During an Eclipse?

When the natural rhythms of the sun and moon are disturbed, it's best to postpone important activities. Be sure to mark eclipse days on your calendar, especially if the eclipse falls in your birth sign. This year, those born under Aries, Pisces, and Virgo should take special note of the feelings that arise. With lunar eclipses, some possibilities

could be a break from attachments or the healing of an illness or substance abuse, which had been triggered by the subconscious. The temporary event could be a healing time, when you gain perspective. During solar eclipses, when you might be in a highly subjective state, pay attention to the hidden subconscious patterns that surface, the emotional truth that is revealed at this time.

The effect of the eclipse can reverberate for some time, often months after the event. But it is especially important to stay cool and make no major moves during the period known as the shadow of the eclipse, which begins about a week before and lasts until at least three days after the eclipse. After three days, the daily rhythms should return to normal, and you can proceed with business as usual.

## This Year's Eclipse Dates

March 3: Lunar eclipse in Virgo
March 18: Solar eclipse in Pisces
August 28: Lunar eclipse in Pisces
September 11: Solar eclipse in Virgo

# Saturn Gives You a Reality Check

When Saturn hits a critical point in your horoscope, you can count on an experience that will make you slow up, pull back, and reexamine your life. It is a call to eliminate what is not working, to shape up, to set priorities, to examine the boundaries and structures in your life (or lack of them) and set new ones. During this process, you may feel restricted, frustrated, or inhibited—not a fun time, but one that will serve you well in the long run. You may need to take on more responsibilities that will test your limits.

By the end of its twenty-eight-year trip around the zodiac, Saturn will have tested you in all areas of your life. The major tests happen in seven-year cycles, when Saturn passes over the angles of your chart, which means your rising sign, the top of your chart or midheaven, your descendant, and the nadir or bottom of your chart. This is when the real life-changing experiences happen. But you

are also in for a testing period whenever Saturn passes a planet in your chart or stresses that planet from a distance. It is useful to check your planetary positions with the timetable of Saturn or prepare in advance, or at least to brace yourself.

When Saturn returns to its location at the time of your birth, at approximately age twenty-eight, you'll have your first Saturn return. At this time, a person usually takes stock or settles down to find his mission in life and assume full adult duties and responsibilities.

Another way Saturn helps us is to reveal the karmic lessons from previous lives and give us the chance to overcome them. So look at Saturn's challenges as much-needed opportunities for self-improvement.

## Outwitting the Planets

Second-guessing Saturn and the eclipses this year is easy if you have a copy of your horoscope calculated by a computer. This enables you to pinpoint the area of your life that will be affected. However, you can make an educated guess, by setting up a rough diagram on your own. If you'd like to find out which area of your life this year's Saturn change is most likely to affect, follow these easy steps.

First, you must know the time of day you were born and look up your rising sign listed on the tables in this book (see chapter 7). Set up an estimated horoscope by drawing a circle, then dividing it into four parts by making a cross directly through the center. Continue to divide each of the parts into thirds, as if you were dividing a cake, until you have twelve slices. Write your rising sign on the middle left-hand slice, which would be the nine o'clock point, if you were looking at your watch. Then write the following signs on the dividing line of each slice, working counterclockwise, until you have listed all twelve signs of the zodiac.

You should now have a basic diagram of your horoscope chart (minus the planets, of course). Starting with your rising-sign slice, number each portion consecutively, again working counterclockwise.

Since this year's eclipses will fall in Pisces and Virgo, find the number of these slices, or houses, on the chart and read the following descriptions for the kinds of issues that are likely to be emphasized. On September 2, Saturn will move from Leo to Virgo, so check those houses in your chart for Saturn-related events.

If an eclipse or Saturn falls in your FIRST HOUSE:
Events cause you to examine the ways you are acting independently and push you to become more visible, to assert yourself. This is a time when you feel compelled to make your own decisions. You may want to change your physical appearance, body image, or style of dress in some way. Under affliction, there might be illness or physical harm.

If an eclipse or Saturn falls in your SECOND HOUSE:
This is the place where you consider all matters of security. You consolidate your resources, earn money, acquire property, and decide what you value and what you want to own. On a deeper level, this house reveals your sense of self-worth.

If an eclipse or Saturn falls in your THIRD HOUSE:
Here you reach out to others, express your ideas, and explore different courses of action. You may feel especially restless or have confrontations with neighbors or siblings. In your search for more knowledge, you may decide to improve your skills, get more education, or sign up for a course that interests you. Local transportation, especially your car, might be affected by an eclipse here.

If an eclipse or Saturn falls in your FOURTH HOUSE:
Here is where you put down roots and establish a base. You'll consider what home really means to you. Issues involving parents, the physical setup or location of your home, and your immediate family demand your attention. You may be especially concerned with parenting or relationships with your own mother. You may consider moving your home to a new location or leaving home.

If an eclipse or Saturn falls in your FIFTH HOUSE:

Here is where you express yourself, either through your personal talents or through procreating children. You are interested in making your special talents visible. This is also the house of love affairs and the romantic aspect of life, where you flirt, have fun, and enjoy the excitement of love. Hobbies and crafts fall in this area.

If an eclipse or Saturn falls in your SIXTH HOUSE:

How well are you doing your job? This is your maintenance department, where you take care of your health, organize your life, and set up a daily routine. It is also the place where you perfect your skills and add polish to your life. The chores you do every day, the skills you learn, and the techniques you use fall here. If something doesn't work in your life, an eclipse is sure to bring this to light. If you've been neglecting your health, diet, and fitness, you'll probably pay the consequences during an eclipse. Or you may be faced with work that requires much routine organization and steady effort, rather than creative ability. Or you may be required to perform services for others.

If an eclipse or Saturn falls in your SEVENTH HOUSE:

This is the area of committed relationships, of those which involve legal agreements, of working in a close relationship with another. Here you'll be dealing with how you relate, what you'll be willing to give up for the sake of a marriage or partnership. Eclipses here can put extra pressure on a relationship and, if it's not working, precipitate a breakup. Lawsuits and open enemies also reside here.

If an eclipse or Saturn falls in your EIGHTH HOUSE:

This area is concerned with power and control. Consider what you are willing to give up in order that something might happen. Power struggles, intense relationships, and desires to penetrate deeper mysteries belong here. Debts, loans, financial matters that involve another party, and wheeling and dealing also come into focus. So does sex, where you surrender your individual power to create a new life together. Matters involving birth and death are also involved here.

If an eclipse or Saturn falls in your NINTH HOUSE:

Here is where you look at the big picture. You'll seek information that helps you find meaning in life: higher education, religion, travel, global issues. Eclipses here can push you to get out of your rut, to explore something you've never done before, and to expand your horizons.

If an eclipse or Saturn falls in your TENTH HOUSE:

This is the high-profile point in your chart. Here is where you consider how society looks at you and your position in the outside world. You'll be concerned about whether you receive proper credit for your work and if you're recognized by higher-ups. Promotions, raises, and other forms of recognition can be given or denied. If you have worked hard, Saturn can give you well-deserved rewards here. Either your standing in your career or in your community can be challenged, or you'll be publicly acknowledged for achieving a goal. An eclipse here can make you famous or burst your balloon if you've been too ambitious or neglecting other areas of your life.

If an eclipse or Saturn falls in your ELEVENTH HOUSE:

Your relationship with groups of people comes under scrutiny during an eclipse: whom you are identified with, whom you socialize with, and how well you are accepted by other members of your team. Activities of clubs and political parties, networking, and other social interactions become important. You'll be concerned about what other people think.

If an eclipse or Saturn falls in your TWELFTH HOUSE:

This is the time when the focus turns to your inner life. An especially favorable eclipse here might bring you great insight and inspiration. On the other hand, events may happen that cause you to retreat from public life. Here is where we go to be alone or to work in retreats, hospitals, or religious institutions, or to explore psychotherapy. Here is where you deliver selfless service, through charitable acts. Good aspects from an eclipse could promote an ability to go with the flow or to rise above the competition to find an inner, almost mystical strength that enables you to connect with the deepest needs of others.

CHAPTER 4

# The Moon and Your Emotions

How do you react to life's problems? What do you care about? What makes you feel comfortable, secure, or romantic? The answers are a few secrets revealed by the moon sign in your horoscope, where the moon represents your receptive, reflective, female, nurturing self. It also reflects who you were nurtured by—the mother or mother figure in your chart. In a man's chart, the moon position describes his receptive, emotional, yin side, as well as the woman in his life who will have the deepest effect, usually his mother. (Venus reveals the kind of woman who will attract him physically.)

It's well worth having an accurate chart cast to determine your moon sign or that of someone you'd like to know better, since this reveals much about your inner life. You can learn what appeals to a person subconsciously by knowing the person's moon sign, which reflects the instinctive emotional nature.

The moon is more at home in some signs than others. It rules maternal Cancer and is exalted in Taurus—both comforting, home-loving signs where the natural emotional energies of the moon are easily and productively expressed. But when the moon is in the opposite signs—Capricorn and Scorpio—it leaves the comfortable nest and deals with emotional issues of power and achievement in the outside world. Those of you with the moon in these signs are likely to find your emotional role more challenging in life.

Since detailed moon tables are too extensive for this book, check through the following listing to find the moon sign that feels most familiar.

## Moon in Aries

This placement makes you both independent and ardent. An idealist, you tend to fall in and out of love easily. You love a challenge but could cool once your quarry is captured. Your emotional reactions are fast and fiery, quickly expressed and quickly forgotten. You may not think before expressing your feelings. It's not easy to hide how you feel. Channeling all your emotional energy could be one of your big challenges.

## Moon in Taurus

A sentimental soul, you are very fond of the good life, and you gravitate toward solid, secure relationships. You like displays of affection and creature comforts—all the tangible trappings of a cozy, safe, calm atmosphere. You are sensual and steady emotionally, but very stubborn, possessive, and determined. You can't be pushed, and you tend to dislike changes. You should make an effort to broaden your horizons and to take a risk sometimes. You may become very attached to your home turf. You may also be a collector of objects that are meaningful to you.

## Moon in Gemini

You crave mental stimulation and variety in life, which you usually get through either an ever-varied social life, the excitement of flirtation and/or multiple professional involvements. You may marry more than once and have a rather chaotic emotional life due to your difficulty with commitment and settling down, as well as your need to be constantly on the go. (Be sure to find a partner who is as outgoing as you are.) You will have to learn at some point to focus your energies because you tend to be somewhat fragmented—to do two things at once, to have two homes or even two lovers. If you can find a creative way to express your many-faceted nature, you'll be ahead of the game.

## Moon in Cancer

This is the most powerful lunar position, which is sure to make a deep imprint on your character. Your needs are very much associated with your reaction to the needs of others. You are very sensitive, caring, and self-protective, though some of you may mask this with a hard shell, like the moon-sensitive crab. This placement also gives an excellent memory, keen intuition, and an uncanny ability to perceive the needs of others. All of the lunar phases will affect you, especially full moons and eclipses, so you would do well to mark them on your calendar. Because you're happiest at home, you may work at home or turn your office into a second home, where you can nurture and comfort people. (You may tend to mother the world.) With natural psychic, intuitive ability, you might be drawn to occult work in some way. Or you may get professionally involved with providing food and shelter to others.

## Moon in Leo

This warm, passionate moon takes everything to heart. You are attracted to all that is noble, generous, and aristocratic in life (and may be a bit of a snob). You have an innate ability to take command emotionally, but you do need strong support, loyalty, and loud applause from those you love. You are possessive of your loved ones and your turf and will roar if anyone threatens to take over your territory.

## Moon in Virgo

You are rather cool until you decide if others measure up. But once someone or something meets your ideal standards, you hold up your end of the arrangement perfectly. You may, in fact, drive yourself too hard to attain some notion of perfection. Try to be a bit easier on yourself and others. Don't always act the censor! You love to be the teacher and are drawn to situations where you can change others for the better, but sometimes you must learn to accept others for what they are—enjoy what you have!

## Moon in Libra

Like other air-sign moons, you think before you feel. Therefore, you may not immediately recognize the emotional needs of others. However, you are relationship oriented and may find it difficult to be alone or to do things alone. After you have learned emotional balance by leaning on yourself first, you can have excellent partnerships. It is best for you to avoid extremes, which set your scales swinging and can make your love life precarious. You thrive in a rather conservative, traditional, romantic relationship, where you receive attention and flattery—but not possessiveness—from your partner. You'll be your most charming in an elegant, harmonious atmosphere.

## Moon in Scorpio

This is a moon that enjoys and responds to intense, passionate feelings. You may go to extremes and have a very dramatic emotional life, full of ardor, suspicion, jealousy, and obsession. It would be much healthier to channel your need for power and control into meaningful work. This is a good position for anyone in the fields of medicine, police work, research, the occult, psychoanalysis, or intuitive work, because life-and-death situations don't faze you. However, you do take personal disappointments very hard.

## Moon in Sagittarius

You take life's ups and downs with good humor and the proverbial grain of salt. You'll love 'em and leave 'em—take off on a great adventure at a moment's notice. Born free could be your slogan. Attracted by the exotic, you have wanderlust mentally and physically. You may be too much in search of new mental and spiritual stimulation to ever settle down.

## Moon in Capricorn

Are you ever accused of being too cool and calculating? You have an earthy side, but you take prestige and position

very seriously. Your strong drive to succeed extends to your romantic life, where you will be devoted to improving your lifestyle, rising to the top. A structured situation where you can advance methodically makes you feel wonderfully secure. You may be attracted to someone older or very much younger or from a different social world. It may be difficult to look at the lighter side of emotional relationships. Though this moon is placed in the sign of its detriment, the good news is that you tend to be very dutiful and responsible to those you care for.

## Moon in Aquarius

You are a people collector with many friends of all backgrounds. You are happiest surrounded by people and may feel uneasy when left alone. Though you usually stay friends with lovers, intense emotions and demanding one-on-one relationships turn you off. You don't like anything to be too rigid or scheduled. Though tolerant and understanding, you can be emotionally unpredictable and may opt for an unconventional love life. With plenty of space, you will be able to sustain relationships with liberal, freedom-loving types.

## Moon in Pisces

You are very responsive and empathetic to others, especially if they have problems or are the underdog. (Be on guard against attracting too many people with sob stories.) You'll be happiest if you can express your creative imagination in the arts or in the spiritual or healing professions. Because you may tend to escape in fantasies or overreact to the moods of others, you need an emotional anchor to help you keep a firm foothold in reality. Steer clear of too much escapism (especially in alcohol) or reclusiveness. Places near water soothe your moods. Working in a field that gives you emotional variety will also help you be productive.

CHAPTER 5

# Basic Astrology: Your Owner's Manual

You probably know your zodiac sign and those of your friends. But do you know the difference between a sign and a constellation? And what is a house? Is yours an earth sign or a water sign? If you'd like to venture around the zodiac into the deeper areas of astrology, this chapter can get you up and running. It's a quick owner's manual, your fast track to understanding the basic principles of this fascinating but often confusing subject.

## Signs and Constellations: What's the Difference?

First, let's get our sign language straight, because for most readers, that's the starting point of astrology.

Signs are actually a type of celestial real estate, located on the zodiac, an imaginary 360-degree belt circling the earth. This belt is divided into twelve equal thirty-degree portions, which are the signs. There's a lot of confusion about the difference between the signs and the constellations of the zodiac. The latter are patterns of stars that originally marked the twelve divisions, like signposts. Though a sign is named after the constellation that once marked the same area, the constellations are no longer in the same place relative to the earth that they were many centuries ago. Over hundreds of years, the earth's orbit has shifted, so that from our point of view here on earth, the

constellations seem to have moved. However, the signs remain in place. (Most Western astrology uses the twelve-equal-part division of the zodiac, though there are some other methods of astrology that still use the constellations instead of the signs.)

Most people think of themselves in terms of their sun sign. A sun sign refers to the sign the sun is orbiting through at a given moment (from our point of view here on earth). For instance, "I'm an Aries" means that the sun was passing through Aries when that person was born. However, there are nine other planets (plus asteroids, fixed stars, and sensitive points) that also form our total astrological personality, and some or many of these will be located in other signs. No one is completely Aries, with all astrological components in one sign! (Please note that, in astrology, the sun and moon are usually referred to as planets, though of course they're not.)

As we mentioned before, the sun signs are places on the zodiac. They do not do anything (the planets are the doers). However, they are associated with many things, depending on their location.

## How We Define the Signs

The definitions of the signs evolved systematically from four components that interrelate. These four different criteria are a sign's element: its quality, its polarity or sex, and its order in the progression of the zodiac. All these factors work together to tell us what the sign is like.

The system is magically mathematical. The number 12—as in the twelve signs of the zodiac—is divisible by 4, by 3, and by 2. There are four elements, three qualities, and two polarities, which follow each other in sequence around the zodiac.

The four elements (earth, air, fire, and water) are the building blocks of astrology. The use of an element to describe a sign probably dates from man's first attempts to categorize what he saw. Ancient sages believed that all things were composed of combinations of these basic elements—earth, air, fire, and water. This included the

human character, which was fiery/choleric, earthy/melancholy, airy/sanguine, or watery/phlegmatic. The elements also correspond to our emotional (water), physical (earth), mental (air) and spiritual (fire) natures. The energies of each of the elements were then observed to be related to the time of year when the sun was passing through a certain segment of the zodiac.

Those born with the sun in fire signs—Aries, Leo, Sagittarius—embody the characteristic of that element. Optimism, warmth, hot tempers, enthusiasm, and spirit are typical of these signs. Taurus, Virgo, and Capricorn are earthy—more grounded, physical, materialistic, organized and deliberate than fire-sign people. Air-sign people—Gemini, Libra, and Aquarius—are mentally oriented communicators. Water signs—Cancer, Scorpio, and Pisces—are emotional, sensitive, and creative.

Think of what each element does to the others. Water puts out fire or evaporates under heat. Air fans the flames or blows them out. Earth smothers fire, drifts and erodes with too much wind, becomes mud or fertile soil with water. Those are often perfect analogies for the relationships between people of different sun-sign elements. This astrochemistry was one of the first ways man described his relationships. Fortunately, no one is entirely air or fire. We all have a bit, or a lot, of each element in our horoscopes. It is this unique mix that defines each astrological personality.

Within each element, there are three qualities that describe types of behavior associated with the sign. Those of cardinal signs are activists, go-getters. These four signs—Aries, Cancer, Libra, and Capricorn—begin each season. Fixed signs, which happen in the middle of the season, are associated with builders, stabilizers. You'll find that sun signs Taurus, Leo, Scorpio, and Aquarius are usually gifted with concentration, stamina, and focus. Mutable signs—Gemini, Virgo, Sagittarius, and Pisces—fall at the end of each season and thus are considered catalysts for change. People born under mutable signs are flexible, adaptable.

The polarity of a sign is either its positive or negative charge. It can be masculine, active, positive, and yang like air or fire signs. Or feminine, reactive, negative, and yin like the water and earth signs.

Finally, we consider the sign's place in the order of the

zodiac. This is vital to the balance of all the forces and the transmission of energy moving through the signs. You may have noticed that your sign is quite different from your neighboring sign on either side. Yet each seems to grow out of its predecessor like links in a chain and transmits a synthesis of energy gathered along the chain to the following sign, beginning with the fire-powered, active, positive charge of Aries.

***How the Signs Add Up***

| SIGN | ELEMENT | QUALITY | POLARITY | PLACE |
|---|---|---|---|---|
| Aries | fire | cardinal | masculine | first |
| Taurus | earth | fixed | feminine | second |
| Gemini | air | mutable | masculine | third |
| Cancer | water | cardinal | feminine | fourth |
| Leo | fire | fixed | masculine | fifth |
| Virgo | earth | mutable | feminine | sixth |
| Libra | air | cardinal | masculine | seventh |
| Scorpio | water | fixed | feminine | eighth |
| Sagittarius | fire | mutable | masculine | ninth |
| Capricorn | earth | cardinal | feminine | tenth |
| Aquarius | air | fixed | masculine | eleventh |
| Pisces | water | mutable | feminine | twelfth |

# Your Sign's Special Planet

Each sign has a ruling planet that is most compatible with its energies. Mars adds its fiery assertive characteristics to

Aries. The sensual beauty and comfort-loving side of Venus rules Taurus, whereas the idealistic side of Venus rules Libra. Quick-moving Mercury rules two mutable signs, Gemini and Virgo. Its mental agility belongs to Gemini while its analytical, critical side is best expressed in Virgo. The changeable emotional moon is associated with Cancer, while the outgoing Leo personality is ruled by the sun. Scorpio originally shared Mars, but when Pluto was discovered in this century, its powerful magnetic energies were deemed more suitable to the intense vibrations of the fixed water sign Scorpio. Disciplined Capricorn is ruled by Saturn, and expansive Sagittarius by Jupiter. Unpredictable Aquarius is ruled by Uranus and creative, imaginative Pisces by Neptune. In a horoscope, if a planet is placed in the sign it rules, it is sure to be especially powerful.

## The Layout of a Horoscope Chart

A horoscope chart is a map of the heavens at a given moment in time. It looks like a wheel divided with twelve spokes. In between each of the spokes is a section called a house.

Each house deals with a different area of life and is influenced by a special sign and a planet. Astrologers look at the house to tell in what area of life an event is happening or about to happen.

The house is governed by the sign passing over the spoke (or cusp of the house) at that particular moment. Though the first house is naturally associated with Aries and Mars, it would also have an additional Capricorn influence if that sign was passing over the house cusp at the time the chart was cast. The sequence of the houses starts with the first house located at the left center spoke (or the number 9 position, if you were reading a clock). The houses are then read counterclockwise around the chart, with the fourth house at the bottom of the chart, the tenth house at the top or twelve o'clock position.

Where do the planets belong? Around the horoscope, planets are placed within the houses according to their location at the time of the chart. That is why it is so important

to have an accurate time; with no specific time, the planets have no specific location in the houses and one cannot determine which area of life they will apply to. Since the signs move across the houses as the earth turns, planets in a house will naturally intensify the importance of that house. The house that contains the sun is naturally one of the most prominent.

## The First House: Home of Aries and Mars

The sign passing over the first house at the time of your birth is known as your *ascendant,* or *rising sign.* The first house is the house of "firsts"—the first impression you make, how you initiate matters, the image you choose to project. This is where you advertise yourself, where you project your personality. Planets that fall here will intensify the way you come across to others.

## The Second House: Home of Taurus and Venus

This house is where you experience the material world—what you value. Here are your attitudes about money, possessions, finances, whatever belongs to you, and what you own, as well as your earning and spending capacity. On a deeper level, this house reveals your sense of self-worth, the inner values that draw wealth in various forms.

## The Third House: Home of Gemini and Mercury

This house describes how you communicate with others, how you reach out to others nearby, and how you interact with the immediate environment. It shows how your thinking process works and the way you express your thoughts. Are you articulate or tongue-tied? Can you think on your feet? This house also shows your first relationships, your experiences with brothers and sisters, and how you deal with people close to you such as your neighbors or pals. It's where you take short trips, write letters, or use the

telephone. It shows how your mind works in terms of left-brain logical and analytical functions.

## The Fourth House: Home of Cancer and the Moon

The fourth house shows the foundation of life, the psychological underpinnings. At the bottom of the chart, this house shows how you are nurtured and made to feel secure—your roots! It shows your early home environment and the circumstances at the end of your life (your final "home") as well as the place you call home now. Astrologers look here for information about the parental nurturers in your life.

## The Fifth House: Home of Leo and the Sun

The fifth house is where the creative potential develops. Here you express yourself and procreate in the sense that children are outgrowths of your creative ability. But this house most represents your inner childlike self who delights in play. If your inner security has been established by the time you reach this house, you are now free to have fun, romance, and love affairs and to give of yourself. This is also the place astrologers look for playful love affairs, flirtations, and brief romantic encounters (rather than long-term commitments).

## The Sixth House: Home of Virgo and Mercury

The sixth house has been called the "care and maintenance" department. This house shows how you take care of your body and organize yourself to perform efficiently in the world. Here is where you get things done, where you look after others, and fulfill service duties such as taking care of pets. Here is what you do to survive on a day-to-day basis. The sixth house demands order in your life; otherwise there would be chaos. This house is your "job" (as opposed to your career, which is the domain of the

tenth house), your diet, and your health and fitness regimens.

## The Seventh House: Home of Libra and Venus

This house shows your attitude toward partners and those with whom you enter into commitments, contracts, or agreements. Here is the way you relate to others, as well as your close, intimate, one-on-one relationships (including open enemies—those you "face off" with). Open hostilities, lawsuits, divorces, and marriages happen here. If the first house represents the "I," the seventh or opposite house is the "not-I"—the complementary partner you attract by the way you come across. If you are having trouble with partnerships, consider what you are attracting by the energies of your first and seventh houses.

## The Eighth House: Home of Scorpio and Pluto (also Mars)

The eighth house refers to how you merge with something or someone, and how you handle power and control. This is one of the most mysterious and powerful houses, where your energy transforms itself from "I" to "we." As you give up power and control by uniting with something or someone, two kinds of energies merge and become something greater, leading to a regeneration of the self on a higher level. Here are your attitudes toward sex, shared resources, taxes (what you share with the government). Because this house involves what belongs to others, you face issues of control and power struggles, or undergo a deep psychological transformation as you bond with another. Here you transcend yourself with dreams, drugs, and occult or psychic experiences that reflect the collective unconscious.

## The Ninth House: Home of Sagittarius and Jupiter

The ninth house shows your search for wisdom and higher knowledge—your belief system. As the third house repre-

sents the "lower mind," its opposite on the wheel, the ninth house, is the "higher mind"—the abstract, intuitive, spiritual mind that asks "big" questions like "Why are we here?" After the third house has explored what was close at hand, the ninth stretches out to broaden you mentally with higher education and travel. Here you stretch spiritually with religious activity. Since you are concerned with how everything is related, you tend to push boundaries, take risks. Here is where you express your ideas in a book or thesis, where you pontificate, philosophize, or preach.

## The Tenth House: Home of Capricorn and Saturn

The tenth house is associated with your public life and high-profile activities. Located directly overhead at the "high noon" position on the horoscope wheel, this is the most "visible" house in the chart, the one where the world sees you. It deals with your career (but not your routine "job") and your reputation. Here is where you go public, take on responsibilities, (as opposed to the fourth house, where you stay home). This will affect the career you choose and your "public relations." This house is also associated with your father figure or the main authority figure in your life.

## The Eleventh House: Home of Aquarius and Uranus

The eleventh house is where you extend yourself to a group, a goal, or a belief system. This house is where you define what you really want, the kinds of friends you have, your political affiliations, and the kind of groups you identify with as an equal. Here is where you become concerned with "what other people think" or where you rebel against social conventions. Here is where you could become a socially conscious humanitarian or a partygoing social butterfly. It's where you look to others to stimulate you and discover your kinship to the rest of humanity. The sign on

this house can help you understand what you gain and lose from friendships.

## The Twelfth House: Home of Pisces and Neptune

Old-fashioned astrologers used to put a rather negative spin on this house, calling it the house of self-undoing. When we undo ourselves, we surrender control, boundaries, limits, and rules. The twelfth house is where the boundaries between yourself and others become blurred and you become selfless. But instead of being self-undoing, the twelfth house can be a place of great creativity and talent. It is the place where you can tap into the collective unconscious, where your imagination is limitless.

In your trip around the zodiac, you've gone from the I of self-assertion in the first house to the final house, which symbolizes the dissolution that happens before rebirth. The twelfth house is where accumulated experiences are processed in the unconscious. Spiritually oriented astrologers look to this house for evidence of past lives and karma. Places where we go for solitude or to do spiritual or reparatory work belong here, such as retreats, religious institutions, or hospitals. Here is also where we withdraw from society voluntarily or involuntarily or are put in prison because of antisocial activity. Selfless giving through charitable acts is part of this house, as is dependence on charity.

In your daily life, the twelfth house reveals your deepest intimacies, your best-kept secrets, especially those you hide from yourself and keep repressed deep in the unconscious. It is where we surrender a sense of a separate self to a deep feeling of wholeness, such as selfless service in religion or any activity that involves merging with the greater whole. Many sports stars have important planets in the twelfth house that enable them to play in the zone, finding an inner, almost mystical, strength that transcends their limits.

# Who's Home in Your Houses?

Houses are stronger or weaker depending on how many planets are inhabiting them. If there are many planets in a

given house, it follows that the activities of that house will be especially important in your life. If the planet that rules the house is also located there, this too adds power to the house.

CHAPTER 6

# Your Planetary Recipe

Besides the sun and moon, there are eight planets in your horoscope. Each is an ingredient representing a basic force in life that interacts with the other planets to make up a recipe that is uniquely yours. The location of a planet in your horoscope can determine how strongly that planet will affect you. A planet that's close to your rising sign will be emphasized in your chart. If two or more planets are grouped together in one sign, they usually operate together, playing off each other, rather than expressing their energy singularly. A lone planet that stands far away from the others is usually outstanding and often calls the shots in a horoscope.

The sign of each planet also has a powerful influence. In some signs, the planetary energies are very much at home and can easily express themselves. In others, the planet has to work harder and is slightly out of sorts. The sign that most corresponds to the energies of a planet is said to be ruled by that planet and obviously is the best place for it to be. The next best place is in a sign where it is exalted, or especially harmonious. On the other hand, there are places in the horoscope where a planet has to work harder to play its role, such as the sign opposite a planet's rulership, which embodies the opposite area of life, and the sign opposite its exaltation. However, a planet that must work harder can actually be more complete, because it must stretch itself to meet the challenges of living in a more difficult sign. Like world leaders who've had to struggle for greatness, this planet may actually develop great strength and character.

Here's a list of the best places for each planet to be. Note that, as new planets were discovered, they replaced

the traditional rulers of signs which best complemented their energies.

ARIES—Mars
TAURUS—Venus, in its most sensual form
GEMINI—Mercury, in its communicative role
CANCER—the moon
LEO—the sun
VIRGO—also Mercury, this time in its more critical capacity
LIBRA—also Venus, in its more aesthetic, judgmental form
SCORPIO—Pluto, replacing Mars, the sign's original ruler
SAGITTARIUS—Jupiter
CAPRICORN—Saturn
AQUARIUS—Uranus, replacing Saturn, its original ruler
PISCES—Neptune, replacing Jupiter, its original ruler

A person who has many planets in exalted signs is lucky indeed, for here is where the planet can accomplish the most and be its most influential and creative.

SUN—exalted in Aries, where its energy creates action
MOON—exalted in Taurus, where instincts and reactions operate on a highly creative level
MERCURY—exalted in Aquarius, where it can reach analytical heights
VENUS—exalted in Pisces, a sign whose sensitivity encourages love and creativity
MARS—exalted in Capricorn, a sign that puts energy to work productively
JUPITER—exalted in Cancer, where it encourages nurturing and growth
SATURN—at home in Libra, where it steadies the scales of justice and promotes balanced, responsible judgment
URANUS—powerful in Scorpio, where it promotes transformation
NEPTUNE—especially favored in Cancer, where it gains the security to transcend to a higher state
PLUTO—exalted in Pisces, where it dissolves the old cycle to make way for transition to the new

# The Personal Planets: Mercury, Venus, and Mars

These planets work in your immediate personal life.

Mercury affects how you communicate and how your mental processes work. Are you a quick study who grasps information rapidly? Or do you learn more slowly and thoroughly? How is your concentration? Can you express yourself easily? Are you a good writer? All these questions can be answered by your Mercury placement.

Venus shows what you react to. What turns you on? What appeals to you aesthetically? Are you charming to others? Are you attractive to look at? Your taste, your refinement, your sense of balance and proportion are all Venus-ruled.

Mars is your outgoing energy, your drive and ambition. Do you reach out for new adventures? Are you assertive? Are you motivated? Self-confident? Hot-tempered? How you channel your energy and drive is revealed by your Mars placement.

# Mercury Shows How Your Mind Works

In our cookbook analogy, Mercury would be the rccipe instructions. Mercury shows how you think and speak, how logical you are. Since it stays close to the sun, read the description for Mercury in your sun sign, then the sign preceding and following it. Then decide which reflects the way you think.

## Mercury in Aries

Your mind is very active and assertive. It approaches a plan aggressively. You never hesitate to say what you think, never shy away from a battle. In fact, you may relish a verbal confrontation. Tact is not your strong point, so you may have to learn not to trip over your tongue.

## Mercury in Taurus

This is a cautious Mercury. Though you may be a slow learner, you have good concentration and mental stamina. You want to make your ideas really happen. You'll attack a problem methodically and consider every angle thoroughly, never jumping to conclusions. You'll stick with a subject until you master it.

## Mercury in Gemini

You are a wonderful communicator with great facility for expressing yourself both verbally and in writing. You love gathering all kinds of information. You probably finish other people's sentences, and express yourself with eloquent hand gestures. You can talk to anybody anytime . . . and probably have phone and e-mail bills to prove it. You read anything from sci-fi to Shakespeare, and might need an extra room just for your book collection. Though you learn fast, you may lack focus and discipline. Watch a tendency to jump from subject to subject.

## Mercury in Cancer

You rely on intuition more than logic. Your mental processes are usually colored by your emotions, so you may seem shy or hesitant to voice your opinions. However, this placement gives you the advantage of great imagination and empathy in the way you communicate with others.

## Mercury in Leo

You are enthusiastic and very dramatic in the way you express yourself. You like to hold the attention of groups, and could be a great public speaker. Your mind thinks big, so you prefer to deal with the overall picture rather than with the details.

## Mercury in Virgo

This is one of the best places for Mercury. It should give you critical ability, attention to details, and thorough analysis. Your mind focuses on the practical side of things. This type of thinking is very well suited to being a teacher or editor.

## Mercury in Libra

You're either a born diplomat who smoothes over ruffled feathers or a talented debater. Many lawyers have this placement. However, since you're forever weighing the pros and cons of a situation, you may vacillate when making decisions.

## Mercury in Scorpio

This is an investigative mind that stops at nothing to get the answers. You may have a sarcastic, stinging wit or a gift for the cutting remark. There's always a grain of truth to your verbal sallies, thanks to your penetrating insight.

## Mercury in Sagittarius

You are a supersalesman with a tendency to expound. Though you are very broad-minded, you can be dogmatic when it comes to telling others what's good for them. You won't hesitate to tell the truth as you see it, so watch a tendency toward tactlessness. On the plus side, you have a great sense of humor. This position of Mercury is often considered by astrologers to be at a disadvantage because Sagittarius opposes Gemini, the sign Mercury rules, and squares off with Virgo, another Mercury-ruled sign. What often happens is that Mercury in Sagittarius oversteps its bounds and loses sight of the facts in a situation. Do a reality check before making promises you may not be able to deliver.

### Mercury in Capricorn

This placement endows good mental discipline. You have a love of learning and a very orderly approach to your subjects. You will patiently plod through the facts and figures until you have mastered the tasks. You grasp structured situations easily, but may be short on creativity.

### Mercury in Aquarius

An independent, original thinker, you'll have more cutting-edge ideas than the average person. You will be quick to check out any unusual opportunities. Your opinions are so well-researched and grounded that once your mind is made up, it is difficult to change.

### Mercury in Pisces

You have the psychic and intuitive mind of a natural poet. Learn to make use of your creative imagination. You may think in terms of helping others, but check a tendency to be vague and forgetful of details.

## Venus: The Sweet Things

In our recipe analogy, Venus would be dessert. Venus shows where you receive pleasure, what you love to do. Find your Venus placement from the charts at the end of this chapter by looking for the year of your birth in the left-hand column. Then follow the line of that year across the page until you reach the time period of your birthday. The sign heading that column will be your Venus. If you were born on a day when Venus was changing signs, check the signs preceding or following that day to determine if that sign feels more like your Venus nature.

### Venus in Aries

You can't stand to be bored, confined, or ordered around. But a good challenge, maybe even a rousing row, turns you

on. Confess—don't you pick a fight now and then just to get someone stirred up? You're attracted by the chase, not the catch, which could cause some problems in your love life if the object of your affection becomes too attainable. You like to wear red, and you can spot a trend before anyone else.

## Venus in Taurus

All your senses work in high gear. You love to be surrounded by glorious tastes, smells, textures, sounds, and visuals. Austerity is not for you! Neither is being rushed. You like time to enjoy your pleasures. Soothing surroundings with plenty of creature comforts are your cup of tea. You like to feel secure in your nest, with no sudden jolts or surprises. You like familiar objects—in fact, you may hate to let anything or anyone go.

## Venus in Gemini

You are a lively, sparkling personality who thrives in a situation that affords a constant variety and a frequent change of scenery. A varied social life is important to you, with plenty of stimulation and a chance to engage in some light flirtation. Commitment may be difficult, because playing the field is so much fun.

## Venus in Cancer

An atmosphere where you feel protected, coddled, and mothered is best for you. You love to be surrounded by children in a cozy, homelike situation. You are attracted to those who are tender and nurturing, who make you feel secure and well provided for. You may be quite secretive about your emotional life, or attracted to clandestine relationships.

## Venus in Leo

First-class attention in large doses turns you on, and so does the glitter of real gold and the flash of mirrors. You

like to feel like a star at all times, surrounded by your admiring audience. The side effect is that you may be attracted to flatterers and tinsel, while the real gold requires some digging.

## Venus in Virgo

Everything neatly in its place? On the surface, you are attracted to an atmosphere where everything is in perfect order, but underneath are some basic, earthy urges. You are attracted to those who appeal to your need to teach, to be of service, or to play out a Pygmalion fantasy. You are at your best when you are busy doing something useful.

## Venus in Libra

Elegance and harmony are your key words. You can't abide an atmosphere of contention. Your taste tends toward the classic, with light harmonies of color—nothing clashing, trendy, or outrageous. You love doing things with a partner, and should be careful to pick one who is decisive but patient enough to let you weigh the pros and cons. And steer clear of argumentative types!

## Venus in Scorpio

Hidden mysteries intrigue you. In fact, anything that is too open and aboveboard is a bit of a bore. You surely have a stack of whodunits by the bed, along with an erotic magazine or two. You like to solve puzzles, and may also be fascinated with the occult, crime, or scientific research. Intense, all-or-nothing situations add spice to your life, and you love to ferret out the secrets of others. But you could get burned by your flair for living dangerously. The color black, spicy food, dark wood furniture, and heady perfume all get you in the right mood.

## Venus in Sagittarius

If you are not actually a world traveler, your surroundings are sure to reflect your love of faraway places. You like a

casual outdoor atmosphere and a dog or two to pet. There should be plenty of room for athletic equipment and suitcases. You're attracted to kindred souls who love to travel and who share your freedom-loving philosophy of life. Athletics and spiritual or New Age pursuits could be other interests.

## Venus in Capricorn

No fly-by-night relationships for you! You want substance in life, and you are attracted to whatever will help you get where you are going. Status objects turn you on. And so do those who have a serious, responsible, businesslike approach as well as those who remind you of a beloved parent. It is characteristic of this placement to be attracted to someone of a different generation. Antiques, traditional clothing, and dignified behavior are becoming to you.

## Venus in Aquarius

This Venus wants to make friends, to be "cool." You like to be in a group, particularly one pushing a worthy cause. You feel quite at home surrounded by people, and could even court fame. Yet all the while you remain detached from any intense commitment. Original ideas and unpredictable people fascinate you. You don't like everything to be planned out in advance, preferring spontaneity and delightful surprises.

## Venus in Pisces

This Venus loves to give of yourself, and you find plenty of takers. Stray animals and people appeal to your heart and your pocketbook, but be careful to look at their motives realistically once in a while. You are extremely vulnerable to sob stories of all kinds. Fantasy, the arts (especially film, dance, and theater), and psychic or spiritual activities also speak to you.

## Mars: Hot and Spicy

In your cosmic recipe, Mars provides the heat and spice. It is the mover and shaker in your life. It shows how you pursue your goals, whether you have energy to burn or proceed at a slow, steady pace. It will also show how you get angry. Do you explode or do a slow burn or hold everything inside, then get revenge later?

To find your Mars, turn to the charts on pages 86–94. Then find your birth year in the left-hand column and trace the line across horizontally until you come to the column headed by the month of your birth. There you will find an abbreviation of your Mars sign. If the description of your Mars sign doesn't ring true, read the description of the sign preceding and following it. You may have been born on a day when Mars was changing signs, in which case your Mars might be in the adjacent sign.

## Mars in Aries

In the sign it rules, Mars shows its brilliant fiery nature. You have an explosive temper and can be quite impatient. On the other hand, you have tremendous courage, energy, and drive. You'll let nothing stand in your way as you race to be first! Obstacles are met head-on and broken through by force. However, those that require patience and persistence can have you exploding in rage. You're a great starter, but not necessarily around for the finish.

## Mars in Taurus

Slow, steady, concentrated energy gives you staying power to last until the finish line. You have great stamina, and you never give up. Your tactic is to wear away obstacles with your persistence. Often you come out a winner because you've had the patience to hang in there. When angered, you do a slow burn.

## Mars in Gemini

You can't sit still for long. This Mars craves variety. You often have two or more things going on at once—it's all an amusing game to you. Your life can get very complicated, but that only adds spice and stimulation. What drives you into a nervous, hyper state? Boredom, sameness, routine, and confinement. You can do wonderful things with your hands, and you have a way with words.

## Mars in Cancer

You rarely attack head-on. Instead, you'll keep things to yourself, make plans in secret, and always cover your actions. This might be interpreted by some as manipulative, but you are only being self-protective. You get furious when anyone knows too much about you. But you do like to know all about others. Your mothering and feeding instincts can be put to good use if you work in the food, hotel, or child-care business. You may have to overcome your fragile sense of security, which prompts you not to take risks and to get physically upset when criticized. Don't take things so personally!

## Mars in Leo

You have a very dominant personality that takes center stage. Modesty is not one of your traits, nor is taking a backseat. You prefer giving the orders, and have been known to make a dramatic scene if they are not obeyed. Properly used, this Mars confers leadership ability, endurance, and courage.

## Mars in Virgo

You are the faultfinder of the zodiac. You notice every detail. Mistakes of any kind make you very nervous. You may worry, even if everything is going smoothly. You may not express your anger directly, but you sure can nag. You have definite likes and dislikes, and you are sure you can do the job better than anyone else. You are certainly more

industrious and detail-oriented than other signs. Your Mars energy is often most positively expressed in some kind of teaching role.

## Mars in Libra

This Mars will have a passion for beauty, justice, and art. Generally, you will avoid confrontations at all costs. You prefer to spend your energy finding diplomatic solutions or weighing pros and cons. Your other techniques are passive aggression or exercising your well-known charm to get people to do what you want.

## Mars in Scorpio

This is a powerful placement, so intense that it demands careful channeling into worthwhile activities. Otherwise, you could become obsessed with your sexuality or might use your need for power and control to manipulate others. You are strong-willed, shrewd, and very private about your affairs, and you'll usually have a secret agenda behind your actions. Your great stamina, focus, and discipline would be excellent assets for careers in the military or medical fields, especially research or surgery. When angry, you don't get mad—you get even!

## Mars in Sagittarius

This expansive Mars often propels people into sales, travel, athletics, or philosophy. Your energies function well when you are on the move. You have a hot temper, and are inclined to say what you think before you consider the consequences. You shoot for high goals—and talk endlessly about them—but you may be weak on groundwork. This Mars needs a solid foundation. Watch a tendency to take unnecessary risks.

## Mars in Capricorn

This is an ambitious Mars with an excellent sense of timing. You have an eye for those who can be of use to you, and

you may dismiss people ruthlessly when you're angry, but you drive yourself hard and deliver full value. This is a good placement for an executive. You'll aim for status and a high material position in life, and you'll keep climbing despite the odds. A great Mars to have!

### Mars in Aquarius

This is the most rebellious Mars. You seem to have a drive to assert yourself against the status quo. You may enjoy provoking people, shocking them out of traditional views. Or this placement could express itself in an offbeat sex life. Somehow you often find yourself in unconventional situations. You enjoy being a leader of an active group, which pursues forward-looking studies, politics, or goals.

### Mars in Pisces

This Mars is a good actor who knows just how to appeal to the sympathies of others. You create and project wonderful fantasies, or you use your sensitive antennae to crusade for those less fortunate. You get what you want through creating a veil of illusion and glamour. This is a good Mars for someone in the creative and imaginative fields—a dancer, performer, photographer, actor. Many famous film stars have this placement. Watch a tendency to manipulate by making others feel sorry for you.

## Jupiter Piles the Plate High

In our recipe analogy, Jupiter would be the high-carb dish that can add on pounds. This big, bright, swirling mass of gases is associated with abundance, prosperity, and the kind of windfall you get without too much hard work. You're optimistic under Jupiter's influence, when anything seems possible. You'll travel, expand your mind with higher education, and publish to share your knowledge widely. On the other hand, Jupiter's influence is neither discriminating nor disciplined. It represents the principle of growth without

judgment, and therefore could result in extravagance, weight gain, laziness, and carelessness, if not kept in check.

Be sure to look up your Jupiter in the tables in this book. When the current position of Jupiter is favorable, you may get that lucky break. This is a great time to try new things, take risks, travel, or get more education. Opportunities seem to open up easily, so take advantage of them.

Once a year, Jupiter changes signs. That means you are due for an expansive time every twelve years, when Jupiter travels through your sun sign. You'll also have up periods every four years, when Jupiter is in the same element as your sun sign.

## Jupiter in Aries

You are the soul of enthusiasm and optimism. Your luckiest times are when you are getting started on an exciting project or selling an idea that you really believe in. You may have to watch a tendency to be arrogant with those who do not share your enthusiasm. You follow your impulses, often ignoring budget or other commonsense limitations. To produce real, solid benefits, you'll need patience and follow-through wherever this Jupiter falls in your horoscope.

## Jupiter in Taurus

You'll spend on beautiful material things, especially those that come from nature—items made of rare woods, natural fabrics, or precious gems, for instance. You can't have too much comfort or too many sensual pleasures. Watch a tendency to overindulge in good food, or to overpamper yourself with nothing but the best. Spartan living is not for you! You may be especially lucky in matters of real estate.

## Jupiter in Gemini

You are the great talker of the zodiac, and you may be a great writer, too. But restlessness could be your weak point. You jump around, talk too much, and could be a jack-of-all-trades. Keeping a secret is especially difficult, so you'll

have to watch a tendency to spill the beans. Since you love to be at the center of a beehive of activity, you'll have a vibrant social life. Your best opportunities will come through your talent for language—speaking, writing, communicating, and selling.

## Jupiter in Cancer

You are luckiest in situations where you can find emotional closeness or deal with basic security needs such as food, nurturing, or shelter. You may be a great collector. Or you may simply love to accumulate things—you are the one who stashes things away for a rainy day. You probably have a very good memory and love children. In fact, you may have many children to care for. The food, hotel, child-care, and shipping businesses hold good opportunities for you.

## Jupiter in Leo

You are a natural showman who loves to live in a larger-than-life way. Yours is a personality full of color that always finds its way into the limelight. You can't have too much attention or applause. Showbiz is a natural place for you, and so is any area where you can play to a crowd. Exercising your flair for drama, your natural playfulness, and your romantic nature brings you good fortune. But watch a tendency to be overly extravagant or to monopolize center stage.

## Jupiter in Virgo

You actually love those minute details others find boring. To you, they make all the difference between the perfect and the ordinary. You are the fine craftsman who spots every flaw. You expand your awareness by finding the most efficient methods and by being of service to others. Many of you will be drawn to medical or teaching fields. You'll also have luck in publishing, crafts, nutrition, and service professions. Watch out for a tendency to overwork.

## Jupiter in Libra

This is an other-directed Jupiter that develops best with a partner. The stimulation of others helps you grow. You are also most comfortable in harmonious, beautiful situations and you work well with artistic people. You have a great sense of fair play and an ability to evaluate the pros and cons of a situation. You usually prefer to play the role of diplomat rather than adversary.

## Jupiter in Scorpio

You love the feeling of power and control, of taking things to their limit. You can't resist a mystery. Your shrewd, penetrating mind sees right through to the heart of most situations and people. You have luck in work that provides for solutions to matters of life and death. You may be drawn to undercover work, behind-the-scenes intrigue, psychotherapy, the occult, and sex-related ventures. Your challenge will be to develop a sense of moderation and tolerance for other beliefs. This Jupiter can be fanatical. You may have luck in handling other people's money—insurance, taxes, and inheritance can bring you a windfall.

## Jupiter in Sagittarius

Independent, outgoing, and idealistic, you'll shoot for the stars. This Jupiter compels you to travel far and wide, both physically and mentally, via higher education. You may have luck while traveling in an exotic place. You also have luck with outdoor ventures, exercise, and animals, particularly horses. Since you tend to be very open about your opinions, watch a tendency to be tactless and to exaggerate. Instead, use your wonderful sense of humor to make your point.

## Jupiter in Capricorn

Jupiter is much more restrained in Capricorn, the sign of rules and authority. Here, Jupiter can make you overwork and heighten any ambition or sense of duty you may have.

You'll expand in areas that advance your position, putting you farther up the social or corporate ladder. You are lucky working within the establishment in a very structured situation where you can show off your ability to organize and reap rewards for your hard work.

### Jupiter in Aquarius

This is another freedom-loving Jupiter, with great tolerance and originality. You are at your best when you are working for a humanitarian cause and in the company of many supporters. This is a good Jupiter for a political career. You'll relate to all kinds of people on all social levels. You have an abundance of original ideas, but you are best off away from routine and any situation that imposes rigid rules. You need mental stimulation!

### Jupiter in Pisces

You are a giver whose feelings and pocketbook are easily touched by others, so choose your companions with care. You could be the original sucker for a hard-luck story. Better find a worthy hospital or a charity that will appreciate your selfless support. You have a great creative imagination. You may attract good fortune in fields related to oil, perfume, pharmaceuticals, petroleum, dance, footwear, and alcohol. But beware of overindulgence in alcohol—focus on a creative outlet instead.

## Saturn Is a Disciplined Diet

Jupiter speeds you up with *lucky breaks* and quick energy. Then along comes Saturn to slow you down with the *disciplinary brakes* and slow-burning energy. It is the part of your planetary diet that helps you achieve lasting goals. Saturn has unfairly been called a malefic planet, one of the bad guys of the zodiac. On the contrary, Saturn is one of our best friends, the kind who tells you what you need to hear even if it's not good news. Under a Saturn transit, we

grow up, take responsibility for our lives, and emerge from whatever test this planet has in store as far wiser, more capable and mature human beings. It is when we are under pressure that we grow stronger.

Look up your natal Saturn in the tables in this book for clues on where you need work.

## Saturn in Aries

Saturn here puts the brakes on Aries' natural drive and enthusiasm. There is often an angry side to this placement. You don't let anyone push you around, and you know what's best for yourself. Following orders is not your strong point, and neither is diplomacy. You tend to be quick to go on the offensive in relationships, attacking first, before anyone attacks you. Because no one quite lives up to your standards, you often wind up doing everything yourself. You'll have to learn to cooperate and tone down self-centeredness. Both Pat Buchanan and Saddam Hussein have this Saturn.

## Saturn in Taurus

A big issue is getting control of the cash flow. There will be lean periods that can be frightening, but you have the patience and endurance to stick them out and the methodical drive to prosper in the end. Learn to take a philosophical attitude, like Ben Franklin, who also had this placement and who said, "A penny saved is a penny earned."

## Saturn in Gemini

You are a serious student of life, but you may have difficulty communicating or sharing your knowledge. You may be shy, speak slowly, or have fears about communicating, like Eleanor Roosevelt. You dwell in the realms of science, theory, or abstract analysis—even when you are dealing with the emotions, like Sigmund Freud, who also had this placement.

## Saturn in Cancer

Your tests come with establishing a secure emotional base. In doing so, you may have to deal with some very basic fears centering on your early home environment. Most of your Saturn tests will have emotional roots in those early childhood experiences. You may have difficulty remaining objective in terms of what you try to achieve. So it will be especially important for you to deal with negative feelings such as guilt, paranoia, jealousy, resentment, and suspicion. Galileo and Michelangelo also navigated these murky waters.

## Saturn in Leo

This is an authoritarian Saturn—a strict, demanding parent who may deny the pleasure principle in your zeal to see that rules are followed. Though you may feel guilty about taking the spotlight, you are very ambitious and loyal. You have to watch a tendency toward rigidity, also toward overwork and holding back affection. Joseph Kennedy and Billy Graham share this placement.

## Saturn in Virgo

This is a cautious, exacting Saturn. You are intensely hard on yourself. Most of all, you give yourself the roughest time with your constant worries about every little detail, often making yourself sick. You may have difficulties setting priorities and getting the job done. Your tests will come in learning tolerance and understanding of others. Charles de Gaulle, Mae West, and Nathaniel Hawthorne had this meticulous Saturn.

## Saturn in Libra

Saturn is exalted here, which makes this planet an ally. You may choose very serious, older partners in life, perhaps stemming from a fear of dependency. You need to learn to stand solidly on your own before you commit to another. You are extremely cautious as you deliberate every

involvement—with good reason. It is best that you find an occupation that makes good use of your sense of duty and honor. Steer clear of fly-by-night situations. Both Khrushchev and Mao Tse-tung had this placement.

## Saturn in Scorpio

You have great staying power. This Saturn tests you in situations involving the control of others. You may feel drawn to some kind of intrigue or undercover work, like J. Edgar Hoover. Or there may be an air of mystery surrounding your life and death, like Marilyn Monroe and Robert Kennedy, who both had this placement. There are lessons to be learned from your sexual involvements. Often sex is used for manipulation or is somehow out of the ordinary. The Roman emperor Caligula and the transsexual Christine Jorgensen are extreme cases.

## Saturn in Sagittarius

Your challenges and lessons will come from tests of your spiritual and philosophical values, as happened to Martin Luther King and Gandhi. You are high-minded and sincere with this reflective, moral placement. Uncompromising in your ethical standards, you could become a benevolent despot.

## Saturn in Capricorn

With the help of Saturn at maximum strength, your judgment will improve with age. And like Spencer Tracy's screen image, you'll be the gray-haired hero with a strong sense of responsibility. You advance in life slowly but steadily, always with a strong hand at the helm and an eye for the advantageous situation. Like Pat Robertson, you're likely to stand for conservative values. Negatively, you may be a loner, prone to periods of melancholy.

## Saturn in Aquarius

Your tests come from relationships with groups. Do you care too much about what others think? Do you feel like an outsider, like Greta Garbo? You may fear being different from others and therefore slight your own unique, forward-looking gifts. Or like Lord Byron and Howard Hughes, you may take the opposite tack and rebel in the extreme. You can apply discipline to accomplish great humanitarian goals, as Albert Schweitzer did.

## Saturn in Pisces

Your fear of the unknown and the irrational may lead you to the safety and protection of an institution. You may go on the run like Jesse James, who had this placement, to avoid looking too deeply inside. Or you might go in the opposite, more positive direction and develop a disciplined psychoanalytic approach, which puts you more in control of your feelings. Some of you will take refuge in work with hospitals, charities, or religious institutions. Queen Victoria, who had this placement, symbolized an era when institutions of all kinds were sustained. Discipline applied to artistic work, especially poetry and dance, or to spiritual work, such as yoga or meditation, might be helpful.

# How Uranus, Neptune, and Pluto Influence a Whole Generation

These three planets remain in signs such a long time that a whole generation bears the imprint of the sign. Mass movements, great sweeping changes, fads that characterize a generation, even the issues of the conflicts and wars of the time are influenced by these "outer three" planets. When one of those distant planets changes signs, there is a definite shift in the atmosphere, the feeling of the end of an era.

Since these planets are so far away from the sun—too distant to be seen by the naked eye—they pick up signals

from the universe at large. These planetary receivers literally link the sun with distant energies, and then perform a similar function in your horoscope by linking your central character with intuitive, spiritual, transformative forces from the cosmos. Each planet has a special domain, and will reflect this in the area of your chart where it falls.

## Uranus Is the Surprise Ingredient

In your cosmic recipe, Uranus is the unexpected ingredient that sets you and your generation apart. There is nothing ordinary about this quirky green planet that seems to be traveling on its side, surrounded by a swarm of moons. Is it any wonder that astrologers assigned it to Aquarius, the most eccentric and gregarious sign? Uranus seems to wend its way around the sun, marching to its own tune.

Significantly, Uranus follows Saturn, the planet of limitations and structures. Often we get caught up in the structures we have created to give ourselves a sense of security. However, if we lose contact with our spiritual roots, then Uranus is likely to jolt us out of our comfortable rut and wake us up.

Uranus energy is electrical, happening in sudden flashes. It is not influenced by karma or past events, nor does it regard tradition, sex, or sentiment. The Uranus key words are surprise and awakening. Suddenly, there's that flash of inspiration, that bright idea, that totally new approach to revolutionize whatever scheme you were undertaking. A Uranus event takes you by surprise; it happens from out of the blue, for better or for worse. The Uranus place in your life is where you awaken and become your own person, leaving the structures of Saturn behind. And it is probably the most unconventional place in your chart.

Look up the sign of Uranus at the time of your birth and see where you follow your own tune.

### Uranus in Aries

Birth Dates:

March 31, 1927–November 4, 1927

January 13, 1928–June 6, 1934
October 10, 1934–March 28, 1935

Your generation is original, creative, pioneering. It developed the computer, the airplane, and the cyclotron. You let nothing hold you back from exploring the unknown, and you have a powerful mixture of fire and electricity behind you. Women of your generation were among the first to be liberated. You were the unforgettable style setters. You have a surprise in store for everyone. Like Yoko Ono, Grace Kelly, and Jacqueline Onassis, your life may be jolted by sudden and violent changes.

## Uranus in Taurus

Birth Dates:
June 6, 1934–October 10, 1934
March 28, 1935–August 7, 1941
October 5, 1941–May 15, 1942

The great territorial shake-ups of World War II began during your generation. You are independent, probably self-employed or would like to be. You have original ideas about making money, and you brace yourself for sudden changes of fortune. This Uranus can cause shake-ups, particularly in finances, but it can also make you a born entrepreneur.

## Uranus in Gemini

Birth Dates:
August 7, 1941–October 5, 1941
May 15, 1942–August 30, 1948
November 12, 1948–June 10, 1949

You were the first children to be influenced by television. Now, in your adult years, your generation stocks up on answering machines, cell phones, computers, and fax machines—any new way you can communicate. You have an inquiring mind, but your interests may be rather short-lived. This Uranus can be easily fragmented if there is no structure and focus.

## Uranus in Cancer

Birth Dates:
August 30, 1948–November 12, 1948
June 10, 1949–August 24, 1955
January 28, 1956–June 10, 1956

This generation came at a time when divorce was becoming commonplace, so your home image is unconventional. You may have an unusual relationship with your parents; you may have come from a broken home or an unconventional one. You'll have unorthodox ideas about parenting, intimacy, food, and shelter. You may also be interested in dreams, psychic phenomena, and memory work.

## Uranus in Leo

Birth Dates:
August 24, 1955–January 28, 1956
June 10, 1956–November 1, 1961
January 10, 1962–August 10, 1962

This generation understood how to use electronic media. Many of your group are now leaders in the high-tech industries, and you also understand how to use the new media to promote yourself. Like Isadora Duncan, you may have a very eccentric kind of charisma and a life that is sparked by unusual love affairs. Your children, too, may have traits that are out of the ordinary. Where this planet falls in your chart, you'll have a love of freedom, be a bit of an egomaniac, and show the full force of your personality in a unique way, like tennis great Martina Navratilova.

## Uranus in Virgo

Birth Dates:
November 1, 1961–January 10, 1962
August 10, 1962–September 28, 1968
May 20, 1969–June 24, 1969

You'll have highly individual work methods. Many of you will be finding newer, more practical ways to use computers. Like Einstein, who had this placement, you'll break the rules brilliantly. Your generation came at a time of student

rebellions, the civil rights movement, and the general acceptance of health foods. Chances are, you're concerned about pollution and cleaning up the environment. You may also be involved with nontraditional healing methods.

## Uranus in Libra

Birth Dates:
September 28, 1968–May 20, 1969
June 24, 1969–November 21, 1974
May 1, 1975–September 8, 1975

Your generation will be always changing partners. Born during the era of women's liberation, you may have come from a broken home and have no clear image of what a marriage entails. There will be many sudden splits and experiments before you settle down. Your generation will be much involved in legal and political reforms and in changing artistic and fashion looks.

## Uranus in Scorpio

Birth Dates:
November 21, 1974–May 1, 1975
September 8, 1975–February 17, 1981
March 20, 1981–November 16, 1981

Interest in transformation, meditation, and life after death signaled the beginning of New Age consciousness. Your generation recognizes no boundaries, no limits, and no external controls. You'll have new attitudes toward death and dying, psychic phenomena, and the occult. Like Mae West and Casanova, you'll shock 'em sexually, too.

## Uranus in Sagittarius

Birth Dates:
February 17, 1981–March 20, 1981
November 16, 1981–February 15, 1988
May 27, 1988–December 2, 1988

Could this generation be the first to travel in outer space? An earlier generation with this placement included Charles Lindbergh and a time when the first zeppelins and

the Wright Brothers were conquering the skies. Uranus here forecasts great discoveries, mind expansion, and long-distance travel. Like Galileo and Martin Luther, those born in these years will generate new theories about the cosmos and mankind's relation to it.

## Uranus in Capricorn

Birth Dates:
December 20, 1904–January 30, 1912
September 4, 1912–November 12, 1912
February 15, 1988–May 27, 1988
December 2, 1988–April 1, 1995
June 9, 1995–January 12, 1996

This generation, now growing up, will challenge traditions with the help of electronic gadgets. In these years, we got organized with the help of technology put to practical use. The Internet was born following the great economic boom of the 1990s. Great leaders who were movers and shakers of history, like Julius Caesar and Henry VIII, were born under this placement.

## Uranus in Aquarius

Birth Dates:
January 30, 1912–September 4, 1912
November 12, 1912–April 1, 1919
August 16, 1919–January 22, 1920
April 1, 1995–June 9, 1995
January 12, 1996–March 10, 2003
September 15, 2003–December 30, 2003

Uranus in Aquarius is the strongest placement for this planet. Recently we've had the opportunity to witness the full force of its power of innovation, as well as its sudden wake-up calls and insistence on humanitarian values. This was a time of high-tech development, when home computers became as ubiquitous as television. It was a time of globalization, of surprise attacks (9/11), and underdeveloped countries demanding attention. The last generation with this placement produced great innovative minds such as Leonard Bernstein and Orson Welles. The next will be-

come another radical breakthrough generation, much concerned with global issues that involve all humanity.

## Uranus in Pisces

Birth Dates:
April 1, 1919–August 16, 1919
January 22, 1920–March 31, 1927
November 4, 1927–January 12, 1928
March 10, 2003–September 15, 2003
December 20, 2003–May 28, 2010

Uranus is now in Pisces, ushering in a new generation. In the past century, Uranus in Pisces focused attention on the rise of electronic entertainment—radio and the cinema—and the secretiveness of Prohibition. This produced a generation of idealists exemplified by Judy Garland's theme "Somewhere over the Rainbow." Uranus in Pisces also hints at stealth activities, at hospital and prison reform, at high-tech drugs and medical experiments, at shake-ups and reforms in the Pisces-ruled petroleum industry. Issues regarding the water and oil supply, water-related storm damage, sudden hurricanes, and floods demand our attention.

# Neptune Is the Magic Solvent

Neptune is the liquid in your horoscope recipe that dissolves other ingredients and creates a magical, inspired result. It is often maligned as the planet of illusions that dissolves reality, enabling you to escape the material world. Under Neptune's influence, you see what you want to see. But Neptune also encourages you to create. It embodies glamour, subtlety, mystery, and mysticism, and it governs anything that takes you beyond the mundane world, including out-of-body experiences.

Neptune acts to transcend your ordinary perceptions to take you to another level, where you experience either confusion or ecstasy. Its force can pull you off course only if you allow this to happen. Those who use Neptune wisely can translate their daydreams into poetry, theater, design,

or inspired moves in the business world, avoiding the tricky "con artist" side of this planet.
Find your Neptune listed below.

## Neptune in Cancer

Birth Dates:
July 19, 1901–December 25, 1901
May 21, 1902–September 23, 1914
December 14, 1914–July 19, 1915
March 19, 1916–May 2, 1916

Dreams of the homeland, idealistic patriotism, and glamorization of the nurturing assets of women characterized this time. You who were born here have unusual psychic ability and deep insights into basic needs of others.

## Neptune in Leo

Birth Dates:
September 23, 1914–December 14, 1914
July 19, 1915–March 19, 1916
May 2, 1916–September 21, 1928
February 19, 1929–July 24, 1929

Neptune in Leo brought us the glamour and high living of the 1920s and the big spenders of that time. The Neptune temptations of gambling, seduction, theater, and lavish entertaining distracted from the realities of the age. Those born in that generation also made great advances in the arts.

## Neptune in Virgo

Birth Dates:
September 21, 1928–February 19, 1929
July 24, 1929–October 3, 1942
April 17, 1943–August 2, 1943

Neptune in Virgo encompassed the 1930s, the Great Depression, and the beginning of World War II, when a new order was born. There was a time of facing "what doesn't work." Many were unemployed and found solace at the movies, watching the great Virgo star Greta Garbo or the

escapist dance films of Busby Berkeley. New public services were born. Those with Neptune in Virgo later spread the gospel of health and fitness. This generation's devotion to spending hours at the office inspired the term *workaholic*.

## Neptune in Libra

Birth Dates:

October 3, 1942–April 17, 1943
August 2, 1943–December 24, 1955
March 12, 1956–October 19, 1956
June 15, 1957–August 6, 1957

This was the time of World War II and the postwar period, when the world regained balance and returned to relative stability. Neptune in Libra was the romantic generation who would later be concerned with relating. As this generation matured, there was a new trend toward marriage and commitment. Racial and sexual equality became important issues, as they redesigned traditional roles to suit modern times.

## Neptune in Scorpio

Birth Dates:

December 24, 1955–March 12, 1956
October 19, 1956–June 15, 1957
August 6, 1957–January 4, 1970
May 3, 1970–November 6, 1970

Neptune in Scorpio brought in a generation that would become interested in transformative power. Born in an era that glamorized sex, drugs, rock and roll, and Eastern religion, they matured in a more sobering time of AIDS, cocaine abuse, and New Age spirituality. As they evolve, they will become active in healing the planet from the results of the abuse of power.

## Neptune in Sagittarius

Birth Dates:

January 4, 1970–May 3, 1970
November 6, 1970–January 19, 1984

June 23, 1984–November 21, 1984

Neptune in Sagittarius was the time when space and astronaut travel became a reality. The Neptune influence glamorized new approaches to mysticism, religion, and mind expansion. This generation will take a new approach to spiritual life, with emphasis on visions, mysticism, and clairvoyance.

## Neptune in Capricorn

Birth Dates:

January 19, 1984–June 23, 1984

November 21, 1984–January 29, 1998

Neptune in Capricorn brought a time when delusions about material power were glamorized in the mid–1980s and 1990s. There was a boom in the stock market, and the Internet era spawned young tycoons who later lost it all. It was also a time when the psychic and occult worlds spawned a new category of business enterprise, and sold services on television.

## Neptune in Aquarius

Birth Dates:

January 29, 1998–April 4, 2011

This should continue to be a time of breakthroughs. Here the creative influence of Neptune reaches a universal audience. This is a time of dissolving barriers, of globalization—when we truly become one world. During this transit of high-tech Aquarius, new kinds of entertainment media reach across cultural differences. However, the transit of Neptune has also raised boundary issues between cultures, especially in Middle Eastern countries with Neptune-ruled oil fields. As Neptune raises issues of social and political structures not being as solid as they seem, this could continue to produce rebellion and chaos in the environment. However, by using imagination (Neptune) in partnership with a global view (Aquarius) we could reach creative solutions.

Those born with this placement should be true citizens of the world with a remarkable creative ability to transcend social and cultural barriers.

## Pluto Can Transform You

Add a small touch of Pluto to your recipe and it will change the dish completely! Though it is a tiny planet, its influence is great. When Pluto zaps a strategic point in your horoscope, your life changes dramatically.

This little planet is the power behind the scenes; it affects you at deep levels of consciousness, causing events to come to the surface that will transform you and your generation. Nothing escapes, or is sacred, with this probing planet. Its purpose is to wipe out the past so something new can happen.

The Pluto place in your horoscope is where you have invisible power (Mars governs the visible power), where you can transform, heal, and affect the unconscious needs of the masses. Pluto tells lots about how your generation projects power, what makes it seem cool to others. And when Pluto changes signs, there is a whole new concept of what's cool. Pluto's strange elliptical orbit occasionally runs inside the orbit of neighboring Neptune. Because of its eccentric path, the length of time Pluto stays in any given sign can vary from thirteen to thirty-two years. It covered only seven signs in the last century.

## Pluto in Gemini

Birth Dates:

Late 1800s–May 26, 1914

This was a time of mass suggestion and breakthroughs in communications, a time when many brilliant writers such as Ernest Hemingway and F. Scott Fitzgerald were born. Henry Miller, D. H. Lawrence, and James Joyce scandalized society by using explicit sexual images and language in their literature. "Muckraking" journalists exposed corruption. Pluto-ruled Scorpio President Theodore Roosevelt said, "Speak softly, but carry a big stick." This generation had an intense need to communicate and made major breakthroughs in knowledge. A compulsive restlessness and a thirst for a variety of experiences characterized many of this generation.

## Pluto in Cancer

Birth Dates:

May 26, 1914–June 14, 1939

Dictators and mass media arose to wield emotional power over the masses. Women's rights was a popular issue. Deep sentimental feelings, acquisitiveness, and possessiveness characterized these times and people. Most of the great stars of the Hollywood era that embodied the American image were born during this period: Grace Kelly, Esther Williams, Frank Sinatra, Lana Turner, to name a few.

## Pluto in Leo

Birth Dates:

June 14, 1939–August, 19, 1957

The performing arts played on the emotions of the masses. Mick Jagger, John Lennon, and rock and roll were born at this time. So were "baby boomers" like Bill and Hillary Clinton. Those born here tend to be self-centered, powerful, and boisterous. This generation does its own thing, for better or for worse.

## Pluto in Virgo

Birth Dates:

August 19, 1957–October 5, 1971
April 17, 1972–July 30, 1972

This is the "yuppie" generation that sparked a mass movement toward fitness, health, and career. It is a much more sober, serious, driven generation than the fun-loving Pluto in Leo. During this time, machines were invented to process detail work efficiently. Inventions took a practical turn with answering machines, fax machines, car phones, and home office equipment—all making the workplace far more efficient.

## Pluto in Libra

Birth Dates:

October 5, 1971–April 17, 1972

July 30, 1972–November 5, 1983
May 18, 1984–August 27, 1984

A mellower generation, people born at this time are concerned with partnerships, working together, and finding diplomatic solutions to problems. Marriage is important to this generation, and they will define it by combining traditional values with equal partnership. This was a time of women's liberation, gay rights, ERA, and legal battles over abortion, all of which transformed our ideas about relationships.

## Pluto in Scorpio

Birth Dates:

November 5, 1983–May 18, 1984
August 27, 1984–January 17, 1995

Pluto was in the sign it rules for a comparatively short period of time. However, this was a time of record achievements, destructive sexually transmitted diseases, nuclear power controversies, and explosive political issues. Pluto destroys in order to create new understanding—the phoenix rising from the ashes—which should be some consolation for those of you who felt Pluto's force before 1995. Sexual shockers were par for the course during these intense years when black clothing, transvestites, body piercing, tattoos, and sexually explicit advertising pushed the boundaries of good taste.

## Pluto in Sagittarius

Birth Dates:

January 17, 1995–April 20, 1995
November 10, 1995–January 26, 2008

During our current Pluto transit, we are being pushed to expand our horizons, to find deeper spiritual meaning in life. Pluto's opposition with Saturn in 2001 brought an enormous conflict between traditional societies and the forces of change. It signals a time when religious convictions will exert more power in our political life as well.

Since Sagittarius is the sign that rules travel, there's a good possibility that Pluto, the planet of extremes, will make space travel a reality for some of us. Already, we are

seeing wealthy adventurers paying for the privilege of travel on space shuttles. Discovery of life-forms on other planets could transform our ideas about where we came from.

New dimensions in electronic publishing, concern with animal rights and the environment, and an increasing emphasis on extreme forms of religion are other signs of these times. Look for charismatic religious leaders to arise now. We'll also be developing far-reaching philosophies designed to elevate our lives with a new sense of purpose.

# VENUS SIGNS 1901–2007

| | Aries | Taurus | Gemini | Cancer | Leo | Virgo |
|---|---|---|---|---|---|---|
| **1901** | 3/29–4/22 | 4/22–5/17 | 5/17–6/10 | 6/10–7/5 | 7/5–7/29 | 7/29–8/23 |
| **1902** | 5/7–6/3 | 6/3–6/30 | 6/30–7/25 | 7/25–8/19 | 8/19–9/13 | 9/13–10/7 |
| **1903** | 2/28–3/24 | 3/24–4/18 | 4/18–5/13 | 5/13–6/9 | 6/9–7/7 | 7/7–8/17 |
| | | | | | | 9/6–11/8 |
| **1904** | 3/13–5/7 | 5/7–6/1 | 6/1–6/25 | 6/25–7/19 | 7/19–8/13 | 8/13–9/6 |
| **1905** | 2/3–3/6 | 3/6–4/9 | 7/8–8/6 | 8/6–9/1 | 9/1–9/27 | 9/27–10/21 |
| | 4/9–5/28 | 5/28–7/8 | | | | |
| **1906** | 3/1–4/7 | 4/7–5/2 | 5/2–5/26 | 5/26–6/20 | 6/20–7/16 | 7/16–8/11 |
| **1907** | 4/27–5/22 | 5/22–6/16 | 6/16–7/11 | 7/11–8/4 | 8/4–8/29 | 8/29–9/22 |
| **1908** | 2/14–3/10 | 3/10–4/5 | 4/5–5/5 | 5/5–9/8 | 9/8–10/8 | 10/8–11/3 |
| **1909** | 3/29–4/22 | 4/22–5/16 | 5/16–6/10 | 6/10–7/4 | 7/4–7/29 | 7/29–8/23 |
| **1910** | 5/7–6/3 | 6/4–6/29 | 6/30–7/24 | 7/25–8/18 | 8/19–9/12 | 9/13–10/6 |
| **1911** | 2/28–3/23 | 3/24–4/17 | 4/18–5/12 | 5/13–6/8 | 6/9–7/7 | 7/8–11/18 |
| **1912** | 4/13–5/6 | 5/7–5/31 | 6/1–6/24 | 6/24–7/18 | 7/19–8/12 | 8/13–9/5 |
| **1913** | 2/3–3/6 | 3/7–5/1 | 7/8–8/5 | 8/6–8/31 | 9/1–9/26 | 9/27–10/20 |
| | 5/2–5/30 | 5/31–7/7 | | | | |
| **1914** | 3/14–4/6 | 4/7–5/1 | 5/2–5/25 | 5/26–6/19 | 6/20–7/15 | 7/16–8/10 |
| **1915** | 4/27–5/21 | 5/22–6/15 | 6/16–7/10 | 7/11–8/3 | 8/4–8/28 | 8/29–9/21 |
| **1916** | 2/14–3/9 | 3/10–4/5 | 4/6–5/5 | 5/6–9/8 | 9/9–10/7 | 10/8–11/2 |
| **1917** | 3/29–4/21 | 4/22–5/15 | 5/16–6/9 | 6/10–7/3 | 7/4–7/28 | 7/29–8/21 |
| **1918** | 5/7–6/2 | 6/3–6/28 | 6/29–7/24 | 7/25–8/18 | 8/19–9/11 | 9/12–10/5 |
| **1919** | 2/27–3/22 | 3/23–4/16 | 4/17–5/12 | 5/13–6/7 | 6/8–7/7 | 7/8–11/8 |
| **1920** | 4/12–5/6 | 5/7–5/30 | 5/31–6/23 | 6/24–7/18 | 7/19–8/11 | 8/12–9/4 |
| **1921** | 2/3–3/6 | 3/7–4/25 | 7/8–8/5 | 8/6–8/31 | 9/1–9/25 | 9/26–10/20 |
| | 4/26–6/1 | 6/2–7/7 | | | | |
| **1922** | 3/13–4/6 | 4/7–4/30 | 5/1–5/25 | 5/26–6/19 | 6/20–7/14 | 7/15–8/9 |
| **1923** | 4/27–5/21 | 5/22–6/14 | 6/15–7/9 | 7/10–8/3 | 8/4–8/27 | 8/28–9/20 |
| **1924** | 2/13–3/8 | 3/9–4/4 | 4/5–5/5 | 5/6–9/8 | 9/9–10/7 | 10/8–11/12 |
| **1925** | 3/28–4/20 | 4/21–5/15 | 5/16–6/8 | 6/9–7/3 | 7/4–7/27 | 7/28–8/21 |

| Libra | Scorpio | Sagittarius | Capricorn | Aquarius | Pisces |
|---|---|---|---|---|---|
| 8/23–9/17 | 9/17–10/12 | 10/12–1/16 | 1/16–2/9 | 2/9–3/5 | 3/5–3/29 |
| | | | 11/7–12/5 | 12/5–1/11 | |
| 10/7–10/31 | 10/31–11/24 | 11/24–12/18 | 12/18–1/11 | 2/6–4/4 | 1/11–2/6 |
| | | | | | 4/4–5/7 |
| 8/17–9/6 | 12/9–1/5 | | | 1/11–2/4 | 2/4–2/28 |
| 11/8–12/9 | | | | | |
| 9/6–9/30 | 9/30–10/25 | 1/5–1/30 | 1/30–2/24 | 2/24–3/19 | 3/19–4/13 |
| | | 10/25–11/18 | 11/18–12/13 | 12/13–1/7 | |
| 10/21–11/14 | 11/14–12/8 | 12/8–1/1/06 | | | 1/7–2/3 |
| 8/11–9/7 | 9/7–10/9 | 10/9–12/15 | 1/1–1/25 | 1/25–2/18 | 2/18–3/14 |
| | 12/15–12/25 | 12/25–2/6 | | | |
| 9/22–10/16 | 10/16–11/9 | 11/9–12/3 | 2/6–3/6 | 3/6–4/2 | 4/2–4/27 |
| | | | 12/3–12/27 | 12/27–1/20 | |
| 11/3–11/28 | 11/28–12/22 | 12/22–1/15 | | | 1/20–2/4 |
| 8/23–9/17 | 9/17–10/12 | 10/12–11/17 | 1/15–2/9 | 2/9–3/5 | 3/5–3/29 |
| | | | 11/17–12/5 | 12/5–1/15 | |
| 10/7–10/30 | 10/31–11/23 | 11/24–12/17 | 12/18–12/31 | 1/1–1/15 | 1/16–1/28 |
| | | | | 1/29–4/4 | 4/5–5/6 |
| 11/19–12/8 | 12/9–12/31 | | 1/1–1/10 | 1/11–2/2 | 2/3–2/27 |
| 9/6–9/30 | 1/1–1/4 | 1/5–1/29 | 1/30–2/23 | 2/24–3/18 | 3/19–4/12 |
| | 10/1–10/24 | 10/25–11/17 | 11/18–12/12 | 12/13–12/31 | |
| 10/21–11/13 | 11/14–12/7 | 12/8–12/31 | | 1/1–1/6 | 1/7–2/2 |
| 8/11–9/6 | 9/7–10/9 | 10/10–12/5 | 1/1–1/24 | 1/25–2/17 | 2/18–3/13 |
| | 12/6–12/30 | 12/31 | | | |
| 9/22–10/15 | 10/16–11/8 | 1/1–2/6 | 2/7–3/6 | 3/7–4/1 | 4/2–4/26 |
| | | 11/9–12/2 | 12/3–12/26 | 12/27–12/31 | |
| 11/3–11/27 | 11/28–12/21 | 12/22–12/31 | | 1/1–1/19 | 1/20–2/13 |
| 8/22–9/16 | 9/17–10/11 | 1/1–1/14 | 1/15–2/7 | 2/8–3/4 | 3/5–3/28 |
| | | 10/12–11/6 | 11/7–12/5 | 12/6–12/31 | |
| 10/6–10/29 | 10/30–11/22 | 11/23–12/16 | 12/17–12/31 | 1/1–4/5 | 4/6–5/6 |
| 11/9–12/8 | 12/9–12/31 | | 1/1–1/9 | 1/10–2/2 | 2/3–2/26 |
| 9/5–9/30 | 1/1–1/3 | 1/4–1/28 | 1/29–2/22 | 2/23–3/18 | 3/19–4/11 |
| | 9/31–10/23 | 10/24–11/17 | 11/18–12/11 | 12/12–12/31 | |
| 10/21–11/13 | 11/14–12/7 | 12/8–12/31 | | 1/1–1/6 | 1/7–2/2 |
| 8/10–9/6 | 9/7–10/10 | 10/11–11/28 | 1/1–1/24 | 1/25–2/16 | 2/17–3/12 |
| | 11/29–12/31 | | | | |
| 9/21–10/14 | 1/1 | 1/2–2/6 | 2/7–3/5 | 3/6–3/31 | 4/1–4/26 |
| | 10/15–11/7 | 11/8–12/1 | 12/2–12/25 | 12/26–12/31 | |
| 11/13–11/26 | 11/27–12/21 | 12/22–12/31 | | 1/1–1/19 | 1/20–2/12 |
| 8/22–9/15 | 9/16–10/11 | 1/1–1/14 | 1/15–2/7 | 2/8–3/3 | 3/4–3/27 |
| | | 10/12–11/6 | 11/7–12/5 | 12/6–12/31 | |

# VENUS SIGNS 1901–2007

| | Aries | Taurus | Gemini | Cancer | Leo | Virgo |
|---|---|---|---|---|---|---|
| **1926** | 5/7–6/2 | 6/3–6/28 | 6/29–7/23 | 7/24–8/17 | 8/18–9/11 | 9/12–10/5 |
| **1927** | 2/27–3/22 | 3/23–4/16 | 4/17–5/11 | 5/12–6/7 | 6/8–7/7 | 7/8–11/9 |
| **1928** | 4/12–5/5 | 5/6–5/29 | 5/30–6/23 | 6/24–7/17 | 7/18–8/11 | 8/12–9/4 |
| **1929** | 2/3–3/7 | 3/8–4/19 | 7/8–8/4 | 8/5–8/30 | 8/31–9/25 | 9/26–10/19 |
| | 4/20–6/2 | 6/3–7/7 | | | | |
| **1930** | 3/13–4/5 | 4/6–4/30 | 5/1–5/24 | 5/25–6/18 | 6/19–7/14 | 7/15–8/9 |
| **1931** | 4/26–5/20 | 5/21–6/13 | 6/14–7/8 | 7/9–8/2 | 8/3–8/26 | 8/27–9/19 |
| **1932** | 2/12–3/8 | 3/9–4/3 | 4/4–5/5 | 5/6–7/12 | 9/9–10/6 | 10/7–11/1 |
| | | | 7/13–7/27 | 7/28–9/8 | | |
| **1933** | 3/27–4/19 | 4/20–5/28 | 5/29–6/8 | 6/9–7/2 | 7/3–7/26 | 7/27–8/20 |
| **1934** | 5/6–6/1 | 6/2–6/27 | 6/28–7/22 | 7/23–8/16 | 8/17–9/10 | 9/11–10/4 |
| **1935** | 2/26–3/21 | 3/22–4/15 | 4/16–5/10 | 5/11–6/6 | 6/7–7/6 | 7/7–11/8 |
| **1936** | 4/11–5/4 | 5/5–5/28 | 5/29–6/22 | 6/23–7/16 | 7/17–8/10 | 8/11–9/4 |
| **1937** | 2/2–3/8 | 3/9–4/13 | 7/7–8/3 | 8/4–8/29 | 8/30–9/24 | 9/25–10/18 |
| | 4/14–6/3 | 6/4–7/6 | | | | |
| **1938** | 3/12–4/4 | 4/5–4/28 | 4/29–5/23 | 5/24–6/18 | 6/19–7/13 | 7/14–8/8 |
| **1939** | 4/25–5/19 | 5/20–6/13 | 6/14–7/8 | 7/9–8/1 | 8/2–8/25 | 8/26–9/19 |
| **1940** | 2/12–3/7 | 3/8–4/3 | 4/4–5/5 | 5/6–7/4 | 9/9–10/5 | 10/6–10/31 |
| | | | 7/5–7/31 | 8/1–9/8 | | |
| **1941** | 3/27–4/19 | 4/20–5/13 | 5/14–6/6 | 6/7–7/1 | 7/2–7/26 | 7/27–8/20 |
| **1942** | 5/6–6/1 | 6/2–6/26 | 6/27–7/22 | 7/23–8/16 | 8/17–9/9 | 9/10–10/3 |
| **1943** | 2/25–3/20 | 3/21–4/14 | 4/15–5/10 | 5/11–6/6 | 6/7–7/6 | 7/7–11/8 |
| **1944** | 4/10–5/3 | 5/4–5/28 | 5/29–6/21 | 6/22–7/16 | 7/17–8/9 | 8/10–9/2 |
| **1945** | 2/2–3/10 | 3/11–4/6 | 7/7–8/3 | 8/4–8/29 | 8/30–9/23 | 9/24–10/18 |
| | 4/7–6/3 | 6/4–7/6 | | | | |
| **1946** | 3/11–4/4 | 4/5–4/28 | 4/29–5/23 | 5/24–6/17 | 6/18–7/12 | 7/13–8/8 |
| **1947** | 4/25–5/19 | 5/20–6/12 | 6/13–7/7 | 7/8–8/1 | 8/2–8/25 | 8/26–9/18 |
| **1948** | 2/11–3/7 | 3/8–4/3 | 4/4–5/6 | 5/7–6/28 | 9/8–10/5 | 10/6–10/31 |
| | | | 6/29–8/2 | 8/3–9/7 | | |
| **1949** | 3/26–4/19 | 4/20–5/13 | 5/14–6/6 | 6/7–6/30 | 7/1–7/25 | 7/26–8/19 |
| **1950** | 5/5–5/31 | 6/1–6/26 | 6/27–7/21 | 7/22–8/15 | 8/16–9/9 | 9/10–10/3 |
| **1951** | 2/25–3/21 | 3/22–4/15 | 4/16–5/10 | 5/11–6/6 | 6/7–7/7 | 7/8–11/9 |

| Libra | Scorpio | Sagittarius | Capricorn | Aquarius | Pisces |
| --- | --- | --- | --- | --- | --- |
| 10/6–10/29 | 10/30–11/22 | 11/23–12/16 | 12/17–12/31 | 1/1–4/5 | 4/6–5/6 |
| 11/10–12/8 | 12/9–12/31 | 1/1–1/7 | 1/8 | 1/9–2/1 | 2/2–2/26 |
| 9/5–9/28 | 1/1–1/3 | 1/4–1/28 | 1/29–2/22 | 2/23–3/17 | 3/18–4/11 |
| | 9/29–10/23 | 10/24–11/16 | 11/17–12/11 | 12/12–12/31 | |
| 10/20–11/12 | 11/13–12/6 | 12/7–12/30 | 12/31 | 1/1–1/5 | 1/6–2/2 |
| 8/10–9/6 | 9/7–10/11 | 10/12–11/21 | 1/1–1/23 | 1/24–2/16 | 2/17–3/12 |
| | 11/22–12/31 | | | | |
| 9/20–10/13 | 1/1–1/3 | 1/4–2/6 | 2/7–3/4 | 3/5–3/31 | 4/1–4/25 |
| | 10/14–11/6 | 11/7–11/30 | 12/1–12/24 | 12/25–12/31 | |
| 11/2–11/25 | 11/26–12/20 | 12/21–12/31 | | 1/1–1/18 | 1/19–2/11 |
| 8/21–9/14 | 9/15–10/10 | 1/1–1/13 | 1/14–2/6 | 2/7–3/2 | 3/3–3/26 |
| | | 10/11–11/5 | 11/6–12/4 | 12/5–12/31 | |
| 10/5–10/28 | 10/29–11/21 | 11/22–12/15 | 12/16–12/31 | 1/1–4/5 | 4/6–5/5 |
| 11/9–12/7 | 12/8–12/31 | | 1/1–1/7 | 1/8–1/31 | 2/1–2/25 |
| 9/5–9/27 | 1/1–1/2 | 1/3–1/27 | 1/28–2/21 | 2/22–3/16 | 3/17–4/10 |
| | 9/28–10/22 | 10/23–11/15 | 11/16–12/10 | 12/11–12/31 | |
| 10/19–11/11 | 11/12–12/5 | 12/6–12/29 | 12/30–12/31 | 1/1–1/5 | 1/6–2/1 |
| 8/9–9/6 | 9/7–10/13 | 10/14–11/14 | 1/1–1/22 | 1/23–2/15 | 2/16–3/11 |
| | 11/15–12/31 | | | | |
| 9/20–10/13 | 1/1–1/3 | 1/4–2/5 | 2/6–3/4 | 3/5–3/30 | 3/31–4/24 |
| | 10/14–11/6 | 11/7–11/30 | 12/1–12/24 | 12/25–12/31 | |
| 11/1–11/25 | 11/26–12/19 | 12/20–12/31 | | 1/1–1/18 | 1/19–2/11 |
| 8/21–9/14 | 9/15–10/9 | 1/1–1/12 | 1/13–2/5 | 2/6–3/1 | 3/2–3/26 |
| | | 10/10–11/5 | 11/6–12/4 | 12/5–12/31 | |
| 10/4–10/27 | 10/28–11/20 | 11/21–12/14 | 12/15–12/31 | 1/1–4/5 | 4/6–5/5 |
| 11/9–12/7 | 12/8–12/31 | | 1/1–1/7 | 1/8–1/31 | 2/1–2/24 |
| 9/3–9/27 | 1/1–1/2 | 1/3–1/27 | 1/28–2/20 | 2/21–3/16 | 3/17–4/9 |
| | 9/28–10/21 | 10/22–11/15 | 11/16–12/10 | 12/11–12/31 | |
| 10/19–11/11 | 11/12–12/5 | 12/6–12/29 | 12/30–12/31 | 1/1–1/4 | 1/5–2/1 |
| 8/9–9/6 | 9/7–10/15 | 10/16–11/7 | 1/1–1/21 | 1/22–2/14 | 2/15–3/10 |
| | 11/8–12/31 | | | | |
| 9/19–10/12 | 1/1–1/4 | 1/5–2/5 | 2/6–3/4 | 3/5–3/29 | 3/30–4/24 |
| | 10/13–11/5 | 11/6–11/29 | 11/30–12/23 | 12/24–12/31 | |
| 11/1–11/25 | 11/26–12/19 | 12/20–12/31 | | 1/1–1/17 | 1/18–2/10 |
| 8/20–9/14 | 9/15–10/9 | 1/1–1/12 | 1/13–2/5 | 2/6–3/1 | 3/2–3/25 |
| | | 10/10–11/5 | 11/6–12/5 | 12/6–12/31 | |
| 10/4–10/27 | 10/28–11/20 | 11/21–12/13 | 12/14–12/31 | 1/1–4/5 | 4/6–5/4 |
| 11/10–12/7 | 12/8–12/31 | | 1/1–1/7 | 1/8–1/31 | 2/1–2/24 |

## VENUS SIGNS 1901–2007

| | Aries | Taurus | Gemini | Cancer | Leo | Virgo |
|---|---|---|---|---|---|---|
| **1952** | 4/10–5/4 | 5/5–5/28 | 5/29–6/21 | 6/22–7/16 | 7/17–8/9 | 8/10–9/3 |
| **1953** | 2/2–3/3 | 3/4–3/31 | 7/8–8/3 | 8/4–8/29 | 8/30–9/24 | 9/25–10/18 |
| | 4/1–6/5 | 6/6–7/7 | | | | |
| **1954** | 3/12–4/4 | 4/5–4/28 | 4/29–5/23 | 5/24–6/17 | 6/18–7/13 | 7/14–8/8 |
| **1955** | 4/25–5/19 | 5/20–6/13 | 6/14–7/7 | 7/8–8/1 | 8/2–8/25 | 8/26–9/18 |
| **1956** | 2/12–3/7 | 3/8–4/4 | 4/5–5/7 | 5/8–6/23 | 9/9–10/5 | 10/6–10/31 |
| | | | 6/24–8/4 | 8/5–9/8 | | |
| **1957** | 3/26–4/19 | 4/20–5/13 | 5/14–6/6 | 6/7–7/1 | 7/2–7/26 | 7/27–8/19 |
| **1958** | 5/6–5/31 | 6/1–6/26 | 6/27–7/22 | 7/23–8/15 | 8/16–9/9 | 9/10–10/3 |
| **1959** | 2/25–3/20 | 3/21–4/14 | 4/15–5/10 | 5/11–6/6 | 6/7–7/8 | 7/9–9/20 |
| | | | | | 9/21–9/24 | 9/25–11/9 |
| **1960** | 4/10–5/3 | 5/4–5/28 | 5/29–6/21 | 6/22–7/15 | 7/16–8/9 | 8/10–9/2 |
| **1961** | 2/3–6/5 | 6/6–7/7 | 7/8–8/3 | 8/4–8/29 | 8/30–9/23 | 9/24–10/17 |
| **1962** | 3/11–4/3 | 4/4–4/28 | 4/29–5/22 | 5/23–6/17 | 6/18–7/12 | 7/13–8/8 |
| **1963** | 4/24–5/18 | 5/19–6/12 | 6/13–7/7 | 7/8–7/31 | 8/1–8/25 | 8/26–9/18 |
| **1964** | 2/11–3/7 | 3/8–4/4 | 4/5–5/9 | 5/10–6/17 | 9/9–10/5 | 10/6–10/31 |
| | | | 6/18–8/5 | 8/6–9/8 | | |
| **1965** | 3/26–4/18 | 4/19–5/12 | 5/13–6/6 | 6/7–6/30 | 7/1–7/25 | 7/26–8/19 |
| **1966** | 5/6–6/31 | 6/1–6/26 | 6/27–7/21 | 7/22–8/15 | 8/16–9/8 | 9/9–10/2 |
| **1967** | 2/24–3/20 | 3/21–4/14 | 4/15–5/10 | 5/11–6/6 | 6/7–7/8 | 7/9–9/9 |
| | | | | | 9/10–10/1 | 10/2–11/9 |
| **1968** | 4/9–5/3 | 5/4–5/27 | 5/28–6/20 | 6/21–7/15 | 7/16–8/8 | 8/9–9/2 |
| **1969** | 2/3–6/6 | 6/7–7/6 | 7/7–8/3 | 8/4–8/28 | 8/29–9/22 | 9/23–10/17 |
| **1970** | 3/11–4/3 | 4/4–4/27 | 4/28–5/22 | 5/23–6/16 | 6/17–7/12 | 7/13–8/8 |
| **1971** | 4/24–5/18 | 5/19–6/12 | 6/13–7/6 | 7/7–7/31 | 8/1–8/24 | 8/25–9/17 |
| **1972** | 2/11–3/7 | 3/8–4/3 | 4/4–5/10 | 5/11–6/11 | | |
| | | | 6/12–8/6 | 8/7–9/8 | 9/9–10/5 | 10/6–10/30 |
| **1973** | 3/25–4/18 | 4/18–5/12 | 5/13–6/5 | 6/6–6/29 | 7/1–7/25 | 7/26–8/19 |
| **1974** | 5/5–5/31 | 6/1–6/25 | 6/26–7/21 | 7/22–8/14 | 8/15–9/8 | 9/9–10/2 |
| **1975** | 2/24–3/20 | 3/21–4/13 | 4/14–5/9 | 5/10–6/6 | 6/7–7/9 | 7/10–9/2 |
| | | | | | 9/3–10/4 | 10/5–11/9 |

| Libra | Scorpio | Sagittarius | Capricorn | Aquarius | Pisces |
|---|---|---|---|---|---|
| 9/4–9/27 | 1/1–1/2 | 1/3–1/27 | 1/28–2/20 | 2/21–3/16 | 3/17–4/9 |
| | 9/28–10/21 | 10/22–11/15 | 11/16–12/10 | 12/11–12/31 | |
| 10/19–11/11 | 11/12–12/5 | 12/6–12/29 | 12/30–12/31 | 1/1–1/5 | 1/6–2/1 |
| 8/9–9/6 | 9/7–10/22 | 10/23–10/27 | 1/1–1/22 | 1/23–2/15 | 2/16–3/11 |
| | 10/28–12/31 | | | | |
| 9/19–10/13 | 1/1–1/6 | 1/7–2/5 | 2/6–3/4 | 3/5–3/30 | 3/31–4/24 |
| | 10/14–11/5 | 11/6–11/30 | 12/1–12/24 | 12/25–12/31 | |
| 11/1–11/25 | 11/26–12/19 | 12/20–12/31 | | 1/1–1/17 | 1/18–2/11 |
| 8/20–9/14 | 9/15–10/9 | 1/1–1/12 | 1/13–2/5 | 2/6–3/1 | 3/2–3/25 |
| | | 10/10–11/5 | 11/6–12/6 | 12/7–12/31 | |
| 10/4–10/27 | 10/28–11/20 | 11/21–12/14 | 12/15–12/31 | 1/1–4/6 | 4/7–5/5 |
| 11/10–12/7 | 12/8–12/31 | | 1/1–1/7 | 1/8–1/31 | 2/1–2/24 |
| 9/3–9/26 | 1/1–1/2 | 1/3–1/27 | 1/28–2/20 | 2/21–3/15 | 3/16–4/9 |
| | 9/27–10/21 | 10/22–11/15 | 11/16–12/10 | 12/11–12/31 | |
| 10/18–11/11 | 11/12–12/4 | 12/5–12/28 | 12/29–12/31 | 1/1–1/5 | 1/6–2/2 |
| 8/9–9/6 | 9/7–12/31 | | 1/1–1/21 | 1/22–2/14 | 2/15–3/10 |
| 9/19–10/12 | 1/1–1/6 | 1/7–2/5 | 2/6–3/4 | 3/5–3/29 | 3/30–4/23 |
| | 10/13–11/5 | 11/6–11/29 | 11/30–12/23 | 12/24–12/31 | |
| 11/1–11/24 | 11/25–12/19 | 12/20–12/31 | | 1/1–1/16 | 1/17–2/10 |
| 8/20–9/13 | 9/14–10/9 | 1/1–1/12 | 1/13–2/5 | 2/6–3/1 | 3/2–3/25 |
| | | 10/10–11/5 | 11/6–12/7 | 12/8–12/31 | |
| 10/3–10/26 | 10/27–11/19 | 11/20–12/13 | 2/7–2/25 | 1/1–2/6 | 4/7–5/5 |
| | | | 12/14–12/31 | 2/26–4/6 | |
| 11/10–12/7 | 12/8–12/31 | | 1/1–1/6 | 1/7–1/30 | 1/31–2/23 |
| 9/3–9/26 | 1/1 | 1/2–1/26 | 1/27–2/20 | 2/21–3/15 | 3/16–4/8 |
| | 9/27–10/21 | 10/22–11/14 | 11/15–12/9 | 12/10–12/31 | |
| 10/18–11/10 | 11/11–12/4 | 12/5–12/28 | 12/29–12/31 | 1/1–1/4 | 1/5–2/2 |
| 8/9–9/7 | 9/8–12/31 | | 1/1–1/21 | 1/22–2/14 | 2/15–3/10 |
| 9/18–10/11 | 1/1–1/7 | 1/8–2/5 | 2/6–3/4 | 3/5–3/29 | 3/30–4/23 |
| | 10/12–11/5 | 11/6–11/29 | 11/30–12/23 | 12/24–12/31 | |
| | 11/25–12/18 | 12/19–12/31 | | 1/1–1/16 | 1/17–2/10 |
| 10/31–11/24 | | | | | |
| 8/20–9/13 | 9/14–10/8 | 1/1–1/12 | 1/13–2/4 | 2/5–2/28 | 3/1–3/24 |
| | | 10/9–11/5 | 11/6–12/7 | 12/8–12/31 | |
| | | | 1/30–2/28 | 1/1–1/29 | |
| 10/3–10/26 | 10/27–11/19 | 11/20–12/13 | 12/14–12/31 | 3/1–4/6 | 4/7–5/4 |
| 11/10–12/7 | 12/8–12/31 | | 1/1–1/6 | 1/7–1/30 | 1/31–2/23 |

# VENUS SIGNS 1901–2007

| | Aries | Taurus | Gemini | Cancer | Leo | Virgo |
|---|---|---|---|---|---|---|
| 1976 | 4/8–5/2 | 5/2–5/27 | 5/27–6/20 | 6/20–7/14 | 7/14–8/8 | 8/8–9/1 |
| 1977 | 2/2–6/6 | 6/6–7/6 | 7/6–8/2 | 8/2–8/28 | 8/28–9/22 | 9/22–10/17 |
| 1978 | 3/9–4/2 | 4/2–4/27 | 4/27–5/22 | 5/22–6/16 | 6/16–7/12 | 7/12–8/6 |
| 1979 | 4/23–5/18 | 5/18–6/11 | 6/11–7/6 | 7/6–7/30 | 7/30–8/24 | 8/24–9/17 |
| 1980 | 2/9–3/6 | 3/6–4/3 | 4/3–5/12 | 5/12–6/5 | 9/7–10/4 | 10/4–10/30 |
| | | | 6/5–8/6 | 8/6–9/7 | | |
| 1981 | 3/24–4/17 | 4/17–5/11 | 5/11–6/5 | 6/5–6/29 | 6/29–7/24 | 7/24–8/18 |
| 1982 | 5/4–5/30 | 5/30–6/25 | 6/25–7/20 | 7/20–8/14 | 8/14–9/7 | 9/7–10/2 |
| 1983 | 2/22–3/19 | 3/19–4/13 | 4/13–5/9 | 5/9–6/6 | 6/6–7/10 | 7/10–8/27 |
| | | | | | 8/27–10/5 | 10/5–11/9 |
| 1984 | 4/7–5/2 | 5/2–5/26 | 5/26–6/20 | 6/20–7/14 | 7/14–8/7 | 8/7–9/1 |
| 1985 | 2/2–6/6 | 6/7–7/6 | 7/6–8/2 | 8/2–8/28 | 8/28–9/22 | 9/22–10/16 |
| 1986 | 3/9–4/2 | 4/2–4/26 | 4/26–5/21 | 5/21–6/15 | 6/15–7/11 | 7/11–8/7 |
| 1987 | 4/22–5/17 | 5/17–6/11 | 6/11–7/5 | 7/5–7/30 | 7/30–8/23 | 8/23–9/16 |
| 1988 | 2/9–3/6 | 3/6–4/3 | 4/3–5/17 | 5/17–5/27 | 9/7–10/4 | 10/4–10/29 |
| | | | 5/27–8/6 | 8/28–9/22 | 9/22–10/16 | |
| 1989 | 3/23–4/16 | 4/16–5/11 | 5/11–6/4 | 6/4–6/29 | 6/29–7/24 | 7/24–8/18 |
| 1990 | 5/4–5/30 | 5/30–6/25 | 6/25–7/20 | 7/20–8/13 | 8/13–9/7 | 9/7–10/1 |
| 1991 | 2/22–3/18 | 3/18–4/13 | 4/13–5/9 | 5/9–6/6 | 6/6–7/11 | 7/11–8/21 |
| | | | | | 8/21–10/6 | 10/6–11/9 |
| 1992 | 4/7–5/1 | 5/1–5/26 | 5/26–6/19 | 6/19–7/13 | 7/13–8/7 | 8/7–8/31 |
| 1993 | 2/2–6/6 | 6/6–7/6 | 7/6–8/1 | 8/1–8/27 | 8/27–9/21 | 9/21–10/16 |
| 1994 | 3/8–4/1 | 4/1–4/26 | 4/26–5/21 | 5/21–6/15 | 6/15–7/11 | 7/11–8/7 |
| 1995 | 4/22–5/16 | 5/16–6/10 | 6/10–7/5 | 7/5–7/29 | 7/29–8/23 | 8/23–9/16 |
| 1996 | 2/9–3/6 | 3/6–4/3 | 4/3–8/7 | 8/7 9/7 | 9/7–10/4 | 10/4–10/29 |
| 1997 | 3/23 4/10 | 4/16–5/10 | 5/10–6/4 | 6/4–6/28 | 6/28–7/23 | 7/23–8/17 |
| 1998 | 5/3–5/29 | 5/29–6/24 | 6/24–7/19 | 7/19–8/13 | 8/13–9/6 | 9/6–9/30 |
| 1999 | 2/21–3/18 | 3/18–4/12 | 4/12–5/8 | 5/8–6/5 | 6/5–7/12 | 7/12–8/15 |
| | | | | | 8/15–10/7 | 10/7–11/9 |
| 2000 | 4/6–5/1 | 5/1–5/25 | 5/25–6/13 | 6/13–7/13 | 7/13–8/6 | 8/6–8/31 |
| 2001 | 2/2–6/6 | 6/6–7/5 | 7/5–8/1 | 8/1–8/26 | 8/26–9/20 | 9/20–10/15 |
| 2002 | 3/7–4/1 | 4/1–4/25 | 4/25–5/20 | 5/20–6/14 | 6/14–7/10 | 7/10–8/7 |
| 2003 | 4/21–5/16 | 5/16–6/9 | 6/9–7/4 | 7/4–7/29 | 7/29–8/22 | 8/22–9/15 |
| 2004 | 2/8–3/5 | 3/5–4/3 | 4/3–8/7 | 8/7–9/6 | 9/6–10/3 | 10/3–10/28 |
| 2005 | 3/22–4/15 | 4/15–5/10 | 5/10–6/3 | 6/3–6/28 | 6/28–7/23 | 7/23–8/17 |
| 2006 | 5/3–5/29 | 5/29–6/24 | 6/24–7/19 | 7/19–8/12 | 8/12–9/6 | 9/6–9/30 |
| 2007 | 2/21–3/16 | 3/17–4/10 | 4/11–5/7 | 5/8–6/4 | 6/5–7/13 | 7/14–8/7 |
| | | | | | 8/8–10/6 | 10/7–11/7 |

| Libra | Scorpio | Sagittarius | Capricorn | Aquarius | Pisces |
|---|---|---|---|---|---|
| 9/1–9/26 | 9/26–10/20 | 1/1–1/26 | 1/26–2/19 | 2/19–3/15 | 3/15–4/8 |
| 10/17–11/10 | 11/10–12/4 | 12/4–12/27 | 12/27–1/20/78 | | 1/4–2/2 |
| 8/6–9/7 | 9/7–1/7 | | | 1/20–2/13 | 2/13–3/9 |
| 9/17–10/11 | 10/11–11/4 | 1/7–2/5 | 2/5–3/3 | 3/3–3/29 | 3/29–4/23 |
| | | 11/4–11/28 | 11/28–12/22 | 12/22–1/16/80 | |
| 10/30–11/24 | 11/24–12/18 | 12/18–1/11/81 | | | 1/16–2/9 |
| 8/18–9/12 | 9/12–10/9 | 10/9–11/5 | 1/11–2/4 | 2/4–2/28 | 2/28–3/24 |
| | | | 11/5–12/8 | 12/8–1/23/82 | |
| 10/2–10/26 | 10/26–11/18 | 11/18–12/12 | 1/23–3/2 | 3/2–4/6 | 4/6–5/4 |
| | | | 12/12–1/5/83 | | |
| 11/9–12/6 | 12/6–1/1/84 | | | 1/5–1/29 | 1/29–2/22 |
| 9/1–9/25 | 9/25–10/20 | 1/1–1/25 | 1/25–2/19 | 2/19–3/14 | 3/14–4/7 |
| | | 10/20–11/13 | 11/13–12/9 | 12/10–1/4 | |
| 10/16–11/9 | 11/9–12/3 | 12/3–12/27 | 12/28–1/19 | | 1/4–2/2 |
| 8/7–9/7 | 9/7–1/7 | | | 1/20–2/13 | 2/13–3/9 |
| 9/16–10/10 | 10/10–11/3 | 1/7–2/5 | 2/5–3/3 | 3/3–3/28 | 3/28–4/22 |
| | | 11/3–11/28 | 11/28–12/22 | 12/22–1/15 | |
| 10/29–11/23 | 11/23–12/17 | 12/17–1/10 | | | 1/15–2/9 |
| 8/18–9/12 | 9/12–10/8 | 10/8–11/5 | 1/10–2/3 | 2/3–2/27 | 2/27–3/23 |
| | | | 11/5–12/10 | 12/10–1/16/90 | |
| 10/1–10/25 | 10/25–11/18 | 11/18–12/12 | 1/16–3/3 | 3/3–4/6 | 4/6–5/4 |
| | | | 12/12–1/5 | | |
| 11/9–12/6 | 12/6–12/31 | 12/31–1/25/92 | | 1/5–1/29 | 1/29–2/22 |
| 8/31–9/25 | 9/25–10/19 | 10/19–11/13 | 1/25–2/18 | 2/18–3/13 | 3/13–4/7 |
| | | | 11/13–12/8 | 12/8–1/3/93 | |
| 10/16–11/9 | 11/9–12/2 | 12/2–12/26 | 12/26–1/19 | | 1/3–2/2 |
| 8/7–9/7 | 9/7–1/7 | | | 1/19–2/12 | 2/12–3/8 |
| 9/16–10/10 | 10/10–11/13 | 1/7–2/4 | 2/4–3/2 | 3/2–3/28 | 3/28–4/22 |
| | | 11/3–11/27 | 11/27–12/21 | 12/21–1/15 | |
| 10/29–11/23 | 11/23–12/17 | 12/17–1/10/97 | | | 1/15–2/9 |
| 8/17–9/12 | 9/12–10/8 | 10/8–11/5 | 1/10–2/3 | 2/3–2/27 | 2/27–3/23 |
| | | | 11/5–12/12 | 12/12–1/9 | |
| 9/30–10/24 | 10/24–11/17 | 11/17–12/11 | 1/9–3/4 | 3/4–4/6 | 4/6–5/3 |
| 11/9–12/5 | 12/5–12/31 | 12/31–1/24 | | 1/4–1/28 | 1/28–2/21 |
| 8/31–9/24 | 9/24–10/19 | 10/19–11/13 | 1/24–2/18 | 2/18–3/12 | 3/13–4/6 |
| | | | 11/13–12/8 | 12/8 | |
| 10/15–11/8 | 11/8–12/2 | 12/2–12/26 | 12/26/01– | 12/8/00–1/3/01 | 1/3–2/2 |
| | | | 1/18/02 | | |
| 8/7–9/7 | 9/7–1/7/03 | | 12/26/01–1/18 | 1/18–2/11 | 2/11–3/7 |
| 9/15–10/9 | 10/9–11/2 | 1/7–2/4 | 2/4–3/2 | 3/2–3/27 | 3/27–4/21 |
| | | 11/2–11/26 | 11/26–12/21 | 12/21–1/14/04 | |
| 10/28–11/22 | 11/22–12/16 | 12/16–1/9/05 | | 1/1–1/14 | 1/14–2/8 |
| 8/17–9/11 | 9/11–10/8 | 10/8–11/15 | 1/9–2/2 | 2/2–2/26 | 2/26–3/22 |
| | | | 11/5–12/15 | 12/15–1/1/06 | |
| 9/30–10/24 | 10/24–11/17 | 11/17–12/11 | 1/1–3/5 | 3/5–4/6 | 4/6–5/3 |
| 11/8–12/4 | 12/5–12/29 | 12/30–1/24/08 | | 1/3–1/26 | 1/27–2/20 |

## How to Use the Mars, Jupiter, and Saturn Tables

Find the year of your birth on the left side of each column. The dates when the planet entered each sign are listed on the right side of each column. (Signs are abbreviated to three letters.) Your birthday should fall on or between each date listed, and your planetary placement should correspond to the earlier sign of that period.

All planet changes are calculated for the Greenwich Mean Time zone.

### MARS SIGNS 1901–2007

| | | | |
|---|---|---|---|
| 1901 | MAR | 1 | Leo |
| | MAY | 11 | Vir |
| | JUL | 13 | Lib |
| | AUG | 31 | Scp |
| | OCT | 14 | Sag |
| | NOV | 24 | Cap |
| 1902 | JAN | 1 | Aqu |
| | FEB | 8 | Pic |
| | MAR | 19 | Ari |
| | APR | 27 | Tau |
| | JUN | 7 | Gem |
| | JUL | 20 | Can |
| | SEP | 4 | Leo |
| | OCT | 23 | Vir |
| | DEC | 20 | Lib |
| 1903 | APR | 19 | Vir |
| | MAY | 30 | Lib |
| | AUG | 6 | Scp |
| | SEP | 22 | Sag |
| | NOV | 3 | Cap |
| | DEC | 12 | Aqu |
| 1904 | JAN | 19 | Pic |
| | FEB | 27 | Ari |
| | APR | 6 | Tau |
| | MAY | 18 | Gem |
| | JUN | 30 | Can |
| | AUG | 15 | Leo |
| | OCT | 1 | Vir |
| | NOV | 20 | Lib |
| 1905 | JAN | 13 | Scp |
| | AUG | 21 | Sag |
| | OCT | 8 | Cap |
| | NOV | 18 | Aqu |
| | DEC | 27 | Pic |
| 1906 | FEB | 4 | Ari |
| | MAR | 17 | Tau |
| | APR | 28 | Gem |
| | JUN | 11 | Can |
| | JUL | 27 | Leo |
| | SEP | 12 | Vir |
| | OCT | 30 | Lib |
| | DEC | 17 | Scp |
| 1907 | FEB | 5 | Sag |
| | APR | 1 | Cap |
| | OCT | 13 | Aqu |
| | NOV | 29 | Pic |
| 1908 | JAN | 11 | Ari |
| | FEB | 23 | Tau |
| | APR | 7 | Gem |
| | MAY | 22 | Can |
| | JUL | 8 | Leo |
| | AUG | 24 | Vir |
| | OCT | 10 | Lib |
| | NOV | 25 | Scp |

| | | | |
|---|---|---|---|
| 1909 | JAN | 10 | Sag |
| | FEB | 24 | Cap |
| | APR | 9 | Aqu |
| | MAY | 25 | Pic |
| | JUL | 21 | Ari |
| | SEP | 26 | Pic |
| | NOV | 20 | Ari |
| 1910 | JAN | 23 | Tau |
| | MAR | 14 | Gem |
| | MAY | 1 | Can |
| | JUN | 19 | Leo |
| | AUG | 6 | Vir |
| | SEP | 22 | Lib |
| | NOV | 6 | Scp |
| | DEC | 20 | Sag |
| 1911 | JAN | 31 | Cap |
| | MAR | 14 | Aqu |
| | APR | 23 | Pic |
| | JUN | 2 | Ari |
| | JUL | 15 | Tau |
| | SEP | 5 | Gem |
| | NOV | 30 | Tau |
| 1912 | JAN | 30 | Gem |
| | APR | 5 | Can |
| | MAY | 28 | Leo |
| | JUL | 17 | Vir |
| | SEP | 2 | Lib |
| | OCT | 18 | Scp |
| | NOV | 30 | Sag |
| 1913 | JAN | 10 | Cap |
| | FEB | 19 | Aqu |
| | MAR | 30 | Pic |
| | MAY | 8 | Ari |
| | JUN | 17 | Tau |
| | JUL | 29 | Gem |
| | SEP | 15 | Can |
| 1914 | MAY | 1 | Leo |
| | JUN | 26 | Vir |
| | AUG | 14 | Lib |
| | SEP | 29 | Scp |
| | NOV | 11 | Sag |
| | DEC | 22 | Cap |
| 1915 | JAN | 30 | Aqu |
| | MAR | 9 | Pic |
| | APR | 16 | Ari |
| | MAY | 26 | Tau |
| | JUL | 6 | Gem |
| | AUG | 19 | Can |
| | OCT | 7 | Leo |
| 1916 | MAY | 28 | Vir |
| | JUL | 23 | Lib |
| | SEP | 8 | Scp |
| | OCT | 22 | Sag |
| | DEC | 1 | Cap |
| 1917 | JAN | 9 | Aqu |
| | FEB | 16 | Pic |
| | MAR | 26 | Ari |
| | MAY | 4 | Tau |
| | JUN | 14 | Gem |
| | JUL | 28 | Can |
| | SEP | 12 | Leo |
| | NOV | 2 | Vir |
| 1918 | JAN | 11 | Lib |
| | FEB | 25 | Vir |
| | JUN | 23 | Lib |
| | AUG | 17 | Scp |
| | OCT | 1 | Sag |
| | NOV | 11 | Cap |
| | DEC | 20 | Aqu |
| 1919 | JAN | 27 | Pic |
| | MAR | 6 | Ari |
| | APR | 15 | Tau |
| | MAY | 26 | Gem |
| | JUL | 8 | Can |
| | AUG | 23 | Leo |
| | OCT | 10 | Vir |
| | NOV | 30 | Lib |
| 1920 | JAN | 31 | Scp |
| | APR | 23 | Lib |
| | JUL | 10 | Scp |
| | SEP | 4 | Sag |
| | OCT | 18 | Cap |
| | NOV | 27 | Aqu |
| 1921 | JAN | 5 | Pic |
| | FEB | 13 | Ari |
| | MAR | 25 | Tau |

| | | | |
|---|---|---|---|
| | MAY | 6 | Gem |
| | JUN | 18 | Can |
| | AUG | 3 | Leo |
| | SEP | 19 | Vir |
| | NOV | 6 | Lib |
| | DEC | 26 | Scp |
| 1922 | FEB | 18 | Sag |
| | SEP | 13 | Cap |
| | OCT | 30 | Aqu |
| | DEC | 11 | Pic |
| 1923 | JAN | 21 | Ari |
| | MAR | 4 | Tau |
| | APR | 16 | Gem |
| | MAY | 30 | Can |
| | JUL | 16 | Leo |
| | SEP | 1 | Vir |
| | OCT | 18 | Lib |
| | DEC | 4 | Scp |
| 1924 | JAN | 19 | Sag |
| | MAR | 6 | Cap |
| | APR | 24 | Aqu |
| | JUN | 24 | Pic |
| | AUG | 24 | Aqu |
| | OCT | 19 | Pic |
| | DEC | 19 | Ari |
| 1925 | FEB | 5 | Tau |
| | MAR | 24 | Gem |
| | MAY | 9 | Can |
| | JUN | 26 | Leo |
| | AUG | 12 | Vir |
| | SEP | 28 | Lib |
| | NOV | 13 | Scp |
| | DEC | 28 | Sag |
| 1926 | FEB | 9 | Cap |
| | MAR | 23 | Aqu |
| | MAY | 3 | Pic |
| | JUN | 15 | Ari |
| | AUG | 1 | Tau |
| 1927 | FEB | 22 | Gem |
| | APR | 17 | Can |
| | JUN | 6 | Leo |
| | JUL | 25 | Vir |
| | SEP | 10 | Lib |
| | OCT | 26 | Scp |
| | DEC | 8 | Sag |
| 1928 | JAN | 19 | Cap |
| | FEB | 28 | Aqu |
| | APR | 7 | Pic |
| | MAY | 16 | Ari |
| | JUN | 26 | Tau |
| | AUG | 9 | Gem |
| | OCT | 3 | Can |
| | DEC | 20 | Gem |
| 1929 | MAR | 10 | Can |
| | MAY | 13 | Leo |
| | JUL | 4 | Vir |
| | AUG | 21 | Lib |
| | OCT | 6 | Scp |
| | NOV | 18 | Sag |
| | DEC | 29 | Cap |
| 1930 | FEB | 6 | Aqu |
| | MAR | 17 | Pic |
| | APR | 24 | Ari |
| | JUN | 3 | Tau |
| | JUL | 14 | Gem |
| | AUG | 28 | Can |
| | OCT | 20 | Leo |
| 1931 | FEB | 16 | Can |
| | MAR | 30 | Leo |
| | JUN | 10 | Vir |
| | AUG | 1 | Lib |
| | SEP | 17 | Scp |
| | OCT | 30 | Sag |
| | DEC | 10 | Cap |
| 1932 | JAN | 18 | Aqu |
| | FEB | 25 | Pic |
| | APR | 3 | Ari |
| | MAY | 12 | Tau |
| | JUN | 22 | Gem |
| | AUG | 4 | Can |
| | SEP | 20 | Leo |
| | NOV | 13 | Vir |
| 1933 | JUL | 6 | Lib |
| | AUG | 26 | Scp |
| | OCT | 9 | Sag |
| | NOV | 19 | Cap |

| | | | |
|---|---|---|---|
| | DEC | 28 | Aqu |
| 1934 | FEB | 4 | Pic |
| | MAR | 14 | Ari |
| | APR | 22 | Tau |
| | JUN | 2 | Gem |
| | JUL | 15 | Can |
| | AUG | 30 | Leo |
| | OCT | 18 | Vir |
| | DEC | 11 | Lib |
| 1935 | JUL | 29 | Scp |
| | SEP | 16 | Sag |
| | OCT | 28 | Cap |
| | DEC | 7 | Aqu |
| 1936 | JAN | 14 | Pic |
| | FEB | 22 | Ari |
| | APR | 1 | Tau |
| | MAY | 13 | Gem |
| | JUN | 25 | Can |
| | AUG | 10 | Leo |
| | SEP | 26 | Vir |
| | NOV | 14 | Lib |
| 1937 | JAN | 5 | Scp |
| | MAR | 13 | Sag |
| | MAY | 14 | Scp |
| | AUG | 8 | Sag |
| | SEP | 30 | Cap |
| | NOV | 11 | Aqu |
| | DEC | 21 | Pic |
| 1938 | JAN | 30 | Ari |
| | MAR | 12 | Tau |
| | APR | 23 | Gem |
| | JUN | 7 | Can |
| | JUL | 22 | Leo |
| | SEP | 7 | Vir |
| | OCT | 25 | Lib |
| | DEC | 11 | Scp |
| 1939 | JAN | 29 | Sag |
| | MAR | 21 | Cap |
| | MAY | 25 | Aqu |
| | JUL | 21 | Cap |
| | SEP | 24 | Aqu |
| | NOV | 19 | Pic |
| 1940 | JAN | 4 | Ari |
| | FEB | 17 | Tau |
| | APR | 1 | Gem |
| | MAY | 17 | Can |
| | JUL | 3 | Leo |
| | AUG | 19 | Vir |
| | OCT | 5 | Lib |
| | NOV | 20 | Scp |
| 1941 | JAN | 4 | Sag |
| | FEB | 17 | Cap |
| | APR | 2 | Aqu |
| | MAY | 16 | Pic |
| | JUL | 2 | Ari |
| 1942 | JAN | 11 | Tau |
| | MAR | 7 | Gem |
| | APR | 26 | Can |
| | JUN | 14 | Leo |
| | AUG | 1 | Vir |
| | SEP | 17 | Lib |
| | NOV | 1 | Scp |
| | DEC | 15 | Sag |
| 1943 | JAN | 26 | Cap |
| | MAR | 8 | Aqu |
| | APR | 17 | Pic |
| | MAY | 27 | Ari |
| | JUL | 7 | Tau |
| | AUG | 23 | Gem |
| 1944 | MAR | 28 | Can |
| | MAY | 22 | Leo |
| | JUL | 12 | Vir |
| | AUG | 29 | Lib |
| | OCT | 13 | Scp |
| | NOV | 25 | Sag |
| 1945 | JAN | 5 | Cap |
| | FEB | 14 | Aqu |
| | MAR | 25 | Pic |
| | MAY | 2 | Ari |
| | JUN | 11 | Tau |
| | JUL | 23 | Gem |
| | SEP | 7 | Can |
| | NOV | 11 | Leo |
| | DEC | 26 | Can |
| 1946 | APR | 22 | Leo |
| | JUN | 20 | Vir |

| | | | |
|---|---|---|---|
| | AUG | 9 | Lib |
| | SEP | 24 | Scp |
| | NOV | 6 | Sag |
| | DEC | 17 | Cap |
| 1947 | JAN | 25 | Aqu |
| | MAR | 4 | Pic |
| | APR | 11 | Ari |
| | MAY | 21 | Tau |
| | JUL | 1 | Gem |
| | AUG | 13 | Can |
| | OCT | 1 | Leo |
| | DEC | 1 | Vir |
| 1948 | FEB | 12 | Leo |
| | MAY | 18 | Vir |
| | JUL | 17 | Lib |
| | SEP | 3 | Scp |
| | OCT | 17 | Sag |
| | NOV | 26 | Cap |
| 1949 | JAN | 4 | Aqu |
| | FEB | 11 | Pic |
| | MAR | 21 | Ari |
| | APR | 30 | Tau |
| | JUN | 10 | Gem |
| | JUL | 23 | Can |
| | SEP | 7 | Leo |
| | OCT | 27 | Vir |
| | DEC | 26 | Lib |
| 1950 | MAR | 28 | Vir |
| | JUN | 11 | Lib |
| | AUG | 10 | Scp |
| | SEP | 25 | Sag |
| | NOV | 6 | Cap |
| | DEC | 15 | Aqu |
| 1951 | JAN | 22 | Pic |
| | MAR | 1 | Ari |
| | APR | 10 | Tau |
| | MAY | 21 | Gem |
| | JUL | 3 | Can |
| | AUG | 18 | Leo |
| | OCT | 5 | Vir |
| | NOV | 24 | Lib |
| 1952 | JAN | 20 | Scp |
| | AUG | 27 | Sag |

| | | | |
|---|---|---|---|
| | OCT | 12 | Cap |
| | NOV | 21 | Aqu |
| | DEC | 30 | Pic |
| 1953 | FEB | 8 | Ari |
| | MAR | 20 | Tau |
| | MAY | 1 | Gem |
| | JUN | 14 | Can |
| | JUL | 29 | Leo |
| | SEP | 14 | Vir |
| | NOV | 1 | Lib |
| | DEC | 20 | Scp |
| 1954 | FEB | 9 | Sag |
| | APR | 12 | Cap |
| | JUL | 3 | Sag |
| | AUG | 24 | Cap |
| | OCT | 21 | Aqu |
| | DEC | 4 | Pic |
| 1955 | JAN | 15 | Ari |
| | FEB | 26 | Tau |
| | APR | 10 | Gem |
| | MAY | 26 | Can |
| | JUL | 11 | Leo |
| | AUG | 27 | Vir |
| | OCT | 13 | Lib |
| | NOV | 29 | Scp |
| 1956 | JAN | 14 | Sag |
| | FEB | 28 | Cap |
| | APR | 14 | Aqu |
| | JUN | 3 | Pic |
| | DEC | 6 | Ari |
| 1957 | JAN | 28 | Tau |
| | MAR | 17 | Gem |
| | MAY | 4 | Can |
| | JUN | 21 | Leo |
| | AUG | 8 | Vir |
| | SEP | 24 | Lib |
| | NOV | 8 | Scp |
| | DEC | 23 | Sag |
| 1958 | FEB | 3 | Cap |
| | MAR | 17 | Aqu |
| | APR | 27 | Pic |
| | JUN | 7 | Ari |
| | JUL | 21 | Tau |

| | | | |
|---|---|---|---|
| | SEP | 21 | Gem |
| | OCT | 29 | Tau |
| 1959 | FEB | 10 | Gem |
| | APR | 10 | Can |
| | JUN | 1 | Leo |
| | JUL | 20 | Vir |
| | SEP | 5 | Lib |
| | OCT | 21 | Scp |
| | DEC | 3 | Sag |
| 1960 | JAN | 14 | Cap |
| | FEB | 23 | Aqu |
| | APR | 2 | Pic |
| | MAY | 11 | Ari |
| | JUN | 20 | Tau |
| | AUG | 2 | Gem |
| | SEP | 21 | Can |
| 1961 | FEB | 5 | Gem |
| | FEB | 7 | Can |
| | MAY | 6 | Leo |
| | JUN | 28 | Vir |
| | AUG | 17 | Lib |
| | OCT | 1 | Scp |
| | NOV | 13 | Sag |
| | DEC | 24 | Cap |
| 1962 | FEB | 1 | Aqu |
| | MAR | 12 | Pic |
| | APR | 19 | Ari |
| | MAY | 28 | Tau |
| | JUL | 9 | Gem |
| | AUG | 22 | Can |
| | OCT | 11 | Leo |
| 1963 | JUN | 3 | Vir |
| | JUL | 27 | Lib |
| | SEP | 12 | Scp |
| | OCT | 25 | Sag |
| | DEC | 5 | Cap |
| 1964 | JAN | 13 | Aqu |
| | FEB | 20 | Pic |
| | MAR | 29 | Ari |
| | MAY | 7 | Tau |
| | JUN | 17 | Gem |
| | JUL | 30 | Can |
| | SEP | 15 | Leo |
| | NOV | 6 | Vir |
| 1965 | JUN | 29 | Lib |
| | AUG | 20 | Scp |
| | OCT | 4 | Sag |
| | NOV | 14 | Cap |
| | DEC | 23 | Aqu |
| 1966 | JAN | 30 | Pic |
| | MAR | 9 | Ari |
| | APR | 17 | Tau |
| | MAY | 28 | Gem |
| | JUL | 11 | Can |
| | AUG | 25 | Leo |
| | OCT | 12 | Vir |
| | DEC | 4 | Lib |
| 1967 | FEB | 12 | Scp |
| | MAR | 31 | Lib |
| | JUL | 19 | Scp |
| | SEP | 10 | Sag |
| | OCT | 23 | Cap |
| | DEC | 1 | Aqu |
| 1968 | JAN | 9 | Pic |
| | FEB | 17 | Ari |
| | MAR | 27 | Tau |
| | MAY | 8 | Gem |
| | JUN | 21 | Can |
| | AUG | 5 | Leo |
| | SEP | 21 | Vir |
| | NOV | 9 | Lib |
| | DEC | 29 | Scp |
| 1969 | FEB | 25 | Sag |
| | SEP | 21 | Cap |
| | NOV | 4 | Aqu |
| | DEC | 15 | Pic |
| 1970 | JAN | 24 | Ari |
| | MAR | 7 | Tau |
| | APR | 18 | Gem |
| | JUN | 2 | Can |
| | JUL | 18 | Leo |
| | SEP | 3 | Vir |
| | OCT | 20 | Lib |
| | DEC | 6 | Scp |
| 1971 | JAN | 23 | Sag |
| | MAR | 12 | Cap |

| | | | |
|---|---|---|---|
| | MAY | 3 | Aqu |
| | NOV | 6 | Pic |
| | DEC | 26 | Ari |
| 1972 | FEB | 10 | Tau |
| | MAR | 27 | Gem |
| | MAY | 12 | Can |
| | JUN | 28 | Leo |
| | AUG | 15 | Vir |
| | SEP | 30 | Lib |
| | NOV | 15 | Scp |
| | DEC | 30 | Sag |
| 1973 | FEB | 12 | Cap |
| | MAR | 26 | Aqu |
| | MAY | 8 | Pic |
| | JUN | 20 | Ari |
| | AUG | 12 | Tau |
| | OCT | 29 | Ari |
| | DEC | 24 | Tau |
| 1974 | FEB | 27 | Gem |
| | APR | 20 | Can |
| | JUN | 9 | Leo |
| | JUL | 27 | Vir |
| | SEP | 12 | Lib |
| | OCT | 28 | Scp |
| | DEC | 10 | Sag |
| 1975 | JAN | 21 | Cap |
| | MAR | 3 | Aqu |
| | APR | 11 | Pic |
| | MAY | 21 | Ari |
| | JUL | 1 | Tau |
| | AUG | 14 | Gem |
| | OCT | 17 | Can |
| | NOV | 25 | Gem |
| 1976 | MAR | 18 | Can |
| | MAY | 16 | Leo |
| | JUL | 6 | Vir |
| | AUG | 24 | Lib |
| | OCT | 8 | Scp |
| | NOV | 20 | Sag |
| 1977 | JAN | 1 | Cap |
| | FEB | 9 | Aqu |
| | MAR | 20 | Pic |
| | APR | 27 | Ari |
| | JUN | 6 | Tau |
| | JUL | 17 | Gem |
| | SEP | 1 | Can |
| | OCT | 26 | Leo |
| 1978 | JAN | 26 | Can |
| | APR | 10 | Leo |
| | JUN | 14 | Vir |
| | AUG | 4 | Lib |
| | SEP | 19 | Scp |
| | NOV | 2 | Sag |
| | DEC | 12 | Cap |
| 1979 | JAN | 20 | Aqu |
| | FEB | 27 | Pic |
| | APR | 7 | Ari |
| | MAY | 16 | Tau |
| | JUN | 26 | Gem |
| | AUG | 8 | Can |
| | SEP | 24 | Leo |
| | NOV | 19 | Vir |
| 1980 | MAR | 11 | Leo |
| | MAY | 4 | Vir |
| | JUL | 10 | Lib |
| | AUG | 29 | Scp |
| | OCT | 12 | Sag |
| | NOV | 22 | Cap |
| | DEC | 30 | Aqu |
| 1981 | FEB | 6 | Pic |
| | MAR | 17 | Ari |
| | APR | 25 | Tau |
| | JUN | 5 | Gem |
| | JUL | 18 | Can |
| | SEP | 2 | Leo |
| | OCT | 21 | Vir |
| | DEC | 16 | Lib |
| 1982 | AUG | 3 | Scp |
| | SEP | 20 | Sag |
| | OCT | 31 | Cap |
| | DEC | 10 | Aqu |
| 1983 | JAN | 17 | Pic |
| | FEB | 25 | Ari |
| | APR | 5 | Tau |
| | MAY | 16 | Gem |
| | JUN | 29 | Can |

| | | | |
|---|---|---|---|
| | AUG | 13 | Leo |
| | SEP | 30 | Vir |
| | NOV | 18 | Lib |
| 1984 | JAN | 11 | Scp |
| | AUG | 17 | Sag |
| | OCT | 5 | Cap |
| | NOV | 15 | Aqu |
| | DEC | 25 | Pic |
| 1985 | FEB | 2 | Ari |
| | MAR | 15 | Tau |
| | APR | 26 | Gem |
| | JUN | 9 | Can |
| | JUL | 25 | Leo |
| | SEP | 10 | Vir |
| | OCT | 27 | Lib |
| | DEC | 14 | Scp |
| 1986 | FEB | 2 | Sag |
| | MAR | 28 | Cap |
| | OCT | 9 | Aqu |
| | NOV | 26 | Pic |
| 1987 | JAN | 8 | Ari |
| | FEB | 20 | Tau |
| | APR | 5 | Gem |
| | MAY | 21 | Can |
| | JUL | 6 | Leo |
| | AUG | 22 | Vir |
| | OCT | 8 | Lib |
| | NOV | 24 | Scp |
| 1988 | JAN | 8 | Sag |
| | FEB | 22 | Cap |
| | APR | 6 | Aqu |
| | MAY | 22 | Pic |
| | JUL | 13 | Ari |
| | OCT | 23 | Pic |
| | NOV | 1 | Ari |
| 1989 | JAN | 19 | Tau |
| | MAR | 11 | Gem |
| | APR | 29 | Can |
| | JUN | 16 | Leo |
| | AUG | 3 | Vir |
| | SEP | 19 | Lib |
| | NOV | 4 | Scp |
| | DEC | 18 | Sag |
| 1990 | JAN | 29 | Cap |
| | MAR | 11 | Aqu |
| | APR | 20 | Pic |
| | MAY | 31 | Ari |
| | JUL | 12 | Tau |
| | AUG | 31 | Gem |
| | DEC | 14 | Tau |
| 1991 | JAN | 21 | Gem |
| | APR | 3 | Can |
| | MAY | 26 | Leo |
| | JUL | 15 | Vir |
| | SEP | 1 | Lib |
| | OCT | 16 | Scp |
| | NOV | 29 | Sag |
| 1992 | JAN | 9 | Cap |
| | FEB | 18 | Aqu |
| | MAR | 28 | Pic |
| | MAY | 5 | Ari |
| | JUN | 14 | Tau |
| | JUL | 26 | Gem |
| | SEP | 12 | Can |
| 1993 | APR | 27 | Leo |
| | JUN | 23 | Vir |
| | AUG | 12 | Lib |
| | SEP | 27 | Scp |
| | NOV | 9 | Sag |
| | DEC | 20 | Cap |
| 1994 | JAN | 28 | Aqu |
| | MAR | 7 | Pic |
| | APR | 14 | Ari |
| | MAY | 23 | Tau |
| | JUL | 3 | Gem |
| | AUG | 16 | Can |
| | OCT | 4 | Leo |
| | DEC | 12 | Vir |
| 1995 | JAN | 22 | Leo |
| | MAY | 25 | Vir |
| | JUL | 21 | Lib |
| | SEP | 7 | Scp |
| | OCT | 20 | Sag |
| | NOV | 30 | Cap |
| 1996 | JAN | 8 | Aqu |
| | FEB | 15 | Pic |

| | | | |
|---|---|---|---|
| | MAR | 24 | Ari |
| | MAY | 2 | Tau |
| | JUN | 12 | Gem |
| | JUL | 25 | Can |
| | SEP | 9 | Leo |
| | OCT | 30 | Vir |
| 1997 | JAN | 3 | Lib |
| | MAR | 8 | Vir |
| | JUN | 19 | Lib |
| | AUG | 14 | Scp |
| | SEP | 28 | Sag |
| | NOV | 9 | Cap |
| | DEC | 18 | Aqu |
| 1998 | JAN | 25 | Pic |
| | MAR | 4 | Ari |
| | APR | 13 | Tau |
| | MAY | 24 | Gem |
| | JUL | 6 | Can |
| | AUG | 20 | Leo |
| | OCT | 7 | Vir |
| | NOV | 27 | Lib |
| 1999 | JAN | 26 | Scp |
| | MAY | 5 | Lib |
| | JUL | 5 | Scp |
| | SEP | 2 | Sag |
| | OCT | 17 | Cap |
| | NOV | 26 | Aqu |
| 2000 | JAN | 4 | Pic |
| | FEB | 12 | Ari |
| | MAR | 23 | Tau |
| | MAY | 3 | Gem |
| | JUN | 16 | Can |
| | AUG | 1 | Leo |
| | SEP | 17 | Vir |
| | NOV | 4 | Lib |
| | DEC | 23 | Scp |
| 2001 | FEB | 14 | Sag |
| | SEP | 8 | Cap |
| | OCT | 27 | Aqu |
| | DEC | 8 | Pic |
| 2002 | JAN | 18 | Ari |
| | MAR | 1 | Tau |
| | APR | 13 | Gem |
| | MAY | 28 | Can |
| | JUL | 13 | Leo |
| | AUG | 29 | Vir |
| | OCT | 15 | Lib |
| | DEC | 1 | Scp |
| 2003 | JAN | 17 | Sag |
| | MAR | 4 | Cap |
| | APR | 21 | Aqu |
| | JUN | 17 | Pic |
| | DEC | 16 | Ari |
| 2004 | FEB | 3 | Tau |
| | MAR | 21 | Gem |
| | MAY | 7 | Can |
| | JUN | 23 | Leo |
| | AUG | 10 | Vir |
| | SEP | 26 | Lib |
| | NOV | 11 | Sep |
| | DEC | 25 | Sag |
| 2005 | FEB | 6 | Cap |
| | MAR | 20 | Aqu |
| | MAY | 1 | Pic |
| | JUN | 12 | Ari |
| | JUL | 28 | Tau |
| 2006 | FEB | 17 | Gem |
| | APR | 14 | Can |
| | JUN | 3 | Leo |
| | JUL | 22 | Vir |
| | SEP | 8 | Lib |
| | OCT | 23 | Scp |
| | DEC | 6 | Sag |
| 2007 | JAN | 16 | Cap |
| | FEB | 25 | Aqu |
| | APR | 6 | Pic |
| | MAY | 15 | Ari |
| | JUNE | 24 | Tau |
| | AUG | 7 | Gem |
| | SEP | 28 | Can |
| | DEC | 31 | Gem* |

*Repeat means planet is retrograde.

## JUPITER SIGNS 1901–2007

| | | | |
|---|---|---|---|
| 1901 | JAN | 19 | Cap |
| 1902 | FEB | 6 | Aqu |
| 1903 | FEB | 20 | Pic |
| 1904 | MAR | 1 | Ari |
| | AUG | 8 | Tau |
| | AUG | 31 | Ari |
| 1905 | MAR | 7 | Tau |
| | JUL | 21 | Gem |
| | DEC | 4 | Tau |
| 1906 | MAR | 9 | Gem |
| | JUL | 30 | Can |
| 1907 | AUG | 18 | Leo |
| 1908 | SEP | 12 | Vir |
| 1909 | OCT | 11 | Lib |
| 1910 | NOV | 11 | Scp |
| 1911 | DEC | 10 | Sag |
| 1913 | JAN | 2 | Cap |
| 1914 | JAN | 21 | Aqu |
| 1915 | FEB | 4 | Pic |
| 1916 | FEB | 12 | Ari |
| | JUN | 26 | Tau |
| | OCT | 26 | Ari |
| 1917 | FEB | 12 | Tau |
| | JUN | 29 | Gem |
| 1918 | JUL | 13 | Can |
| 1919 | AUG | 2 | Leo |
| 1920 | AUG | 27 | Vir |
| 1921 | SEP | 25 | Lib |
| 1922 | OCT | 26 | Scp |
| 1923 | NOV | 24 | Sag |
| 1924 | DEC | 18 | Cap |
| 1926 | JAN | 6 | Aqu |
| 1927 | JAN | 18 | Pic |
| | JUN | 6 | Ari |
| | SEP | 11 | Pic |
| 1928 | JAN | 23 | Ari |
| | JUN | 4 | Tau |
| 1929 | JUN | 12 | Gem |
| 1930 | JUN | 26 | Can |
| 1931 | JUL | 17 | Leo |
| 1932 | AUG | 11 | Vir |
| 1933 | SEP | 10 | Lib |
| 1934 | OCT | 11 | Scp |
| 1935 | NOV | 9 | Sag |
| 1936 | DEC | 2 | Cap |
| 1937 | DEC | 20 | Aqu |
| 1938 | MAY | 14 | Pic |
| | JUL | 30 | Aqu |
| | DEC | 29 | Pic |
| 1939 | MAY | 11 | Ari |
| | OCT | 30 | Pic |
| | DEC | 20 | Ari |
| 1940 | MAY | 16 | Tau |
| 1941 | MAY | 26 | Gem |
| 1942 | JUN | 10 | Can |
| 1943 | JUN | 30 | Leo |
| 1944 | JUL | 26 | Vir |
| 1945 | AUG | 25 | Lib |
| 1946 | SEP | 25 | Scp |
| 1947 | OCT | 24 | Sag |
| 1948 | NOV | 15 | Cap |
| 1949 | APR | 12 | Aqu |
| | JUN | 27 | Cap |
| | NOV | 30 | Aqu |
| 1950 | APR | 15 | Pic |
| | SEP | 15 | Aqu |
| | DEC | 1 | Pic |
| 1951 | APR | 21 | Ari |
| 1952 | APR | 28 | Tau |
| 1953 | MAY | 9 | Gem |
| 1954 | MAY | 24 | Can |
| 1955 | JUN | 13 | Leo |
| | NOV | 17 | Vir |
| 1956 | JAN | 18 | Leo |
| | JUL | 7 | Vir |
| | DEC | 13 | Lib |

| | | | |
|---|---|---|---|
| 1957 | FEB | 19 | Vir |
| | AUG | 7 | Lib |
| 1958 | JAN | 13 | Scp |
| | MAR | 20 | Lib |
| | SEP | 7 | Scp |
| 1959 | FEB | 10 | Sag |
| | APR | 24 | Scp |
| | OCT | 5 | Sag |
| 1960 | MAR | 1 | Cap |
| | JUN | 10 | Sag |
| | OCT | 26 | Cap |
| 1961 | MAR | 15 | Aqu |
| | AUG | 12 | Cap |
| | NOV | 4 | Aqu |
| 1962 | MAR | 25 | Pic |
| 1963 | APR | 4 | Ari |
| 1964 | APR | 12 | Tau |
| 1965 | APR | 22 | Gem |
| | SEP | 21 | Can |
| | NOV | 17 | Gem |
| 1966 | MAY | 5 | Can |
| | SEP | 27 | Leo |
| 1967 | JAN | 16 | Can |
| | MAY | 23 | Leo |
| | OCT | 19 | Vir |
| 1968 | FEB | 27 | Leo |
| | JUN | 15 | Vir |
| | NOV | 15 | Lib |
| 1969 | MAR | 30 | Vir |
| | JUL | 15 | Lib |
| | DEC | 16 | Scp |
| 1970 | APR | 30 | Lib |
| | AUG | 15 | Scp |
| 1971 | JAN | 14 | Sag |
| | JUN | 5 | Scp |
| | SEP | 11 | Sag |
| 1972 | FEB | 6 | Cap |
| | JUL | 24 | Sag |
| | SEP | 25 | Cap |
| 1973 | FEB | 23 | Aqu |
| 1974 | MAR | 8 | Pic |
| 1975 | MAR | 18 | Ari |
| 1976 | MAR | 26 | Tau |
| | AUG | 23 | Gem |
| | OCT | 16 | Tau |
| 1977 | APR | 3 | Gem |
| | AUG | 20 | Can |
| | DEC | 30 | Gem |
| 1978 | APR | 12 | Can |
| | SEP | 5 | Leo |
| 1979 | FEB | 28 | Can |
| | APR | 20 | Leo |
| | SEP | 29 | Vir |
| 1980 | OCT | 27 | Lib |
| 1981 | NOV | 27 | Scp |
| 1982 | DEC | 26 | Sag |
| 1984 | JAN | 19 | Cap |
| 1985 | FEB | 6 | Aqu |
| 1986 | FEB | 20 | Pic |
| 1987 | MAR | 2 | Ari |
| 1988 | MAR | 8 | Tau |
| | JUL | 22 | Gem |
| | NOV | 30 | Tau |
| 1989 | MAR | 11 | Gem |
| | JUL | 30 | Can |
| 1990 | AUG | 18 | Leo |
| 1991 | SEP | 12 | Vir |
| 1992 | OCT | 10 | Lib |
| 1993 | NOV | 10 | Scp |
| 1994 | DEC | 9 | Sag |
| 1996 | JAN | 3 | Cap |
| 1997 | JAN | 21 | Aqu |
| 1998 | FEB | 4 | Pic |
| 1999 | FEB | 13 | Ari |
| | JUN | 28 | Tau |
| | OCT | 23 | Ari |
| 2000 | FEB | 14 | Tau |
| | JUN | 30 | Gem |
| 2001 | JUL | 14 | Can |
| 2002 | AUG | 1 | Leo |

| | | | | | | | |
|---|---|---|---|---|---|---|---|
| 2003 | AUG | 27 | Vir | 2006 | NOV | 24 | Sag |
| 2004 | SEP | 24 | Lib | 2007 | DEC | 17 | Cap |
| 2005 | OCT | 26 | Scp | | | | |

## SATURN SIGNS 1903–2007

| | | | | | | | |
|---|---|---|---|---|---|---|---|
| 1903 | JAN | 19 | Aqu | | SEP | 22 | Ari |
| 1905 | APR | 13 | Pic | 1940 | MAR | 20 | Tau |
| | AUG | 17 | Aqu | 1942 | MAY | 8 | Gem |
| 1906 | JAN | 8 | Pic | 1944 | JUN | 20 | Can |
| 1908 | MAR | 19 | Ari | 1946 | AUG | 2 | Leo |
| 1910 | MAY | 17 | Tau | 1948 | SEP | 19 | Vir |
| | DEC | 14 | Ari | 1949 | APR | 3 | Leo |
| 1911 | JAN | 20 | Tau | | MAY | 29 | Vir |
| 1912 | JUL | 7 | Gem | 1950 | NOV | 20 | Lib |
| | NOV | 30 | Tau | 1951 | MAR | 7 | Vir |
| 1913 | MAR | 26 | Gem | | AUG | 13 | Lib |
| 1914 | AUG | 24 | Can | 1953 | OCT | 22 | Scp |
| | DEC | 7 | Gem | 1956 | JAN | 12 | Sag |
| 1915 | MAY | 11 | Can | | MAY | 14 | Scp |
| 1916 | OCT | 17 | Leo | | OCT | 10 | Sag |
| | DEC | 7 | Can | 1959 | JAN | 5 | Cap |
| 1917 | JUN | 24 | Leo | 1962 | JAN | 3 | Aqu |
| 1919 | AUG | 12 | Vir | 1964 | MAR | 24 | Pic |
| 1921 | OCT | 7 | Lib | | SEP | 16 | Aqu |
| 1923 | DEC | 20 | Scp | | DEC | 16 | Pic |
| 1924 | APR | 6 | Lib | 1967 | MAR | 3 | Ari |
| | SEP | 13 | Scp | 1969 | APR | 29 | Tau |
| 1926 | DEC | 2 | Sag | 1971 | JUN | 18 | Gem |
| 1929 | MAR | 15 | Cap | 1972 | JAN | 10 | Tau |
| | MAY | 5 | Sag | | FEB | 21 | Gem |
| | NOV | 30 | Cap | 1973 | AUG | 1 | Can |
| 1932 | FEB | 24 | Aqu | 1974 | JAN | 7 | Gem |
| | AUG | 13 | Cap | | APR | 18 | Can |
| | NOV | 20 | Aqu | 1975 | SEP | 17 | Leo |
| 1935 | FEB | 14 | Pic | 1976 | JAN | 14 | Can |
| 1937 | APR | 25 | Ari | | JUN | 5 | Leo |
| | OCT | 18 | Pic | 1977 | NOV | 17 | Vir |
| 1938 | JAN | 14 | Ari | 1978 | JAN | 5 | Leo |
| 1939 | JUL | 6 | Tau | | JUL | 26 | Vir |

| | | | | | | | |
|---|---|---|---|---|---|---|---|
| 1980 | SEP | 21 | Lib | 1994 | JAN | 28 | Pic |
| 1982 | NOV | 29 | Scp | 1996 | APR | 7 | Ari |
| 1983 | MAY | 6 | Lib | 1998 | JUN | 9 | Tau |
| | AUG | 24 | Scp | | OCT | 25 | Ari |
| 1985 | NOV | 17 | Sag | 1999 | MAR | 1 | Tau |
| 1988 | FEB | 13 | Cap | 2000 | AUG | 10 | Gem |
| | JUN | 10 | Sag | | OCT | 16 | Tau |
| | NOV | 12 | Cap | 2001 | APR | 21 | Gem |
| 1991 | FEB | 6 | Aqu | 2003 | JUN | 3 | Can |
| 1993 | MAY | 21 | Pic | 2005 | JUL | 16 | Leo |
| | JUN | 30 | Aqu | 2007 | SEP | 2 | Vir |

CHAPTER 7

# Your Rising Sign Tells Where the Action Is

You can learn much about a person by the signs and interactions of the sun, moon, and planets in the horoscope, but you can't tell where in that person's life the activity will take place. Knowing the rising sign, which is based on the exact moment in time of an event such as a birth, will provide information that enables the astrologer to make predictions. For example, you might know that a person has Mars in Aries, which will describe that person's dynamic fiery energy. But if you also know that the person has a Capricorn rising sign, this Mars will fall in the fourth house of home and family, so you know where that energy will operate.

Your rising sign is the degree of the zodiac ascending over the eastern horizon when you were born. (That's why it's often called the ascendant.) It marks the first point in the horoscope, the beginning of the first house, one of twelve divisions of the horoscope, each of which represents a different area of your life. After the rising sign sets up the first house, the other houses parade around the chart in sequence, with the following sign on the house cusp. Due to the earth's rotation, the rising sign changes every two hours, which means that other babies, who may have been born later or earlier on the same day in the same hospital as you were (and will be sure to have most planets in the same signs as you do) may not have the same rising sign and their planets may fall in different houses in the chart.

For instance, if Mars is in Gemini and your rising sign is Taurus, Mars will most likely be active in the second or financial house of your chart. Someone born later in the day when the rising sign is Virgo would have Mars positioned at the top of the chart, energizing the tenth house of career.

Most astrologers insist on knowing the exact time of a client's birth before analyzing a chart. The more accurate your birth time, the more accurately an astrologer can position the planets in your chart. Without a valid rising sign, your collection of planets would have no homes. One would have no idea which area of your life would be influenced by a particular planet.

## How Your Rising Sign Can Influence Your Sun Sign

Your rising sign has an important relationship with your sun sign. Some will complement the sun sign; others hide it under a totally different mask, as if playing an entirely different role, making it difficult to guess the person's sun sign from outer appearances. This may be the reason why you might not look or act like your sun sign's archetype. For example, a Leo with a conservative Capricorn ascendant would come across as much more serious than a Leo with a fiery Aries or Sagittarius ascendant.

Though the rising sign usually creates the first impression you make, there are exceptions. When the sun sign is reinforced by other planets in the same sign, this might overpower the impression of the rising sign. For instance, a Leo sun plus a Leo Venus and Leo Jupiter would counteract the more conservative image that would otherwise be conveyed by the person's Capricorn ascendant.

Those born early in the morning when the sun was on the horizon will be most likely to project the image of their sun sign. These people are often called a "double Aries" or a "double Virgo" because the same sun sign and ascendant reinforce each other.

## Find Your Rising Sign

Look up your rising sign from the chart at the end of this chapter. Since rising signs change every two hours, it is important to know your birth time as close to the minute

as possible. Even a few minutes' difference could change the rising sign and therefore the setup of your chart. If you are unsure about the exact time, but know within a few hours, check the following descriptions to see which is most like the personality you project.

## Aries Rising: Alpha Energy

You are the most aggressive version of your sun sign, with boundless energy that can be used productively if it's channeled in the right direction. Watch a tendency to overreact emotionally and blow your top. You come across as openly competitive, a positive asset in business or sports. Be on guard against impatience, which could lead to head injuries. Your walk and bearing could have the telltale head-forward Aries posture. You may wear more bright colors, especially red, than others of your sign. You may also have a tendency to drive your car faster.

Can you see the alpha Aries tendency in Barbra Streisand (a sun-sign Taurus) and Bette Midler (a sun-sign Sagittarius)?

## Taurus Rising: Down to Earth

You're slow-moving, with a beautiful (or distinctive) speaking or singing voice that can be especially soothing or melodious. You probably surround yourself with comfort, good food, luxurious environments, and other sensual pleasures. You prefer welcoming others into your home to gadding about. You may have a talent for business, especially in trading, appraising, and real estate. A Taurus ascendant gives a well-padded physique that gains weight easily, like Liza Minnelli. This ascendant can also endow females with a curvaceous beauty.

## Gemini Rising: A Way with Words

You're naturally sociable, with lighter, more ethereal mannerisms than others of your sign, especially if you're female.

You love to communicate with people, and express your ideas and feelings easily, like British prime minister Tony Blair. You may have a talent for writing or public speaking. You thrive on variety, a constantly changing scene, and a lively social life. However, you may relate to others at a deeper level than might be suspected. And you will be far more sympathetic and caring than you project. You will probably travel widely, changing partners and jobs several times (or juggle two at once). Physically, your nerves are quite sensitive. Occasionally, you would benefit from a calm, tranquil atmosphere away from your usual social scene.

## Cancer Rising: Nurturing Instincts

You are naturally acquisitive, possessive, private, a moneymaker, like Bill Gates or Michael Bloomberg. You easily pick up on others' needs and feelings—a great gift in business, the arts, and personal relationships. But you must guard against overreacting or taking things too personally, especially during full moon periods. Find creative outlets for your natural nurturing gifts, such as helping the less fortunate, particularly children. Your insights would be helpful in psychology. Your desire to feed and care for others would be useful in the restaurant, hotel, or child-care industries. You may be especially fond of wearing romantic old clothes, collecting antiques, and, of course, dining on exquisite food. Since your body may retain fluids, pay attention to your diet. To relax, escape to places near water.

## Leo Rising: Diva Dazzle

You may come across as more poised than you really feel. However, you play it to the hilt, projecting a proud royal presence. A Leo ascendant gives you a natural flair for drama, like Marilyn Monroe, and you might be accused of stealing the spotlight. You'll also project a much more outgoing, optimistic, sunny personality than others of your sign. You take care to please your public by always projecting

your best star quality, probably tossing a luxuriant mane of hair, sporting a striking hairstyle, or dressing to impress. Females often dazzle with spectacular jewelry. Since you may have a strong parental nature, you could well be the regal family matriarch or patriarch, like George W. Bush.

## Virgo Rising: High Standards

Virgo rising masks your inner nature with a practical, analytical outer image. You seem neat, orderly, more particular than others of your sign. Others in your life may feel they must live up to your high standards. Though at times you may be openly critical, this masks a well-meaning desire to have only the best for loved ones. Your sharp eye for details could be used in the financial world, or your literary skills could draw you to teaching or publishing. The healing arts, health care, and service-oriented professions attract many with a Virgo ascendant. You're likely to take good care of yourself, with great attention to health, diet, and exercise, like Madonna. You might even show some hypochondriac tendencies, like Woody Allen. Physically, you may have a very sensitive digestive system.

## Libra Rising: The Charmer

Libra rising gives you a charming, social public persona, like Bill Clinton. You tend to avoid confrontations in relationships, preferring to smooth the way or negotiate diplomatically rather than give in to an emotional reaction. Because you are interested in all aspects of a situation, you may be slow to reach decisions. Physically, you'll have good proportions and symmetry. You will move with natural grace and balance. You're likely to have pleasing, if not beautiful, facial features, with a winning smile, like Cary Grant. You'll show natural good taste and harmony in your clothes and home decor. Legal, diplomatic, or public relations professions could draw your interest.

## Scorpio Rising: An Air of Mystery

You project an intriguing air of mystery with this ascendant, as the Scorpio secretiveness and sense of underlying power combines with your sun sign. As with Jackie O, there's more to you than meets the eye. You seem like someone who is always in control and who can move comfortably in the world of power. Your physical look comes across as intense. Many of you have remarkable eyes, with a direct, penetrating gaze. But you'll never reveal your private agenda, and you tend to keep your true feelings under wraps (watch a tendency toward paranoia). You may have an interesting romantic history with secret love affairs, like Grace Kelly. Many of you heighten your air of mystery by wearing black. You're happiest near water and should provide yourself with a seaside retreat.

## Sagittarius Rising: The Explorer

You travel with this ascendant. You may also be a more outdoor, sportive type, with an athletic, casual, outgoing air. Your moods are camouflaged with cheerful optimism or a philosophical attitude. Though you don't hesitate to speak your mind, like Ted Turner, who was called the Mouth of the South, you can also laugh at your troubles or crack a joke more easily than others of your sign. A Sagittarius ascendant can also draw you to the field of higher education or to spiritual life. You'll seem to have less attachment to things and people, and may explore the globe. Your strong, fast legs are a physical bonus.

## Capricorn Rising: Serious Business

This rising sign makes you come across as serious, goal-oriented, disciplined, and careful with cash. You are not one of the zodiac's big spenders, though you might splurge occasionally on items with good investment value. You're the traditional, conservative type in dress and environment,

and you might come across as quite normal and business-like, like Rupert Murdoch. You'll function well in a structured or corporate environment where you can climb to the top. (You are always aware of who's the boss.) In your personal life, you could be a loner or a single parent who is "father and mother" to your children.

## Aquarius Rising: One of a Kind

You come across as less concerned about what others think and could even be a bit eccentric. You're more at ease with groups of people than others in your sign, and you may be attracted to public life, like Jay Leno. Your appearance may be unique, either unconventional or unimportant to you. Those of you whose sun is in a water sign (Cancer, Scorpio, Pisces) may exercise your nurturing qualities with a large group, an extended family, or a day-care or community center.

## Pisces Rising: Romantic Roles

Your creative, nurturing talents are heightened and so is your ability to project emotional drama. And, like Antonio Banderas, your dreamy eyes and poetic air bring out the protective instinct in others. You could be attracted to the arts, especially theater, dance, film, and photography, or to psychology, spiritual practice, and charity work. You are happiest when you are using your creative ability to help others. Since you are vulnerable to mood swings, it is especially important for you to find interesting, creative work where you can express your talents and heighten your self-esteem. Accentuate the positive. Be wary of escapist tendencies, particularly involving alcohol or drugs to which you are supersensitive, like Whitney Houston.

# RISING SIGNS—A.M. BIRTHS

| | 1 AM | 2 AM | 3 AM | 4 AM | 5 AM | 6 AM | 7 AM | 8 AM | 9 AM | 10 AM | 11 AM | 12 NOON |
|---|---|---|---|---|---|---|---|---|---|---|---|---|
| Jan 1 | Lib | Sc | Sc | Sc | Sag | Sag | Cap | Cap | Aq | Aq | Pis | Ar |
| Jan 9 | Lib | Sc | Sc | Sag | Sag | Sag | Cap | Cap | Aq | Pis | Ar | Tau |
| Jan 17 | Sc | Sc | Sc | Sag | Sag | Cap | Cap | Aq | Aq | Pis | Ar | Tau |
| Jan 25 | Sc | Sc | Sag | Sag | Sag | Cap | Cap | Aq | Pis | Ar | Tau | Tau |
| Feb 2 | Sc | Sc | Sag | Sag | Cap | Cap | Aq | Pis | Pis | Ar | Tau | Gem |
| Feb 10 | Sc | Sag | Sag | Sag | Cap | Cap | Aq | Pis | Ar | Tau | Tau | Gem |
| Feb 18 | Sc | Sag | Sag | Cap | Cap | Aq | Pis | Pis | Ar | Tau | Gem | Gem |
| Feb 26 | Sag | Sag | Sag | Cap | Aq | Aq | Pis | Ar | Tau | Tau | Gem | Gem |
| Mar 6 | Sag | Sag | Cap | Cap | Aq | Pis | Pis | Ar | Tau | Gem | Gem | Can |
| Mar 14 | Sag | Cap | Cap | Aq | Aq | Pis | Ar | Tau | Tau | Gem | Gem | Can |
| Mar 22 | Sag | Cap | Cap | Aq | Pis | Ar | Ar | Tau | Gem | Gem | Can | Can |
| Mar 30 | Cap | Cap | Aq | Pis | Pis | Ar | Tau | Tau | Gem | Can | Can | Can |
| Apr 7 | Cap | Cap | Aq | Pis | Ar | Ar | Tau | Gem | Gem | Can | Can | Leo |
| Apr 14 | Cap | Aq | Aq | Pis | Ar | Tau | Tau | Gem | Gem | Can | Can | Leo |
| Apr 22 | Cap | Aq | Pis | Ar | Ar | Tau | Gem | Gem | Gem | Can | Leo | Leo |
| Apr 30 | Aq | Aq | Pis | Ar | Tau | Tau | Gem | Can | Can | Can | Leo | Leo |
| May 8 | Aq | Pis | Ar | Ar | Tau | Gem | Gem | Can | Can | Leo | Leo | Leo |
| May 16 | Aq | Pis | Ar | Tau | Gem | Gem | Can | Can | Can | Leo | Leo | Vir |
| May 24 | Pis | Ar | Ar | Tau | Gem | Gem | Can | Can | Leo | Leo | Leo | Vir |
| June 1 | Pis | Ar | Tau | Gem | Gem | Can | Can | Can | Leo | Leo | Vir | Vir |
| June 9 | Ar | Ar | Tau | Gem | Gem | Can | Can | Leo | Leo | Leo | Vir | Vir |
| June 17 | Ar | Tau | Gem | Gem | Can | Can | Can | Leo | Leo | Vir | Vir | Vir |
| June 25 | Tau | Tau | Gem | Gem | Can | Can | Leo | Leo | Leo | Vir | Vir | Lib |
| July 3 | Tau | Gem | Gem | Can | Can | Can | Leo | Leo | Vir | Vir | Vir | Lib |
| July 11 | Tau | Gem | Gem | Can | Can | Leo | Leo | Leo | Vir | Vir | Lib | Lib |
| July 18 | Gem | Gem | Can | Can | Can | Leo | Leo | Vir | Vir | Vir | Lib | Lib |
| July 26 | Gem | Gem | Can | Can | Leo | Leo | Vir | Vir | Vir | Lib | Lib | Lib |
| Aug 3 | Gem | Can | Can | Can | Leo | Leo | Vir | Vir | Vir | Lib | Lib | Sc |
| Aug 11 | Gem | Can | Can | Leo | Leo | Leo | Vir | Vir | Lib | Lib | Lib | Sc |
| Aug 18 | Can | Can | Can | Leo | Leo | Vir | Vir | Vir | Lib | Lib | Sc | Sc |
| Aug 27 | Can | Can | Leo | Leo | Leo | Vir | Vir | Lib | Lib | Lib | Sc | Sc |
| Sept 4 | Can | Can | Leo | Leo | Leo | Vir | Vir | Vir | Lib | Lib | Sc | Sc |
| Sept 12 | Can | Leo | Leo | Leo | Vir | Vir | Lib | Lib | Lib | Sc | Sc | Sag |
| Sept 20 | Leo | Leo | Leo | Vir | Vir | Vir | Lib | Lib | Sc | Sc | Sc | Sag |
| Sept 28 | Leo | Leo | Leo | Vir | Vir | Lib | Lib | Lib | Sc | Sc | Sag | Sag |
| Oct 6 | Leo | Leo | Vir | Vir | Vir | Lib | Lib | Sc | Sc | Sc | Sag | Sag |
| Oct 14 | Leo | Vir | Vir | Vir | Lib | Lib | Lib | Sc | Sc | Sag | Sag | Cap |
| Oct 22 | Leo | Vir | Vir | Lib | Lib | Lib | Sc | Sc | Sc | Sag | Sag | Cap |
| Oct 30 | Vir | Vir | Vir | Lib | Lib | Sc | Sc | Sc | Sag | Sag | Cap | Cap |
| Nov 7 | Vir | Vir | Lib | Lib | Lib | Sc | Sc | Sc | Sag | Sag | Cap | Cap |
| Nov 15 | Vir | Vir | Lib | Lib | Sc | Sc | Sc | Sag | Sag | Cap | Cap | Aq |
| Nov 23 | Vir | Lib | Lib | Lib | Sc | Sc | Sag | Sag | Sag | Cap | Cap | Aq |
| Dec 1 | Vir | Lib | Lib | Sc | Sc | Sc | Sag | Sag | Cap | Cap | Aq | Aq |
| Dec 9 | Lib | Lib | Lib | Sc | Sc | Sag | Sag | Sag | Cap | Cap | Aq | Pis |
| Dec 18 | Lib | Lib | Sc | Sc | Sc | Sag | Sag | Cap | Cap | Aq | Aq | Pis |
| Dec 28 | Lib | Lib | Sc | Sc | Sag | Sag | Sag | Cap | Aq | Aq | Pis | Ar |

# RISING SIGNS—P.M. BIRTHS

| | 1 PM | 2 PM | 3 PM | 4 PM | 5 PM | 6 PM | 7 PM | 8 PM | 9 PM | 10 PM | 11 PM | 12 MID-NIGHT |
|---|---|---|---|---|---|---|---|---|---|---|---|---|
| Jan 1 | Tau | Gem | Gem | Can | Can | Can | Leo | Leo | Vir | Vir | Vir | Lib |
| Jan 9 | Tau | Gem | Gem | Can | Can | Leo | Leo | Leo | Vir | Vir | Vir | Lib |
| Jan 17 | Gem | Gem | Can | Can | Can | Leo | Leo | Vir | Vir | Vir | Lib | Lib |
| Jan 25 | Gem | Gem | Can | Can | Leo | Leo | Leo | Vir | Vir | Lib | Lib | Lib |
| Feb 2 | Gem | Can | Can | Can | Leo | Leo | Vir | Vir | Vir | Lib | Lib | Sc |
| Feb 10 | Gem | Can | Can | Leo | Leo | Leo | Vir | Vir | Lib | Lib | Lib | Sc |
| Feb 18 | Can | Can | Can | Leo | Leo | Vir | Vir | Vir | Lib | Lib | Sc | Sc |
| Feb 26 | Can | Can | Leo | Leo | Leo | Vir | Vir | Lib | Lib | Lib | Sc | Sc |
| Mar 6 | Can | Leo | Leo | Leo | Vir | Vir | Vir | Lib | Lib | Sc | Sc | Sc |
| Mar 14 | Can | Leo | Leo | Vir | Vir | Vir | Lib | Lib | Lib | Sc | Sc | Sag |
| Mar 22 | Leo | Leo | Leo | Vir | Vir | Lib | Lib | Lib | Sc | Sc | Sc | Sag |
| Mar 30 | Leo | Leo | Vir | Vir | Vir | Lib | Lib | Sc | Sc | Sc | Sag | Sag |
| Apr 7 | Leo | Leo | Vir | Vir | Lib | Lib | Lib | Sc | Sc | Sc | Sag | Sag |
| Apr 14 | Leo | Vir | Vir | Vir | Lib | Lib | Sc | Sc | Sc | Sag | Sag | Cap |
| Apr 22 | Leo | Vir | Vir | Lib | Lib | Lib | Sc | Sc | Sc | Sag | Sag | Cap |
| Apr 30 | Vir | Vir | Vir | Lib | Lib | Sc | Sc | Sc | Sag | Sag | Cap | Cap |
| May 8 | Vir | Vir | Lib | Lib | Lib | Sc | Sc | Sag | Sag | Sag | Cap | Cap |
| May 16 | Vir | Vir | Lib | Lib | Sc | Sc | Sc | Sag | Sag | Cap | Cap | Aq |
| May 24 | Vir | Lib | Lib | Lib | Sc | Sc | Sag | Sag | Sag | Cap | Cap | Aq |
| June 1 | Vir | Lib | Lib | Sc | Sc | Sc | Sag | Sag | Cap | Cap | Aq | Aq |
| June 9 | Lib | Lib | Lib | Sc | Sc | Sag | Sag | Sag | Cap | Cap | Aq | Pis |
| June 17 | Lib | Lib | Sc | Sc | Sc | Sag | Sag | Cap | Cap | Aq | Aq | Pis |
| June 25 | Lib | Lib | Sc | Sc | Sag | Sag | Sag | Cap | Cap | Aq | Pis | Ar |
| July 3 | Lib | Sc | Sc | Sc | Sag | Sag | Cap | Cap | Aq | Aq | Pis | Ar |
| July 11 | Lib | Sc | Sc | Sag | Sag | Sag | Cap | Cap | Aq | Pis | Ar | Tau |
| July 18 | Sc | Sc | Sc | Sag | Sag | Cap | Cap | Aq | Aq | Pis | Ar | Tau |
| July 26 | Sc | Sc | Sag | Sag | Sag | Cap | Cap | Aq | Pis | Ar | Tau | Tau |
| Aug 3 | Sc | Sc | Sag | Sag | Cap | Cap | Aq | Aq | Pis | Ar | Tau | Gem |
| Aug 11 | Sc | Sag | Sag | Sag | Cap | Cap | Aq | Pis | Ar | Tau | Tau | Gem |
| Aug 18 | Sc | Sag | Sag | Cap | Cap | Aq | Pis | Pis | Ar | Tau | Gem | Gem |
| Aug 27 | Sag | Sag | Sag | Cap | Cap | Aq | Pis | Ar | Tau | Tau | Gem | Gem |
| Sept 4 | Sag | Sag | Cap | Cap | Aq | Pis | Pis | Ar | Tau | Gem | Gem | Can |
| Sept 12 | Sag | Sag | Cap | Aq | Aq | Pis | Ar | Tau | Tau | Gem | Gem | Can |
| Sept 20 | Sag | Cap | Cap | Aq | Pis | Pis | Ar | Tau | Gem | Gem | Can | Can |
| Sept 28 | Cap | Cap | Aq | Aq | Pis | Ar | Tau | Tau | Gem | Gem | Can | Can |
| Oct 6 | Cap | Cap | Aq | Pis | Ar | Ar | Tau | Gem | Gem | Can | Can | Leo |
| Oct 14 | Cap | Aq | Aq | Pis | Ar | Tau | Tau | Gem | Gem | Can | Can | Leo |
| Oct 22 | Cap | Aq | Pis | Ar | Ar | Tau | Gem | Gem | Can | Can | Leo | Leo |
| Oct 30 | Aq | Aq | Pis | Ar | Tau | Tau | Gem | Can | Can | Can | Leo | Leo |
| Nov 7 | Aq | Aq | Pis | Ar | Tau | Tau | Gem | Can | Can | Can | Leo | Leo |
| Nov 15 | Aq | Pis | Ar | Tau | Gem | Gem | Can | Can | Can | Leo | Leo | Vir |
| Nov 23 | Pis | Ar | Ar | Tau | Gem | Gem | Can | Can | Leo | Leo | Leo | Vir |
| Dec 1 | Pis | Ar | Tau | Gem | Gem | Can | Can | Can | Leo | Leo | Vir | Vir |
| Dec 9 | Ar | Tau | Tau | Gem | Gem | Can | Can | Leo | Leo | Leo | Vir | Vir |
| Dec 18 | Ar | Tau | Gem | Gem | Can | Can | Can | Leo | Leo | Vir | Vir | Vir |
| Dec 28 | Tau | Tau | Gem | Gem | Can | Can | Leo | Leo | Vir | Vir | Vir | Lib |

CHAPTER 8

# Learn the Glyphs and Read Your Own Chart!

If you get to a certain point in astrology, you'll want to read your own chart (or someone else's). Or perhaps you'll have a reading and be given a copy of your chart by an astrologer. In either case, you'll be confronted by a circular chart covered with mysterious symbols—unreadable except by someone who has learned these glyphs.

Breaking into astrology requires cracking the ancient code that is a type of picture writing universally understood by astrologers. It's well worth the effort to learn these symbols. You'll not only be able to read a chart, but you will be able to make use of free charts available on any number of Internet sites and astrology software programs. This year, you can even take astrology with you on your PDA and read a chart on the go. But almost none of these programs show the planetary positions written in plain English, so you'll miss out if you don't learn the glyphs.

Each little symbol has built-in clues to help you decipher not only which sign or planet it represents, but what the object means in a more esoteric sense. Actually the physical act of writing the symbol is a mystical experience in itself, a way to invoke the deeper meaning of the sign or planet through age-old visual elements that have been with us since time began.

Since there are only twelve signs and ten planets (not counting a few asteroids and other space objects some astrologers use), it's a lot easier than learning to read a foreign language. Here's a code cracker for the glyphs, beginning with the glyphs for the planets. To those who already know their glyphs, don't just skim over the chapter.

These familiar graphics have hidden meanings you will discover!

## The Glyphs for the Planets

The glyphs for the planets are easy to learn. They're simple combinations of the most basic visual elements: the circle, the semicircle or arc, and the cross. However, each component of a glyph has a special meaning in relation to the other parts of the symbol.

The circle, which has no beginning or end, is one of the oldest symbols of spirit or spiritual forces. Early diagrams of the heavens—spiritual territory—are shown in circular form. The never-ending line of the circle is the perfect symbol for eternity. The semicircle or arc is an incomplete circle, symbolizing the receptive, finite soul, which contains spiritual potential in the curving line.

The vertical line of the cross symbolizes movement from heaven to earth. The horizontal line describes temporal movement, here and now, in time and space. Combined in a cross, the vertical and horizontal planes symbolize manifestation in the material world.

## The Sun Glyph ☉

The sun is always shown by this powerful solar symbol, a circle with a point in the center. The center point is you, your spiritual center, and the symbol represents your infinite personality incarnating (the point) into the finite cycles of birth and death.

The sun has been represented by a circle or disk since ancient Egyptian times when the solar disk represented the sun god, Ra. Some archaeologists believe the great stone circles found in England were centers of sun worship. This particular version of the symbol was brought into common use in the sixteenth century after German occultist and scholar Cornelius Agrippa (1486–1535) wrote a book called *Die Occulta Philosophia,* which became accepted as the authority in the field. Agrippa collected many medieval astro-

logical and magical symbols in this book, which have been used by astrologers since then.

## The Moon Glyph ☽

The moon glyph is the most recognizable symbol on a chart, a left-facing arc stylized into the crescent moon. As part of a circle, the arc symbolizes the potential fulfillment of the entire circle, the life force that is still incomplete. Therefore, it is the ideal representation of the reactive, receptive, emotional nature of the moon.

## The Mercury Glyph ☿

Mercury contains all three elemental symbols: the crescent, the circle, and the cross in vertical order. This is the "Venus with a hat" glyph (compare with the symbol of Venus). With another stretch of the imagination, can't you see the winged cap of Mercury the messenger? Think of the upturned crescent as antennae that tune in and transmit messages from the sun, reminding you that Mercury is the way you communicate, the way your mind works. The upturned arc is receiving energy into the spirit or solar circle, which will later be translated into action on the material plane, symbolized by the cross. All the elements are equally sized because Mercury is neutral; it doesn't play favorites! This planet symbolizes objective, detached, unemotional thinking.

## The Venus Glyph ♀

Here the relationship is between two components: the circle of spirit and the cross of matter. Spirit is elevated over matter, pulling it upward. Venus asks, "What is beautiful? What do you like best? What do you love to have done to you?" Consequently, Venus determines both your ideal of beauty and what feels good sensually. It governs your own allure and power to attract, as well as what attracts and pleases you.

## The Mars Glyph ♂

In this glyph, the cross of matter is stylized into an arrowhead pointed up and outward, propelled by the circle of spirit. With a little imagination, you can visualize it as the shield and spear of Mars, the ancient god of war. You can deduce that Mars embodies your spiritual energy projected into the outer world. It's your assertiveness, your initiative, your aggressive drive, what you like to do to others, your temper. If you know someone's Mars, you know whether they'll blow up when angry or do a slow burn. Your task is to use your outgoing Mars energy wisely and well.

## The Jupiter Glyph ♃

Jupiter is the basic cross of matter, with a large stylized crescent perched on the left side of the horizontal, temporal plane. You might think of the crescent as an open hand, because one meaning of Jupiter is "luck," what's handed to you. You don't have to work for what you get from Jupiter; it comes to you, if you're open to it.

The Jupiter glyph might also remind you of a jumbo jet plane, with a huge tail fin, about to take off. This is the planet of travel, mental and spiritual, of expanding your horizons via new ideas, new spiritual dimensions, and new places. Jupiter embodies the optimism and enthusiasm of the traveler about to embark on an exciting adventure.

## The Saturn Glyph ♄

Flip Jupiter over, and you've got Saturn. This might not be immediately apparent because Saturn is usually stylized into an "h" form like the one shown here. The principle it expresses is the opposite of Jupiter's expansive tendencies. Saturn pulls you back to earth: the receptive arc is pushed down underneath the cross of matter. Before there are any rewards or expansion, the duties and obligations of the material world must be considered. Saturn says, "Stop, wait, finish your chores before you take off!"

Saturn's glyph also resembles the sickle of old "Father Time." Saturn was first known as Chronos, the Greek god

of time, for time brings all matter to an end. When it was the most distant planet (before the discovery of Uranus), Saturn was believed to be the place where time stopped. After the soul departed from earth, it journeyed back to the outer reaches of the universe and finally stopped at Saturn, or at "the end of time."

## The Uranus Glyph ♅

The glyph for Uranus is often stylized to form a capital *H* after Sir William Herschel, who discovered the planet. But the more esoteric version curves the two pillars of the H into crescent antennae, or "ears," like satellite disks receiving signals from space. These are perched on the horizontal material line of the cross of matter and pushed from below by the circle of the spirit. To many sci-fi fans, Uranus looks like an orbiting satellite.

Uranus channels the highest energy of all, the white electrical light of the universal spiritual force that holds the cosmos together. This pure electrical energy is gathered from all over the universe. Because Uranus energy doesn't follow any ordinary celestial drumbeat, it can't be controlled or predicted (which is also true of those who are strongly influenced by this eccentric planet). In the symbol, this energy is manifested through the balance of polarities (the two opposite arms of the glyph) like the two polarized wires of a lightbulb.

## The Neptune Glyph ♆

Neptune's glyph is usually stylized to look like a trident, the weapon of the Roman god Neptune. However, on a more esoteric level, it shows the large upturned crescent of the soul pierced through by the cross of matter. Neptune nails down, or materializes, soul energy, bringing impulses from the soul level into manifestation. That is why Neptune is associated with imagination or "imagining in," making an image of the soul. Neptune works through feelings, sensitivity, and the mystical capacity to bring the divine into the earthly realm.

## The Pluto Glyph ♇

Pluto is written two ways. One is a composite of the letters *PL*, the first two letters of the word Pluto and coincidentally the initials of Percival Lowell, one of the planet's discovers. The other, more esoteric symbol is a small circle above a large open crescent that surmounts the cross of matter. This depicts Pluto's power to regenerate. Imagine a new little spirit emerging from the sheltering cup of the soul. Pluto rules the forces of life and death. After this planet has passed a sensitive point in your chart, you are transformed, reborn in some way.

Sci-fi fans might visualize this glyph as a small satellite (the circle) being launched. It was shortly after Pluto's discovery that we learned how to harness the nuclear forces that made space exploration possible. Pluto rules the transformative power of atomic energy, which totally changed our lives and from which there is no turning back.

## The Glyphs for the Signs

On an astrology chart, the glyph for the sign will appear after that of the planet. For example, when you see the moon glyph followed first by a number and then by another glyph representing the sign, this means that the moon was passing over a certain degree of that astrological sign at the time of the chart. On the dividing lines between the houses on your chart, you'll find the symbol for the sign that rules the house.

Because sun sign symbols do not contain the same basic geometric components of the planetary glyphs, we must look elsewhere for clues to their meanings. Many have been passed down from ancient Egyptian and Chaldean civilizations with few modifications. Others have been adapted over the centuries.

In deciphering many of the glyphs, you'll often find that the symbols reveal a dual nature of the sign, which is not always apparent in the usual sun sign descriptions. For instance, the Gemini glyph is similar to the Roman numeral for two, and reveals this sign's longing to discover a twin soul. The Cancer glyph may be interpreted as resembling

either the nurturing breasts or the self-protective claws of a crab, both symbols associated with the contrasting qualities of this sign. Libra's glyph embodies the duality of the spirit balanced with material reality. The Sagittarius glyph shows that the aspirant must also carry along the earthly animal nature in his quest. The Capricorn sea goat is another symbol with dual emphasis. The goat climbs high, yet is always pulled back by the deep waters of the unconscious. Aquarius embodies the double waves of mental detachment, balanced by the desire for connection with others, in a friendly way. Finally, the two fishes of Pisces, which are forever tied together, show the duality of the soul and the spirit that must be reconciled.

## The Aries Glyph ♈

Since the symbol for Aries is the Ram, this glyph is obviously associated with a ram's horns, which characterize one aspect of the Aries personality—an aggressive, me-first, leaping-headfirst attitude. But the symbol can be interpreted in other ways as well. Some astrologers liken it to a fountain of energy, which Aries people also embody. The first sign of the zodiac bursts on the scene eagerly, ready to go. Another analogy is to the eyebrows and nose of the human head, which Aries rules, and the thinking power that is initiated by the brain.

One theory of this symbol links it to the Egyptian god Amun, represented by a ram in ancient times. As Amun-Ra, this god was believed to embody the creator of the universe, the leader of all the other gods. This relates easily to the position of Aries as the leader (or first sign) of the zodiac, which begins at the spring equinox, a time of the year when nature is renewed.

## The Taurus Glyph ♉

This is another easy glyph to draw and identify. It takes little imagination to decipher the bull's head with long curving horns. Like its symbol the Bull, the archetypal Taurus is slow to anger but ferocious when provoked, as well as stubborn, steady, and sensual. Another association is the

larynx (and thyroid) of the throat area (ruled by Taurus) and the eustachian tubes running up to the ears, which coincides with the relationship of Taurus to the voice, song, and music. Many famous singers, musicians, and composers have prominent Taurus influences.

Many ancient religions involved a bull as the central figure in fertility rites or initiations, usually symbolizing the victory of man over his animal nature. Another possible origin is in the sacred bull of Egypt, who embodied the incarnate form of Osiris, god of death and resurrection. In early Christian imagery, the Taurus Bull represented St. Luke.

## The Gemini Glyph ♊

The standard glyph immediately calls to mind the Roman numeral for two (II) and the Twins symbol, as it is called, for Gemini. In almost all drawings and images used for this sign, the relationship between two persons is emphasized. Usually one twin will be touching the other, which signifies communication, human contact, the desire to share.

The top line of the Gemini glyph indicates mental communication, while the bottom line indicates shared physical space.

The most famous Gemini legend is that of the twin sons, Castor and Pollux, one of whom had a mortal father while the other was the son of Zeus, king of the gods. When it came time for the mortal twin to die, his grief-stricken brother pleaded with Zeus, who agreed to let them spend half the year on earth in mortal form and half in immortal life, with the gods on Mount Olympus. This reflects a basic duality of humankind, which possesses an immortal soul yet is also subject to the limits of mortality.

## The Cancer Glyph ♋

Two convenient images relate to the Cancer glyph. It is easiest to decode the curving claws of the Cancer symbol, the Crab. Like the crab's, Cancer's element is water. This sensitive sign also has a hard protective shell to protect its tender interior. The crab must be wily to escape predators,

scampering sideways and hiding under rocks. The crab also responds to the cycles of the moon, as do all shellfish. The other image is that of two female breasts, which Cancer rules, showing that this is a sign that nurtures and protects others as well as itself.

In ancient Egypt, Cancer was also represented by the scarab beetle, a symbol of regeneration and eternal life.

## The Leo Glyph ♌

Notice that the Leo glyph seems to be an extension of Cancer's glyph, with a significant difference. In the Cancer glyph, the lines curve inward protectively. The Leo glyph expresses energy outwardly. And there is no duality in the symbol, the Lion, or in Leo, the sign.

Lions have belonged to the sign of Leo since earliest times. It is not difficult to imagine the king of beasts with his sweeping mane and curling tail from this glyph. The upward sweep of the glyph easily describes the positive energy of Leo: the flourishing tail, their flamboyant qualities. Anther analogy, perhaps a stretch of the imagination, is that of a heart leaping up with joy and enthusiasm, also very typical of Leo, which also rules the heart. In early Christian imagery, the Leo Lion represented St. Mark.

## The Virgo Glyph ♍

You can read much into this mysterious glyph. For instance, it could represent the initials of "Mary Virgin," or a young woman holding a staff of wheat, or stylized female genitalia, all common interpretations. The M shape might also remind you that Virgo is ruled by Mercury. The cross beneath the symbol reveals the grounded, practical nature of this earth sign.

The earliest zodiacs link Virgo with the Egyptian goddess Isis, who gave birth to the god Horus after her husband Osiris had been killed, in the archetype of a miraculous conception. There are many ancient statues of Isis nursing her baby son, which are reminiscent of medieval Virgin and Child motifs. This sign has also been associated with the

image of the Holy Grail, when the Virgo symbol was substituted with a chalice.

## The Libra Glyph ♎

It is not difficult to read the standard image for Libra, the Scales, into this glyph. There is another meaning, however, that is equally relevant: the setting sun as it descends over the horizon. Libra's natural position on the zodiac wheel is the descendant, or sunset position (as the Aries natural position is the ascendant, or rising sign). Both images relate to Libra's personality. Libra is always weighing pros and cons for a balanced decision. In the sunset image, the sun (male) hovers over the horizontal earth (female) before setting. Libra is the space between these lines, harmonizing yin and yang, spiritual and material, male and female, ideal and real worlds. The glyph has also been linked to the kidneys, which are ruled by Libra.

## The Scorpio Glyph ♏

With its barbed tail, this glyph is easy to identify as the Scorpion for the sign of Scorpio. It also represents the male sexual parts, over which the sign rules. From the arrowhead, you can draw the conclusion that Mars was once its ruler. Some earlier Egyptian glyphs for Scorpio represent it as an erect serpent, so the Serpent is an alternate symbol.

Another symbol for Scorpio, which is not identifiable in this glyph, is the Eagle. Scorpios can go to extremes, either in soaring like the eagle or self-destructing like the scorpion. In early Christian imagery, which often used zodiacal symbols, the Scorpio Eagle was chosen to symbolize the intense apostle St. John the Evangelist.

## The Sagittarius Glyph ♐

This is one of the easiest to spot and draw: an upward pointing arrow lifting up a cross. The arrow is pointing skyward, while the cross represents the four elements of the material world, which the arrow must convey. Elevating materiality into spirituality is an important Sagittarius qual-

ity, which explains why this sign is associated with higher learning, religion, philosophy, travel—the aspiring professions. Sagittarius can also send barbed arrows of frankness in the pursuit of truth, so the Archer symbol for Sagittarius is apt. (Sagittarius is also the sign of the supersalesman.)

Sagittarius is symbolically represented by the centaur, a mythological creature who is half man, half horse, aiming his arrow toward the skies. Though Sagittarius is motivated by spiritual aspiration, it also must balance the powerful appetites of the animal nature. The centaur Chiron, a figure in Greek mythology, became a wise teacher who, after many adventures and world travels, was killed by a poisoned arrow.

## The Capricorn Glyph ♑

One of the most difficult symbols to draw, this glyph may take some practice. It is a representation of the sea goat: a mythical animal that is a goat with a curving fish's tail. The goat part of Capricorn wants to leave the waters of the emotions and climb to the elevated areas of life. But the fish tail is the unconscious, the deep chaotic psychic level that draws the goat back. Capricorn is often trying to escape the deep, feeling part of life by submerging himself in work, steadily ascending to the top. To some people, the glyph represents a seated figure with a bent knee, a reminder that Capricorn governs the knee area of the body.

An interesting aspect of this glyph is the contrast of the sharp pointed horns—which represent the penetrating, shrewd, conscious side of Capricorn—with the swishing tail—which represents its serpentine, unconscious, emotional force. One Capricorn legend, which dates from Roman times, tells of the earthy fertility god, Pan, who tried to save himself from uncontrollable sexual desires by jumping into the Nile. His upper body then turned into a goat, while the lower part became a fish. Later, Jupiter gave him a safe haven as a constellation in the skies.

## The Aquarius Glyph ♒

This ancient water symbol can be traced back to an Egyptian hieroglyph representing streams of life force. Symbol-

ized by the Water Bearer, Aquarius is distributor of the waters of life—the magic liquid of regeneration. The two waves can also be linked to the positive and negative charges of the electrical energy that Aquarius rules, a sort of universal wavelength. Aquarius is tuned in intuitively to higher forces via this electrical force. The duality of the glyph could also refer to the dual nature of Aquarius, a sign that runs hot and cold and that is friendly but also detached in the mental world of air signs.

In Greek legends, Aquarius is represented by Ganymede, who was carried to heaven by an eagle in order to become the cupbearer of Zeus and to supervise the annual flooding of the Nile. The sign later became associated with aviation and notions of flight.

## The Pisces Glyph ♓

Here is an abstraction of the familiar image of Pisces, two Fishes swimming in opposite directions yet bound together by a cord. The Fishes represent the spirit—which yearns for the freedom of heaven—and the soul—which remains attached to the desires of the temporal world. During life on earth, the spirit and the soul are bound together. When they complement each other, instead of pulling in opposite directions, they facilitate the Pisces creativity. The ancient version of this glyph, taken from the Egyptians, had no connecting line, which was added in the fourteenth century.

In another interpretation, it is said that the left fish indicates the direction of involution or the beginning of a cycle, while the right fish signifies the direction of evolution, the way to completion of a cycle. It's an appropriate grand finale for Pisces, the last sign of the zodiac.

## CHAPTER 9

# Astrology on Your Computer: Where to Find Software That Suits Your Budget and Ability

Once you've learned the basics of astrology, you'll be ready to practice reading charts. It's great fun to start out by analyzing the charts of friends and family so you can see how the planets manifest in real life. If you have a computer, there's no easier way than to use astrology software, which can calculate a chart in seconds and even help you interpret it.

When it comes to astrology software, there are endless options. How do you make the right choice? First, define your goals. Do you want to do charts of friends and family, study celebrity charts, or check the aspects every day on your Palm Pilot? Do you want to invest in a more comprehensive program that adapts to your changing needs as you learn astrology?

The good news is that there's a program for every level of interest in all price points—starting with free. For the dabbler, there are the affordable Winstar Express and the Astroscan shareware. For the serious student, there are Astrolog (free), Solar Fire, Kepler, Winstar Plus—software that does every technique on planets and gives you beautiful chart printouts. You can do a chart of someone you've just met on your PDA with Astracadabra. If you're a Mac user, you'll be satisfied with the wonderful IO and Time Passages software.

However, since all the programs use the astrology symbols, or glyphs, for planets and signs, rather than written words, you should learn the glyphs before you purchase

your software. Our chapter on the glyphs in this book will help you do just that. Here are some software options for you to explore.

# Easy for Beginners

## Time Passages

Designed for either a Macintosh or Windows computer, Time Passages is straightforward and easy to use. It allows you to generate charts and interpretation reports for yourself or friends and loved ones at the touch of a button. If you haven't yet learned the astrology symbols, this might be the program for you; just roll your mouse over any symbol of the planets, signs, or house cusps, and you'll be shown a description in plain English below the chart. Then click on the planet, sign, or house cusp and up pops a detailed interpretation. It couldn't be easier. A new basic edition, under fifty dollars at this writing, is bargain priced and ideal for beginners.

Time Passages
(866) 772-7876 (866-77-ASTRO)
Web site: www.astrograph.com

# Growth Opportunities

## Astrolabe

Astrolabe is one of the top astrology software resources. Check out the latest version of their powerful Solar Fire software for Windows. A breeze to use, it will grow with your increasing knowledge of astrology to the most sophisticated levels. This company also markets a variety of programs for all levels of expertise and a wide selection of computer-generated astrology readings. This is a good resource for innovative software as well as applications for older computers.

The Astrolabe Web site is a great place to start your astrology tour of the Internet. Visitors to the site are greeted with a chart of the time you log on. And you can get your chart calculated, also free, with an interpretation e-mailed to you.

Astrolabe
Box 1750-R
Brewster, MA 02631
Phone: (800) 843-6682
Web site: www.alabe.com

## Matrix Software

You'll find a wide variety of software at student and advanced levels in all price ranges, demo disks, and lots of interesting readings. Check out Winstar Express, a powerful but reasonably priced program suitable for all skill levels. The Matrix Web site offers lots of fun activities for Web surfers, such as free readings from the *I Ching,* the runes, and the tarot. There are many free desktop backgrounds with astrology themes. Go here to connect with news groups and online discussions. Their online almanac helps you schedule the best day to sign on the dotted line, ask for a raise, or plant your tomatoes.

Matrix Software
126 South Michigan Ave.
Big Rapids, MI 49307
Phone: (800) 752-6387
Web site: www.astrologysoftware.com

## Astro Communications Services (ACS)

Books, software for Mac and IBM compatibles, individual charts, and telephone readings are offered by this California company. Their freebies include astrology greeting cards and new moon reports. Find technical astrology materials here, such as *The American Ephemeris* and PC atlases. ACS will calculate and send charts to you, a valuable service if you do not have a computer.

ACS Publications
P.O. box 1646
El Cajon, CA 72022-1646
Phone: (800) 514-5070
Fax: (619) 631-0185
Web site: www.astrocom.com

## Air Software

Here you'll find powerful, creative astrology software, and current stock market analysis. Financial astrology programs for stock market traders are a specialty. There are some interesting freebies at this site; check out the maps of eclipse paths for any year and a free astrology clock program.

Air Software
115 Caya Avenue
West Hartford, CT 06110
Phone: (800) 659-1247
Web site: www.alphee.com

## Kepler: State of the Art

Here's a program that has everything. Gorgeous graphic images, audio-visual effects, and myriad sophisticated chart options are built into this fascinating software. It's even got an astrological encyclopedia, plus diagrams and images to help you understand advanced concepts. This program is expensive, but if you're serious about learning astrology, it's an investment that will grow with you! There's a cheaper scaled-down version called Pegasus for those who don't want all the features. Check out its features at www.astrologysoftwareshop.com.

## Time Cycles Research: For Mac Users

Here's where Mac users can find astrology software that's as sophisticated as it gets. If you have a Mac, you'll love their beautiful graphic IO Series programs.

Time Cycles Research
P.O. Box 797
Waterford, CT 06385
Web site: www.timecycles.com

# Shareware and Freeware: The Price Is Right!

## Halloran Software: A Super Shareware Program

Check out Halloran Software's Web site (www.halloran.com), which offers several levels of Windows astrology software. Beginners should consider their Astrology for Windows shareware program, which is available in unregistered demo form as a free download and in registered form for a very reasonable price.

## Astrolog

If you're computer-savvy, you can't go wrong with Walter Pullen's amazingly complete Astrolog program, which is offered absolutely free at the site. The Web address is www.astrolog.org/astrolog.htm.

Astrolog is an ultrasophisticated program with all the features of much more expensive programs. It comes in versions for all formats—DOS, Windows, Mac, UNIX—and has some cool features, such as a revolving globe and a constellation map. If you are looking for astrology software with bells and whistles that doesn't cost big bucks, this program has it all!

## Astroscan

Surf to www.astroscan.ca for a free program called Astroscan. Stunning graphics and ease of use make this basic

program a winner. Astroscan has a fun list of celebrity charts you can call up with a few clicks.

## Programs for the Pocket PDA and Palm Pilot

Would you like to have astrology at your fingertips everywhere you go? No need to drag along your laptop. You can check the chart of the moment or of someone you've just met on your pocket PDA or Palm Pilot. As with most other programs, you'll need to know the astrological symbols in order to read the charts.

For the pocket PC that has the Microsoft Pocket PC 2002 or the Microsoft Windows Mobile 2003 operating system, there is the versatile Astracadabra, which can interchange charts with the popular Solar Fire software. It can be ordered at www.leelehman.com or www.astrologysoftwareshop.com.

For the Palm OS5 and compatible handheld devices, there is Astropocket from www.yves.robert.org/features.html. This is a shareware program, which allows you to use all the features free. However, you cannot store more than one chart at a time until you pay a mere twenty-eight-dollar registration fee for the complete version.

CHAPTER 10

# How to Connect with Astrology Fans Around the Globe

Are you interested in connecting with other astrology fans? How about expanding your knowledge by studying with a famous astrologer or by attending international lectures and conferences, even astrological workshops in exotic places? The astrological community is ready to welcome you.

You need only type the word astrology into any Internet search engine and watch hundreds of listings of astrology-related sites pop up. There are local meetings and international conferences where you can connect with other astrologers, and books and tapes to help you study at home.

To help you sort out the variety of options available, here are our top picks of the Internet and the astrological community at large.

## Nationwide Astrology Organizations and Conferences

### National Council for Geocosmic Research (NCGR)

Whether you'd like to know more about such specialties as financial astrology or techniques for timing events, or if you'd prefer the psychological or mythological approach, you'll meet the top astrologers at conferences sponsored by the National Council for Geocosmic Research. NCGR is

dedicated to providing quality education, bringing astrologers and astrology fans together at conferences, and promoting fellowship. Their course structure provides a systematized study of the many facets of astrology. The organization sponsors educational workshops, taped lectures, conferences, and a directory of professional astrologers. For an annual membership fee, you get their excellent publications and newsletters, plus the opportunity to network with other astrology buffs at local chapter events. (At this writing there are chapters in twenty-six states and four countries.)

To join NCGR for the latest information on upcoming events and chapters in your city, consult their Web site: www.geocosmic.org.

## American Federation of Astrologers (AFA)

Established in 1938, this is one of the oldest astrological organizations in the United States. AFA offers conferences, conventions, and a thorough correspondence course. If you are looking for a reading, their interesting Web site will refer you to an accredited AFA astrologer.

AFA
P.O. Box 22040
Tempe, AZ 85285-2040
Phone: (888) 301-7630 or (480) 838-1751
Fax: (480) 838-8293
Web site: www.astrologers.com

## Association for Astrological Networking (AFAN)

Did you know that astrologers are still being harassed for practicing astrology? AFAN provides support and legal information and works toward improving the public image of astrology. AFAN's network of local astrologers links with the international astrological community. Here are the people who will go to bat for astrology when it is attacked in the media. Everyone who cares about astrology should join!

AFAN
8306 Wilshire Boulevard
PMB 537
Beverly Hills, CA 90211
Phone: (800) 578-2326
E-mail: info@afan.org
Web site: www.afan.org

### International Society for Astrology Research (ISAR)

An international organization of professional astrologers dedicated to encouraging the highest standards of quality in the field of astrology with an emphasis on research. Among ISAR's benefits are a quarterly journal, a weekly e-mail newsletter, frequent conferences, and a free membership directory.

ISAR
P.O. Box 38613
Los Angeles, CA 90038
Fax: (805) 933-0301
Web site: www.isarastrology.com

## Astrology Magazines

In addition to articles by top astrologers, most of these have listings of astrology conferences, events, and local happenings.

*Horoscope Guide*
Kappa Publishing Group
Dept. 4
P.O. Box 2085
Marion, OH 43306-8121

*Dell Horoscope*
P.O. Box 54097
Boulder, CO 80322-4907

### The Mountain Astrologer

A favorite magazine of astrology fans! *The Mountain Astrologer* also has an interesting Web site featuring the latest news from an astrological point of view, plus feature articles from the magazine.

*The Mountain Astrologer*
P.O. Box 970
Cedar Ridge, CA 95924
Phone: (800) 247-4828
Web site: www.mountainastrologer.com

## Astrology College

### Kepler College of Astrological Arts and Sciences

A degree-granting college, which is also a center of astrology, has long been the dream of the astrological community and is a giant step forward in providing credibility to the profession. Therefore, the opening of Kepler College in 2000 was a historical event for astrology. It is the only college in the western hemisphere authorized to issue B.A. and M.A. degrees in Astrological Studies. Here is where to study with the best scholars, teachers, and communicators in the field. A long-distance study program is available for those interested.

For more information, contact:

Kepler College of Astrological Arts and Sciences
4630 200th Street SW
Suite A-1
Lynnwood, WA 98036
Phone: (425) 673-4292
Fax: (425) 673-4983
Web site: www.kepler.edu

## Our Favorite Web Sites

Of the thousands of astrological Web sites that come and go on the Internet, these have stood the test of time and are likely to still be operating when this book is published.

### Astrodienst (www.astro.com)

Don't miss this fabulous international site that has long been one of the best astrology resources on the Internet. It's also a great place to view and download your own astrology chart. The world atlas on this site will give you the accurate longitude and latitude of your birthplace for setting up your horoscope. Then you can print out your free chart in a range of easy-to-read formats. Other attractions: a list of famous people born on your birth date, a feature that helps you choose the best vacation spot, plus articles by world-famous astrologers.

### AstroDatabank (www.astrodatabank.com)

When the news is breaking, you can bet this site will be the first to get accurate birthdays of the headliners. The late astrologer Lois Rodden was a stickler for factual information and her meticulous research is being continued, much to the benefit of the astrological community. The Web site specializes in charts of current newsmakers, political figures, and international celebrities. You can also participate in discussions and analysis of the charts and see what some of the world's best astrologers have to say about them. Their AstroDatabank program, which you can purchase at the site, provides thousands of verified birthdays sorted into categories. It's an excellent research tool.

### StarIQ (www.stariq.com)

Find out how top astrologers view the latest headlines at the must-see StarIQ site. Many of the best minds in astrology comment on the latest news, stock market ups and downs, political contenders. You can sign up to receive e-mail forecasts at the most important times keyed to your

individual chart. (This is one of the best of the many online forecasts.)

## Astrology Books (www.astroamerica.com)

The Astrology Center of America sells a wide selection of books on all aspects of astrology, from the basics to the most advanced, at this online bookstore. Also available are many hard-to-find and recycled books.

## Astrology Scholars' Sites

See what one of astrology's great teachers, Robert Hand, has to offer on his site: www.robhand.com. A leading expert on the history of astrology, he's on the cutting edge of the latest research.

The Project Hindsight group of astrologers is devoted to restoring the astrology of the Hellenistic period, the primary source for all later Western astrology. There are fascinating articles for astrology fans on this site, www.projecthindsight.com.

## Financial Astrology Sites

Financial astrology is a hot specialty, with many tipsters, players, and theorists. There are online columns, newsletters, specialized financial astrology software, and mutual funds run by astrology seers. One of the more respected financial astrologers is Ray Merriman, whose column on www.stariq.com is a must read for those following the bulls and bears. Other top financial astrologers offer tips and forecasts at the www.afund.com and www.alphee.com sites.

CHAPTER 11

# Got a Big Question? A Personal Reading Might Give You the Answer

Life can sometimes leave you feeling bewitched, bothered, and bewildered, as the song goes. Whether you're faced with a seemingly insurmountable problem or would simply like an objective opinion, it might be helpful to consult a professional astrologer who will take all the facets of your astrological chart into consideration. A good reading can give you peace of mind by confirming those mysterious intuitive feelings that you can't quite identify. It can give you insights on your situation that will lead you to better choices, perhaps ones that have been blocked by a blind spot.

A reading can answer some very practical questions as well, such as setting the perfect date for a wedding, a crucial job interview, or a real estate closing. If a partnership is turning sour, insights from a reading might help you put the relationship back on track. Or, after a reading, you might understand the compromises and adjustments needed to make it work. For example, one astrologically minded business team has charts done to help them work well together. Charts for family members might be done to help improve home life or figure out some complicated family dynamics.

Another good reason for a reading is to improve your personal knowledge of astrology by consulting someone who has years of experience analyzing charts. You might choose someone with a special technique that intrigues you. Armed with the knowledge of your chart that you have

acquired so far, you can learn to interpret subtle nuances or gain perspective on your talents and abilities.

But what kind of reading should you have? Besides one-on-one readings with a professional astrologer, there are personal readings by mail, telephone, Internet, and tape. Well-advertised computer-generated reports and celebrity-sponsored readings are sure to attract your attention.

Done by a qualified astrologer, the personal reading can be an empowering experience if you want to reach your full potential, size up a lover or business situation, or find out what the future has in store. There are astrologers who are specialists in certain areas such as finance or medical astrology. And, unfortunately, there are many questionable practitioners who range from streetwise gypsy fortune-tellers to unscrupulous scam artists.

The following basic guidelines can help you sort out your options to find the reading that's right for you.

## One-on-One Consultations with a Professional Astrologer

Nothing compares to a one-on-one consultation with a professional astrologer who has analyzed thousands of charts and can pinpoint the potential in yours. During your reading, you can get your specific questions answered. For instance, how to get along better with your mate or coworker. There are many astrologers who now combine their skills with training in psychology and are well-suited to help you examine your alternatives.

To give you an accurate reading, an astrologer needs certain information from you: the date, time, and place where you were born. (A horoscope can be cast about anyone or anything that has a specific time and place.) Most astrologers will then enter this information into a computer, which will calculate a chart in seconds. From the resulting chart, the astrologer will do an interpretation.

If you don't know your exact birth time, you can usually locate it at the Bureau of Vital Statistics at the city hall or county seat of the state where you were born. If you still

have no success in getting your time of birth, some astrologers can estimate an approximate birth time by using past events in your life to determine the chart. This technique is called *rectification.*

## How to Find an Astrologer

Choose your astrologer with the same care as you would any trusted adviser such as a doctor, lawyer, or banker. Unfortunately, anyone can claim to be an astrologer—to date, there is no licensing of astrologers or universally established professional criteria. However, there are nationwide organizations of serious, committed astrologers that can help you in your search.

Good places to start your investigation are organizations such as the American Federation of Astrologers (AFA) or the National Council for Geocosmic Research (NCGR), which offer a program of study and certification. If you live near a major city, there is sure to be an active NCGR chapter or astrology club in your area; many are listed in astrology magazines available at your local newsstand. In response to many requests for referrals, both the AFA and the NCGR have directories of professional astrologers listed on their Web sites; these directories include a glossary of terms and an explanation of specialties within the astrological field. Contact the NCGR and AFA headquarters for information (see chapter 10 in this book).

## Warning Signals

As a potentially lucrative freelance business, astrology has always attracted self-styled experts who may not have the knowledge or the counseling experience to give a helpful reading. These astrologers can range from the well-meaning amateur to the charlatan or street-corner gypsy who has for many years given astrology a bad name. Be very wary of astrologers who claim to have occult powers or who make pretentious claims of celebrated clients or miraculous

achievements. You can often tell from the initial phone conversation if the astrologer is legitimate. He or she should ask for your birthday time and place, then conduct the conversation in a professional manner. Any astrologer who gives a reading based only on your sun sign is highly suspect.

When you arrive at the reading, the astrologer should be prepared. The consultation should be conducted in a private, quiet place. The astrologer should be interested in your problems of the moment. A good reading involves feedback on your part. So if the reading is not relating to your concerns, you should let the astrologer know. You should feel free to ask questions and get clarifications of technical terms. The more you actively participate, rather than expecting the astrologer to carry the reading or come forth with oracular predictions, the more meaningful your experience will be. An astrologer should help you validate your current experience and be frank about possible negative happenings, but also suggest a positive course of action.

In their approach to a reading, some astrologers may be more literal, others more intuitive. Those who have had counseling training may take a more psychological approach. Though some astrologers may seem to have an almost psychic ability, extrasensory perception or any other parapsychological talent is not essential. A very accurate picture can be drawn from the data in your horoscope chart.

An astrologer may do several charts for each client, including one for the time of birth and a *progressed chart,* showing the evolution from birth to the present time. According to your individual needs, there are many other possibilities, such as a chart for a different location if you are contemplating a change of place. Relationships between any two people, things, or events can be interpreted with a chart that compares one partner's horoscope with the other's. A composite chart, which uses the midpoint between planets in two individual charts to describe the relationship, is another commonly used device.

An astrologer will be particularly interested in transits, those times when cycling planets activate the planets or sensitive points in your birth chart. These indicate important events in your life.

Many astrologers offer tape-recorded readings, another option to consider, especially if the astrologer you choose lives at a distance. In this case, you'll be mailed a taped reading based on your birth chart. This type of reading is more personal than a computer printout and can give you valuable insights, though it is not equivalent to a live dialogue with the astrologer when you can discuss your specific interests and issues of the moment.

## The Telephone Reading

Telephone readings come in two varieties: a dial-in taped reading, usually recorded in advance by an astrologer, or a live consultation with an "astrologer" on the other end of the line. The taped readings are general daily or weekly forecasts, applied to all members of your sign and charged by the minute. The quality depends on the astrologer. One caution: Be aware that these readings can run up quite a telephone bill, especially if you get into the habit of calling every day. Be sure that you are aware of the per-minute cost of each call beforehand.

Live telephone readings also vary with the expertise of the astrologer. Ideally, the astrologer at the other end of the line enters your birth date into a computer, which then quickly calculates your chart. This chart will be referred to during the consultation. The advantage of a live telephone reading is that your individual chart is used and you can ask about a specific problem. However, before you invest in any reading, be sure that your astrologer is qualified and that you fully understand in advance how much you will be charged. There should be no unpleasant financial surprises later.

## Computer-Generated Reports

Companies that offer computer programs (such as ACS, Matrix, Astrolabe) also offer a variety of computer-generated horoscope readings. These can be quite compre-

hensive, offering a beautiful printout of the chart plus many pages of detailed information about each planet and aspect of the chart. You can then study it at your convenience. Of course, the interpretations will be general, since there is no personal input from you, and may not cover your immediate concerns. Since computer-generated horoscopes are much lower in cost than live consultations, you might consider one as either a supplement or a preparation for an eventual live reading. You'll then be more familiar with your chart and able to plan specific questions in advance. They also make terrific gifts for astrology fans. There are several companies, listed in chapter 9, that offer computerized readings prepared by reputable astrologers.

Whichever option you decide to pursue, may your reading be an empowering one!

CHAPTER 12

# Your Pet-scope for 2007: How to Choose Your Best Friend for Life

With both Jupiter, the planet of luck and expansion, and powerful Pluto in the animal-loving sign of Sagittarius, this is sure to be a year of pets and a great time to bring joy into your life by adopting an animal friend. At this writing, 63 percent of all American households have at least one pet, according to a recent survey by the American Pet Product Manufacturers Association. And we spend billions of dollars on the care and feeding of our beloved pets. Our pets are counted as part of the family, often sharing our beds and accompanying us on trips.

Whether you choose to adopt an animal from a local shelter or buy a thoroughbred from a breeder, try for an optimal time of adoption and the sun sign of your new friend. If you're rescuing an animal, however, it's difficult to know the sun sign of the animal, but you can adopt on a day when the moon is compatible with yours, which should bless the emotional relationship. Using the moon signs listed in the daily forecasts in this book, choose a day when the moon is in your sign, a sign of the same element, or a compatible element. This means fire and air signs should go for a day when the moon is in fire signs—Aries, Leo, Sagittarius—or air signs—Gemini, Libra, or Aquarius. Water and earth signs should choose a day when the moon is in water signs—Cancer, Scorpio or Pisces—or earth signs—Taurus, Virgo, or Capricorn. If possible, aim for a new moon, good for beginning a new relationship.

Here are some sign-specific tips for adopting an animal that will become your best friend for life.

## Aries: The Rescuer

Aries gets special pleasure from rescuing animals in distress and rehabing them, so check your local shelters if you're thinking of adopting an animal. As an active fire sign, you'd be happiest with a lively animal, and you might do well with a rescue animal, such as a German shepherd or Labrador retriever. You'd also enjoy training such an animal. Otherwise look for intelligence, alertness, playfulness, and obedience in your friend. Since Aries tend to have an active life, look for a sleek, low-maintenance coat on your dog or cat. Cat lovers would enjoy the more active breeds such as the Siamese or Abyssinian.

An Aries sun-sign dog or cat would be ideal. Aries animals have a brave, energetic, rather combative nature. They can be mischievous, so the kittens and puppies should be monitored for safety. They'll dare to jump higher, run faster, and chase more animals than their peers. They may require stronger words and more obedience training than other signs. Give them plenty of toys and play active games with them often.

## Taurus: The Toucher

Taurus is a touchy-feely sign; this tendency extends to your animal relationships. Look for a dog or cat that enjoys being petted and groomed, is affectionate, and adapts well to family life. As one of the great animal-loving signs, Taurus is likely to have several pets, so it is important that they all get along together. Give each one its own special safe space to minimize turf wars.

Taurus animals are calm and even tempered, but do not like being teased and could retaliate, so be sure to instruct children how to handle and play with their pet. Since this sign has strong appetites and tends to put on weight easily,

be careful not to overindulge the animals in high-calorie treats and table snacks.

Taurus female animals are excellent mothers and make good breeders. They tend to be clean and less destructive of home furnishings than other animals.

## Gemini: The Companion

A bright, quick-witted sign like yours requires an equally interesting and communicative pet. Choose a social animal that adapts well to different environments, since you may travel or have homes in different locations.

Gemini animals can put up with noise, telephones, music, and people coming and going. They'll want to be part of the action, so place a pillow or roost in a public place. They do not like being left alone. If you will be away for long periods, find them an animal companion to play with. You might consider adopting two Gemini pets from the same litter.

Animals born under this sign are easy to teach and some enjoy doing tricks or retrieving. They may be more vocal than other animals, especially if they are confined without companionship.

## Cancer: The Nurturer

Cancer enjoys a devoted, obedient animal who demonstrates loyalty to its master. An affectionate home-loving dog or cat that welcomes you and sits on your lap would be ideal. The emotional connection with your pet is most important; therefore, you may depend on your powerful psychic powers when choosing an animal. Wait until you feel a strong bond of psychic communication. The moon sign of the day you adopt is very important for moon-ruled Cancer, so choose a water sign, if possible.

Cancer animals need a feeling of security; they don't like changes of environment or too much chaos at home. If

you intend to breed your animal, the Cancer pet makes a wonderful and fertile mother.

## Leo: The Prideful Owner

The Leo owner may choose a pet that reminds you of your own physical characteristics, such as similar coloring or build. You will be proud of your pet, will keep the animal groomed to perfection, and will choose the most spectacular example of the breed. Noble animals with a regal attitude, beautiful fur, or striking markings are often preferred, such as the Himalayan or the red tabby Persian cat, the standard poodle or the chow chow. An attention getter is a must.

Under the sign of the king of beasts, Leo-born animals have proud noble natures. They usually have a cheerful, magnanimous disposition and rule their domains regardless of their breed, holding their heads with pride and walking with great authority. They enjoy being groomed, like to show off, and enjoy the attention of fans. Leo animals thrive in the spotlight.

## Virgo: The Caregiver

Virgo owners will be very particular about their pets, paying special attention to requirements for care and maintenance. You need a pet who is clean, obedient, intelligent, yet rather quiet. A highly active, barking or meowing pet that might get on your nerves is a no-no.

Cats are usually very good pets for Virgo. Choose one of the calm breeds, such as a Persian. Though this is a high-maintenance cat, its beauty and personality will be rewarding. You are compassionate with animals in need, and you might find it rewarding to volunteer at a local shelter or veterinary clinic or to train service dogs.

Virgo animals can be fussy eaters and very particular about their environment. They are gentle and intelligent; they respond to kind words and quiet commands, never harsh treatment. Virgo is an excellent sign for dogs that

are trained to do service work, since they seem to enjoy being useful and are intelligent enough to be easily trained.

## Libra: The Beautifier

The Libra owner responds to beauty and elegance in your pet. You require a well-mannered, but social companion, who can be displayed in all of nature's finery. An exotic variety such as a graceful curly-haired Devon Rex cat would be a show stopper. Libra often prefers the smaller varieties, such as a miniature schnauzer, a mini greyhound, or a teacup poodle.

Pets born under Libra are usually charming and well-mannered. They tend to be more careful than those of other signs. They'll avoid confrontations and harsh sounds, but respond to words of love and gentle corrections.

## Scorpio: The Powerful

Scorpios enjoy a powerful animal with a strong character. They enjoy training animals and do well with service dogs, guard dogs, or police animals. Some Scorpios enjoy exotic, edgy pets, such as hairless Sphynx cats or Chinese Chin dogs. Rescuing animals in dire circumstances and finding them new homes are especially rewarding for Scorpios, as Matthew McConaughey did during Hurricane Katrina.

Animals born under this sign tend to be one-person pets, very strongly attached to their owners and extremely loyal and possessive. They are natural guard animals that will take extreme risks to protect their owners. They are best ruled by love and with consistent behavior training. They need to respect their owners and will return their love with great devotion.

## Sagittarius: The Jovial Freedom Lover

Sagittarius is a traveler and one of the great animal lovers of the zodiac. The horse is especially associated with your

sign, and you could well be a horse whisperer. You generally respond most to large, active animals. If a small animal, like a chihuahua, steals your heart, be sure it's one that travels well or tolerates your absence. Outdoor dogs like hunting dogs, retrievers, and border collies would be good companions on your outdoor adventures.

Sagittarius animals are freedom-loving, jovial, happy-go-lucky types. They may be wanderers, however, so be sure they have the proper identification tags and consider embedded microchip identification. These animals tend to be openly affectionate, companionable, and untemperamental. They enjoy socializing and playing with humans and other animals and are especially good with active children.

## Capricorn: The Thoroughbred

Capricorn is a discriminating owner, with a great sense of responsibility toward your animal. You will be concerned with maintenance and care; you will rarely neglect or overlook any health issues with your pet. You will also discipline your pet wisely, not tolerating any destructive or outrageous antics. You will be attracted to good breeding, good manners, and deep loyalty from your pet.

The Capricorn pet tends to be more quiet and serious than other pets, perhaps a lone wolf who prefers the company of its owner rather than a sociable or mischievous type. This is another good sign for a working dog, such as a herder, because Capricorn animals enjoy this outlet for their energy.

## Aquarius: The Independent Original

Aquarius owners tend to lead active, busy lives and need an animal who can either accompany them cheerfully or who won't make waves. Demanding or high-maintenance dogs are not for you. You might prefer unusual or oddball pets, such as dressed-up chihuahuas that travel in your tote bag or scene-stealing, rather shocking hairless cats. Or you

will acquire a group of animals that can play with one another when you are pursuing outside activities. You can relate to the independence of cats.

Aquarius animals are not loners. They enjoy the companionship of humans or groups of other animals. They tend to be more independent and may require more training to follow the house rules.

## Pisces: The Soul-Mate

This is the sign that can talk to the animals. Pisces owners enjoy deep communication with their pets, love having their animals accompany them, sleep with them, and show affection. Pisces will often rescue an animal in distress or adopt an animal from a shelter. Tropical fish are often recommended as a Pisces pet, and they seem to have a natural tranquilizing effect on this sign. However, Pisces may require an animal that shows more affection than do their fish friends.

Pisces animals are creative types; they can be sensually seductive and mysterious, mischievous and theatrical. They make fine house pets, do not usually like to roam far from their owners, and have winning personalities, especially with the adults in the home. Naturally sensitive and seldom vicious, they should be treated gently and given much praise and encouragement.

CHAPTER 13

# Your Baby-scope: Children Born in 2007

Will the babies born this year be easy to raise or will they require a time-out mat or supernanny? Astrology answers these questions by looking beyond sun signs to the planets that describe a whole generation.

Children born this year will belong to one of the most spiritual generations in history. The three outer planets—Uranus, Neptune, and Pluto, which stay in a sign for at least seven years—are the ones that most affect each generation. Now passing through Pisces, Aquarius, and Sagittarius respectively, the three most visionary signs are sure to imprint the children of 2007.

In the past century, Uranus in Pisces coincided with enormous creativity, which should impact this year's children. Neptune in Aquarius and Pluto in Sagittarius are bringing a time of dissolving barriers, of globalization, of interest in religion and spirituality . . . breaking away from the materialism of the last century. In contrast, the members of this generation will truly be children of the world, searching for deeper meanings to existence.

Astrology can be an especially helpful tool that can be used to design an environment that will enhance and encourage each child's positive qualities. Some parents start before conception, planning the birth of their child as far as possible to harmonize with the signs of other family members. However, each baby has its own schedule, so if yours arrives a week early or late, or elects a different sign than you'd planned, recognize that the new sign may be more in line with the mission your child is here to accomplish. In other words, if you were hoping for a Libra child

and he arrives during Virgo, that Virgo energy may be just what is needed to stimulate or complement your family. Remember that there are many astrological elements besides the sun sign that indicate strong family ties. Usually each child will share a particular planetary placement, an emphasis on a particular sign or house, or a certain chart configuration with his parents and other family members. Often there is a significant planetary angle that will define the parent-child relationship, such as family sun signs that form a T-square or a triangle.

One important thing you can do is to be sure the exact moment of birth is recorded. This will be essential in calculating an accurate astrological chart. The following descriptions can be applied to the sun or moon sign (if known) of a child—the sun sign will describe basic personality and the moon sign indicates the child's emotional needs.

## The Aries Child

Baby Aries is quite a handful! This energetic child will walk—and run—as soon as possible and perform daring feats of exploration. Caregivers should be vigilant. Little Aries seems to know no fear (and is especially vulnerable to head injuries). Many Aries children, in their rush to get on with life, seem hyperactive and are easily frustrated when they can't get their own way. Violent temper tantrums and dramatic physical displays are par for the course with these children, necessitating a time-out chair.

The very young Aries should be monitored carefully, since he is prone to take risks and may injure himself. An Aries loves to take things apart and may break toys easily, but with encouragement, the child will develop formidable coordination. Aries's bossy tendencies should be molded into leadership qualities, rather than bullying. Otherwise, the me-first Aries will have many clashes with other strong-willed youngsters. Encourage these children to take out aggressions and frustrations in active, competitive sports, where they usually excel. When a young Aries learns to focus his energies long enough to master a subject and

learns consideration for others, the indomitable Aries spirit will rise to the head of the class.

Aries born in 2007 will benefit from the jovial rays of Jupiter in Sagittarius until December of that year, which should give this child a sunny, optimistic personality.

## The Taurus Child

This is a cuddly, affectionate child who eagerly explores the world of the senses, especially the senses of taste and touch. The Taurus child can be a big eater and will put on weight easily if not encouraged to exercise. Since this child likes comfort and gravitates to beauty, try coaxing little Taurus to exercise to music or take him outdoors for hikes or long walks. Though Taurus may be a slow learner, this sign has an excellent retentive memory and generally masters a subject thoroughly. Taurus is interested in results and will see each project patiently through to completion, continuing long after others have given up.

Choose Taurus toys carefully to help develop innate talents. Construction toys, such as blocks or erector sets, appeal to their love of building. Paints or crayons develop their sense of color. Many Taurus have musical talents and love to sing, which is apparent at a young age.

This year's Taurus will want a pet or two and a few plants of his own. Give little Taurus a minigarden and watch the natural green thumb develop. This child has a strong sense of acquisition and an early grasp of material value. After filling a piggy bank, Taurus graduates to a savings account, before other children have started to learn the value of money. Jupiter in their house of joint ventures this year should give Taurus another edge in financial matters.

## The Gemini Child

Little Gemini will talk as soon as possible, filing the air with questions and chatter. This is a friendly child who

enjoys social contact, seems to require company, and adapts quickly to different surroundings. Geminis have quick minds that easily grasp the use of words, books, and telephones and will probably learn to talk and read at an earlier age than most. Though they are fast learners, Gemini may have a short attention span, darting from subject to subject. Projects and games that help focus the mind could be used to help them concentrate. Musical instruments, typewriters, and computers help older Gemini children combine mental with manual dexterity. Geminis should be encouraged to finish what they start before they go on to another project. Otherwise, they can become jack-of-all-trade types who have trouble completing anything they do. Their dispositions are usually cheerful and witty, making these children popular with their peers and delightful company at home.

This year's Gemini baby should go to the head of the class. Uranus in Pisces could inspire Gemini to make an unusual career choice, perhaps in a high-tech field. When he grows up, this year's Gemini may change fields several times before he finds a job that satisfies his need for stimulation and variety.

## The Cancer Child

This emotional, sensitive child is especially influenced by patterns set early in life. Young Cancers cling to their first memories as well as their childhood possessions. They thrive in calm emotional waters, with a loving, protective mother, and usually remain close to her (even if their relationship with her was difficult) throughout their lives. Divorce, death—anything that disturbs the safe family unit—are devastating to Cancers, who may need extra support and reassurance during a family crisis.

They sometimes need a firm hand to push the positive, creative side of their personality and discourage them from getting swept away by emotional moods or resorting to emotional manipulation to get their way. Praised and encouraged to find creative expression, Cancer will be able

to express his positive side consistently on a firm, secure foundation.

This year's Cancer child should be more grounded and practical, thanks to Jupiter in Sagittarius. This also brings the blessing of good health!

## The Leo Child

Leo children love the limelight and will plot to get the lion's share of attention. These children assert themselves with flair and drama and can behave like tiny tyrants to get their way. But in general, they have sunny, positive dispositions and are rarely subject to blue moods. At school, they're the ones who are voted most popular, head cheerleader, or homecoming queen. Leo is sure to be noticed for personality, if not for stunning looks or academic work; the homely Leo will be a class clown and the unhappy Leo may be the class bully.

Above all, a Leo child cannot tolerate being ignored for long. Drama or performing-arts classes, sports, and school politics are healthy ways for Leo to be a star. But Leos must learn to take lesser roles occasionally, or they will have some painful put-downs in store. Usually, the popularity of Leos is well earned; they are hard workers who try to measure up to their own high standards—and usually succeed.

The Leo baby born this year is likely to be more serious than the typical Leo, thanks to the taskmaster planet Saturn finishing up its two-year stay in Leo. This endows the child with self-discipline and the ability to function well in structured situations. With enhanced focusing ability, little Leo can be a high achiever.

## The Virgo Child

The young Virgo can be a quiet, rather serious child, with a quick, intelligent mind. Early on, little Virgo shows far more attention to detail and concern with small things than

other children do. Little Virgo has a built-in sense of order and a fascination with how things work. It is important for these children to have a place of their own, which they can order as they wish and where they can read or busy themselves with crafts and hobbies.

This child's personality can be very sensitive. Little Virgo may get hyper and overreact to seemingly small irritations, which can take the form of stomach upsets or delicate digestive systems. But this child will flourish where there is mental stimulation and a sense of order. Virgos thrive in school, especially in writing or language skills, and seem truly happy when buried in books. Chances are, young Virgo will learn to read ahead of classmates. Hobbies that involve detail work or that develop fine craftsmanship are especially suited to young Virgos.

Baby Virgo of 2007 is likely to be an especially active, intelligent child, since there are at least five planets in mutable signs during this period. With Saturn, also in Virgo beginning on September 2, he should respond to discipline. However, there should be plenty of mental and social stimulation in his environment to tame his restless nature.

## The Libra Child

The Libra child learns early about the power of charm and appearance. This is often a very physically appealing child with an enchanting dimpled smile, who is naturally sociable and enjoys the company of both children and adults. It is a rare Libra child who is a discipline problem, but when their behavior is unacceptable, they respond better to calm discussion than displays of emotion, especially if the discussion revolves around fairness. Because young Libras without a strong direction tend to drift with the mood of the group, these children should be encouraged to develop their unique talents and powers of discrimination so they can later stand on their own.

In school, this child is usually popular and will often have to choose between social invitations and studies. In the teen years, social pressures mount as the young Libra begins to look for a partner. This is the sign of best friends, so Libra's

choice of companions can have a strong effect on his future direction. Beautiful Libra girls may be tempted to go steady or have an unwise early marriage. Chances are, both sexes will fall in and out of love several times in their search for the ideal partner.

Little Libra of 2007 should have a way with words, thanks to Jupiter and Pluto in Sagittarius, which will enhance verbal and communications skills. This is an especially social, talkative child, who gets along well with siblings and classmates. Later in life, this Libra could choose a career in writing or the communication field.

## The Scorpio Child

The Scorpio child may seem quiet and shy, but will surprise others with intense feelings and formidable willpower. Scorpio children are single-minded when they want something and intensely passionate about whatever they do. One of a caregiver's tasks is to teach this child to balance activities and emotions, yet at the same time to make the most of his or her great concentration and intense commitment.

Since young Scorpios do not show their depth of feelings easily, parents will have to learn to read almost imperceptible signs that troubles are brewing beneath the surface. Both Scorpio boys and girls enjoy games of power and control on or off the playground. Scorpio girls may take an early interest in the opposite sex, masquerading as tomboys, while Scorpio boys may be intensely competitive and loners. When their powerful energies are directed into work, sports, or challenging studies, Scorpio is a superachiever, focused on a goal. With trusted friends, young Scorpio is devoted and caring—the proverbial friend through thick and thin, loyal for life.

Jupiter and Pluto in Sagittarius should give this year's baby Scorpio a more carefree personality plus a flair for finance. There's lots of water in their horoscope, with Pisces and Cancer planets endowing these babies with plenty of imagination and creativity to be developed. Mars in Cancer will ignite a spirit of adventure and a love of water sports. Long journeys could be in the future.

## The Sagittarius Child

This restless, athletic child will be out of the playpen and off on adventures as soon as possible. Little Sagittarius is remarkably well-coordinated, attempting daredevil feats on any wheeled vehicle from scooters to skateboards. These natural athletes need little encouragement to channel their energies into sports. Their cheerful, friendly dispositions earn them popularity in school, and once they have found a subject where their talent and imagination can soar, they will do well academically. They love animals, especially horses, and will be sure to have a pet or two, if not a home zoo. When they are old enough to take care of themselves, they'll clamor to be off on adventures of their own, away from home, if possible.

This child loves to travel, will not get homesick at summer camp, and may sign up to be a foreign-exchange student or spend summers abroad. Outdoor adventure appeals to little Sagittarius, especially if it involves an active sport, such as skiing, cycling, or mountain climbing. Give them enough space and encouragement, and their fiery spirit will propel them to achieve high goals.

Baby Sagittarius of 2007 is a freedom-loving child with a bonanza of luck and charisma, thanks to potent Pluto and lucky Jupiter in Sagittarius. This child has a natural generosity of spirit and an optimistic, expansive nature. He may need reality checks from time to time, since he may also be a big risk taker. He will also demand a great deal of freedom.

## The Capricorn Child

These purposeful, goal-oriented children will work to capacity if they feel this will bring results. They're not ones who enjoy work for its own sake—there must be an end in sight. Authority figures can do much to motivate these children, but once set on an upward path, young Capricorns will mobilize energy and talent and work harder, and with more perseverance, then any other sign. Capricorn has

built-in self-discipline that can achieve remarkable results, even if lacking the flashy personality, quick brain power, or penetrating insight of others. Once involved, young Capricorn will stick to a task until it is mastered. These children also know how to use others to their advantage and may well become team captains or class presidents.

A wise parent will set realistic goals for the Capricorn child, paving the way for the early thrill of achievement. Youngsters should be encouraged to express their caring, feeling side to others, as well as their natural aptitude for leadership. Capricorn children may be especially fond of grandparents and older relatives and will enjoy spending time with them and learning from them. It is not uncommon for young Capricorns to have an older mentor or teacher who guides them. With their great respect for authority, Capricorn children will take this influence very much to heart.

The Capricorn born in 2007 will have serious and responsible alliances, thanks to Saturn in the house of mutual ventures. This placement also hints at financial savvy—so give the child a savings account early on. Jupiter in Sagittarius promises a deep inner life and a generous nature.

## The Aquarius Child

The Aquarius child has an innovative, well-focused mind that often streaks so far ahead of those of peers that this child seems like an oddball. Routine studies never hold the restless youngster for long; he will look for another, more experimental place to try out his ideas and develop his inventions. Life is a laboratory to the inquiring Aquarius mind. School politics, sports, science, and the arts offer scope for such talents. But if there is no room for expression within approved social limits, Aquarius is sure to rebel. Questioning institutions and religions comes naturally, so these children may find an outlet elsewhere, becoming rebels with a cause. It is better not to force this child to conform, but rather to channel forward-thinking young minds into constructive group activities.

This year's Aquarius will have far-out glamour as well as

charisma, thanks to his ruler, Uranus, in a friendly bond with Neptune. This child could be a rock star, a statesman, or a scientist.

## The Pisces Child

Give young Pisces praise, applause, and a gentle, but firm, push in the right direction. Lovable Pisces children may be abundantly talented, but may be hesitant to express themselves, because they are quite sensitive and easily hurt. It is a parent's challenge to help them gain self-esteem and self-confidence. However, this same sensitivity makes them trusted friends who'll have many confidants as they develop socially. It also endows many Pisces with spectacular creative talent.

Pisces adores drama and theatrics of all sorts; therefore, encourage them to channel their creativity into art forms rather than indulging in emotional dramas. Understand that they may need more solitude than other children, as they develop their creative ideas. But though daydreaming can be creative, it is important that these natural dreamers not dwell too long in the world of fantasy. Teach them practical coping skills for the real world. Since Pisces are physically sensitive, parents should help them build strong bodies with proper diet and regular exercise. Young Pisces may gravitate to more individual sports, such as swimming, sailing, and skiing, rather than to team sports. Or they may prefer more artistic physical activities like dance or ice skating.

Born givers, these children are often drawn to the underdog (they fall quickly for sob stories) and attract those who might take advantage of their emphatic nature. Teach them to choose friends wisely and to set boundaries in relationships, to protect their emotional vulnerability—invaluable lessons in later life.

With the planet Uranus now in Pisces, the 2007 baby belongs to a generation of Pisces movers and shakers. This child may have a rebellious streak that rattles the status quo. But this generation also has a visionary nature, which will be much concerned with the welfare of the world at large.

CHAPTER 14

# Is This the Right Time to Fall in Love?

Astrology gives you a power tool for discovering why you are attracted to a certain person and how that person might act or react toward you. It also gives you the times when you are at your most attractive to the opposite sex. Although astrology can't guarantee that you'll have a problem-free relationship, it can give you a romantic timetable and road map to guide you over the rough spots and reveal what you might expect in the future with your partner, after the initial glow has given way to day-to-day reality. Working in your favor is the fact that no one totally embodies any one sign; we're a combination of all the signs in different proportions. So there will always be some naturally compatible (as well as incompatible) aspects between two people's charts.

## The Right Time to Reunite with an Old Lover or Reignite Passion in Your Current Relationship

An old love might resurface in your life when the planet Mercury, which rules communications, is in retrograde motion, about three times each year. (Check this information in chapter 2.) This planet often brings back people from the past, as well as old issues that should be resolved. It's an ideal time to troubleshoot existing relationships in which passion has cooled and to take action to reignite the flame

of love. Heart-to-heart talks about what went wrong could help you understand each other better. Retrograde Venus is another good time to set a relationship back on course; it happens briefly in Virgo this year, from July 27 until September 8, when it turns direct in Leo. Those especially affected will have the sun or moon in Leo or Virgo. It is not a good idea to begin a new romantic relationship when either Venus or Mercury is retrograding.

## Take a Chance on Love

Jupiter, the planet of risk, is in the risk-taking sign Sagittarius, which it rules this year. This could inspire fire signs (Aries, Leo, Sagittarius), in particular, to take a chance on love, perhaps choosing someone from a distant land or different culture. The mood of love is adventurous, exciting, daring, flirtatious. You could be swept off your feet, but this is not necessarily a time for long-term monogamous relationships. Jupiter encourages exploration in all areas!

## Make the First Move

Venus is the planet that makes others respond favorably to you. When it's in your sun sign or a favorable sign, you have a terrific opportunity to attract the opposite sex, so turn on the charm. Ideally both the sun and Venus in your sun sign make you catnip to others.

## Go Out and Meet Someone New

New activities of all kinds are favored during the new moon, especially if it's the new moon in your sun sign (or a sign in the same or complementary element). You'll also want a favorable Mercury (not retrograde) to give you the right words and a good Venus so that hot new prospect gets your message.

## When to Break Up

Breaking up may be easier to do during a waning moon, in the last quarter, when we're gearing up for a new cycle. However, some planetary aspects such as eclipses could force emotional issues out into the open and thus cause a breakup. As Mars transits your sun sign, you may become impatient with long-standing irritations in a relationship and be tempted to move on. Check the Mars tables after chapter 6 and the new and full moon list in chapter 2.

## Is This Person the Right One?

Here's a three-step technique for determining if your lover is the right one for a lasting relationship.

### How to Predict Your Romantic Success

Consider the other planets in your lover's chart, not just the sun sign (you can look up most of them using the charts in this book). Venus will tell what attracts you both. Mars reveals your temper and sex drive, Mercury how you'll communicate, and the moon your emotional nature. (For the moon and Mercury signs, consult one of the free charts available on the Internet. See chapter 10.)

### Step One: Size Up the Overall Relationship

To do an instant take on your relationship, compare the elements of the sun, moon, Mercury, Mars, and Venus—each a key planet in compatibility, in both charts. The interaction of elements (earth, air, fire, water) is the fastest way to size up a relationship. Planets of the same element will have the smoothest chemistry.

Earth element: Taurus Virgo, Capricorn
Air element: Gemini, Libra, Aquarius

Fire element: Aries, Leo, Sagittarius
Water element: Cancer, Scorpio, Pisces

When your partner has the same planet in the same element as your planet in question, the energy will flow freely. Complementary elements (fire signs with air signs or earth signs with water signs) also get along easily.

What if many planets are in other combinations? That's where you'll probably have to work at the relationship. There is tension and possible combustion between fire and water signs or earth and air signs. Take the analogies literally. Fire brings water to a boil; earth and air create a dust storm or tornado. If both your Venus signs are clashing, you will probably have very different tastes, something that could adversely affect a long-term relationship. However, challenges can be stimulating as well, adding spice to a relationship, especially when planets of sexual attraction—Mars relating to Venus—are involved.

## Step Two: Find Out How the Individual Planets Relate

Find out and compare how each planet operates in both your horoscopes (sun, moon, Mercury, Venus, and Mars) by comparing its quality or mode. Planets in cardinal signs are active, assertive; planets in fixed signs are tenacious, stubborn; planets in mutable signs are adaptable, easily changeable. Two planets of the same quality (but different signs) do not easily relate—there is usually a conflict of interests—but they can challenge each other to be more flexible or they can open up new areas in each other's lives. This is where you have to make compromises to reconcile different points of view. You'll have to be flexible or give in often.

*Cardinal signs* (active): Aries, Cancer, Libra, Capricorn
*Fixed signs* (static): Taurus, Leo, Scorpio, Aquarius
*Mutable signs* (changeable): Gemini, Virgo, Pisces, Sagittarius

## Step Three: Rate Your Overall Compatibility

The planets closest to the earth (sun, moon, Mercury, Mars, Venus) are those most likely to affect close relationships. Where possible, look up your planets and those of your partner in this book and grade them as follows. (The more A's and B's, the better! Y's and Z's indicate where you'll have to compromise to work things out.)

Grade A: for the same element (earth, air, fire, water)
Grade B: for complementary elements (air with fire, earth with water)
Grade Y: for challenging elements (air with water, earth with fire)
Grade Z: for the same quality, but different signs

By now, you should have a good idea where your relationship stands astrologically. A further check of the individual planets can answer some all-important questions.

Here's what the individual planets in your charts can reveal about your relationship:

***Are you basically attracted? Compare sun signs.***

The sun sign gives the big picture. Though it is not the whole story, and can be modified by other factors, the sun sign will always have an overall effect.

***Are you emotionally compatible? Check your moon signs.***

Emotional compatibility is strong enough to offset many other stressful factors in your horoscopes. Compare moon and sun signs too. There is an especially strong bond if your partner's moon is in your sun sign or vice versa.

***How well do you communicate? Check Mercury.***

Mercury in the same quality (cardinal, fixed, or mutable) could give you mental stimulation or irritation. Mercury in the same sign or element could be a meeting of minds.

***Do you have similar tastes? Check Venus.***

An incompatible Venus relationship can be very difficult over the long run, if other factors do not balance this out, because it has so much to do with the kind of atmosphere that makes you happy. One of you likes modern; the other likes traditional. One of you has an elegant style; the other is casual. It can be difficult to find the middle ground where you both win. Sometimes you just don't want to compromise that much.

***Sexually sizzling or fizzling? Check Mars.***

It is also useful to compare both Mars and Venus signs. Mars and Venus in the same sign or element is strong chemistry. Your partner's Mars or Venus in your sun sign is another big plus. Sometimes if Mars and Venus are in different modes, it can add sizzle to the relationship.

***Will your partner be faithful?***

Some sun signs tend to more monogamous than others. Fixed signs like a steady relationship and tend not to have multiple lovers. However, if a person with a fixed sign is unhappy, he will tend to have lovers on the side. The chief culprit here is Leo, which needs to be treated like royalty or else it will exercise royal rights elsewhere. Mutable signs tend to be the least monogamous. Gemini, Sagittarius, and Pisces are difficult to tie down and more difficult to hold. Sharing common interests and providing a stable home base can be a big help here, especially with Gemini.

***Where can you meet the sign of your dreams?***

If you have a sun sign in mind, here are places where they are likely to be (and like to go):

**Aries:** Try a sports event, martial arts display, action movie, cooking school, adventure sports vacation, the trendy new hot spot in town, the jogging or bike path.

**Taurus:** Meet them at a gourmet restaurant, auction house, farm or place where there are animals, flower show, garden shop, art classes, stores—especially food or jewelry stores.

**Gemini:** Meet them working for a newspaper or radio station, at parties or social events, writing courses, lectures, watering holes where there's good talk.

**Cancer:** Family dinners, boating or boat shows, cruises, on the beach, at seafood dinners, fishing, cooking schools, gourmet food stores, photography classes, art exhibits.

**Leo:** Big parties, country clubs, golfing, tanning salons, acting classes, theatrical events, movies, dancing, nightclubs, fine department stores, classy restaurants, VIP lounges at the airport, first-class hotels and travel.

**Virgo:** Craft stores, craft shows, flea markets, adult education courses, your local college, libraries, book stores, health food stores, doctors' offices, your local hospital or medical centers, health lectures, concerts, fine art events.

**Libra:** Art shows, fine restaurants, shopping centers, tennis matches, social events, parties and entertainment, the most fashionable stores, exhibits of beautiful objects, antique shows, decorating centers, ballet and the theater.

**Scorpio:** In banks, tax-preparation offices, police stations, sports events, motorcycle rallies, at the beach or swimming pool, doing water sports, at the gym, at action movies or mysteries, psychic fairs, ghostbusting.

**Sagittarius:** At a comedy club or laugh-a-minute film, at horse races or horse shows, pet stores or animal breeders, walking your dog, taking night courses at your local college, at a political debate, traveling to an exotic place, at a car show, mountain climbing, jogging, skiing, discussion group.

**Capricorn:** At a country music show, decorator show house, investment seminar, prestigious country club, exclusive resort, mountain climbing, party for a worthy cause, self-improvement course.

**Aquarius:** At a political rally, sci-fi convention, restaurant off the beaten path, union meeting, working for a worthy cause, campaigning for your candidate, fund-raising, flying lessons or airport.

**Pisces:** At any waterside place, at the theater or acting class, arts class, dancing, ballet, swimming pool, seafood restaurant, psychic event, church or other spiritual gathering, visiting at a hospital, at your local watering hole.

For your sun sign's compatibility with every other sign, see chapter 21.

# How to Keep Your Relationship Sizzling

## The Aries Lover

To keep your Aries mate red-hot, be sure to maintain your own energy level. This is one sign that shows little sympathy for aches, pains, and physical complaints. Curb any tendency toward self-pity—whining is one sure Aries turnoff (water signs take note). This is an open, direct sign. Don't expect your lover to probe your innermost needs. Intense psychological discussions that would thrill a Cancer or Scorpio only make Aries restless. Aries is not the stay-at-home type. This sign is sure to have plenty of activities going on at once. Share them (or they'll find someone else who will)!

Always be a bit of a challenge to your Aries mate—this sign loves the chase almost as much as the conquest. So don't be too easy or accommodating—let them feel a sense of accomplishment when they've won your heart.

Stay up-to-date in your interests and appearance. You

can wear the latest style off the fashion show runway with an Aries, especially if it's bright red. Aries is a pioneer, an adventurer, always ahead of the pack. Play up your frontier spirit. Present the image of the two of you as an unbeatable team that can conquer the world, and you'll keep this courageous sign at your side.

Since they tend to idealize their lovers, Aries partners are especially disillusioned when their mates flirt. So tone down your roving eye to make sure they always feel like number one in your life.

## The Taurus Lover

Taurus is an extremely sensual, affectionate, nurturing lover, but can be quite possessive. Taurus likes to own you. Don't hold back with them or play power games. If you need more space in the relationship, be sure to set clear boundaries, letting them know exactly where they stand. When ambiguity in a relationship makes Taurus uneasy, they may go searching for someone more solid and substantial. A Taurus romance works best where the limits are clearly spelled out.

Taurus needs physical demonstrations of affection—don't hold back on hugs. Together you should create an atmosphere of comfort, good food, and beautiful surroundings. In fact, Taurus is often seduced by surface physical beauty alone. Their five senses are highly susceptible, so find ways to appeal to all of them! Your home should be a restful haven from the outside world. Get a great sound system and some comfortable furniture to sink into and keep the refrigerator stocked with treats. Most Taurus would rather entertain on their own turf than gad about town, so it helps if you're a good host or hostess.

Taurus likes a calm, contented, committed relationship. This is not a sign to trifle with. Don't flirt or tease if you want to please. Don't rock the boat or try to make this sign jealous. Instead, create a steady, secure environment with lots of shared pleasures.

## The Gemini Lover

Keeping Gemini faithful is like walking a tightrope. This sign needs stability and a strong home base to accomplish

their goals. But they also require a great deal of personal freedom.

A great role model is Barbara Bush, a Gemini married to another Gemini. This is a sign that loves to communicate. Sit down and talk things over. Don't interfere: Be interested in your partner's doings, but have a life of your own and ideas to contribute. Since this is a social sign, don't insist on quiet nights at home when your Gemini is in a party mood.

Gemini needs plenty of rope but a steady hand. Focus on common goals and abstract ideals. Gemini likes to share—be a twin soul and do things together. Keep up on their latest interests. Stay in touch mentally and physically. Use both your mind and your hands to communicate.

Variety is the spice of life to this flirtatious sign. Guard against jealousy—it is rarely justified. Provide a stimulating sex life—this is a very experimental sign—to keep them interested. Be a bit unpredictable. Don't let lovemaking become a routine. Most of all, sharing lots of laughs can make Gemini take your relationship very seriously.

## The Cancer Lover

This is probably the water sign that requires the most TLC. Cancers tend to be very private people who may take time to open up. They are extremely self-protective and will rarely tell you what is truly bothering them. They operate indirectly, like the movements of the crab. You may have to divine problems by following subtle clues. Draw them out gently and try to voice any criticism in the most tactful, supportive way possible.

Family ties are especially strong for Cancer. They will rarely break a strong family bond. Create an intimate family atmosphere, with an emphasis on food and family get-togethers. You can get valuable clues to Cancer appeal from their mothers and their family situation. Whatever you do, don't compete with a mother! Get her to teach you the favorite family recipes; take her out to dinner. If your lover's early life was unhappy, it's important that Cancer feels there is a close family with you.

Encouraging creativity can counter Cancer's moodiness,

which is also a sure sign of emotional insecurity. Find ways to distract them from negative moods. Calm them with a good meal or a trip to the seashore. Cancers are usually quite nostalgic and attached to the past. So be careful not to throw out their old treasures or photos.

## The Leo Lover

Whether the Leo is a sunny, upbeat partner or reveals cat-like claws could depend on how you handle the royal Leo pride. A relationship is for two people—a fact that ego-centered Leo can forget. You must gently remind them. Appearances are important to Leo, so try to always look your best.

Leo thinks big—so don't you be petty or miserly—and likes to live like a king. Remember special occasions with a beautifully wrapped gift or flowers. Make an extra effort to treat them royally. Keep a sense of fun and playfulness and loudly applaud Leo's creative efforts. React, respond, and be a good audience! If Leo's ignored, this sign will seek a more appreciative audience fast! Cheating Leos are almost always looking for an ego boost.

Be generous with compliments. You can't possibly overdo here. Always accentuate the positive. Make them feel important by asking for advice and consulting them often. Leo enjoys a charming sociable companion, but be sure to make them the center of attention in your life. If you have a demanding job or outside schedule, make a point to pull out all the stops once in a while, to create special events that keep romance alive.

## The Virgo Lover

Virgo may seem cool and conservative on the surface, but underneath, you'll find a sensual romantic. Think of Raquel Welch, Sophia Loren, Jacqueline Bisset, and Garbo! It's amazing how seductive this practical sign can be!

They are idealists, however, looking for someone who meets their high standards. If you've measured up, they'll do anything to serve and please you. Virgos love to feel needed, so give them a job to do in your life. They are

great fixer-uppers. Take their criticism as a form of love and caring, of noticing what you do. Bring them out socially—they're often very shy. Calm their nerves with good food, a healthy environment, and trips to the country.

Mental stimulation is a turn-on to this Mercury-ruled sign. An intellectual discussion could lead to romantic action, so stay on your toes and keep well-informed. This sign often mixes business with pleasure, so it helps if you share the same professional interests—you'll get to see more of your busy mate. With Virgo, the couple who works as well as plays together stays together.

## The Libra Lover

Libra enjoys life with a mate and needs the harmony of a steady relationship. Outside affairs can throw them off balance. However, members of this sign are natural charmers who love to surround themselves with admirers, and this can cause a very possessive partner to feel insecure. Most of the time, Libras, who love to be the belles of the ball, are only testing their allure with harmless flirtations and will rarely follow through, unless they are not getting enough attention or there is an unattractive atmosphere at home.

Mental compatibility is what keeps Libra in tune. Unfortunately this sign, like Taurus, often falls for physical beauty or someone who provides an elegant lifestyle, rather than someone who shares their ideals and activities, which is the kind of sharing that will keep you together in the long run.

Do not underestimate Libra's need for beauty and harmony. To keep them happy, avoid scenes. Opt for calm, impersonal discussion of problems (or a well-reasoned debate) over an elegant dinner. Pay attention to the niceties of life. Send little gifts on Valentine's Day and don't forget birthdays and anniversaries. Play up the romance to the hilt—with all the lovely gestures and trimmings—but tone down intensity and emotional drama (Aries and Scorpio take note). Libra needs to be surrounded by a physically tasteful atmosphere—elegant, well-designed furnishings, calm colors, good manners, and good grooming at all times.

## The Scorpio Lover

Scorpios are often deceptively cool and remote on the outside, but don't be fooled. This sign always has a hidden agenda and feels very intense about most things. The disguise is necessary because Scorpio does not trust easily; but when they do, they are devoted and loyal. You can lean on this very focused sign. The secret is in first establishing that basic trust through mutual honesty and respect.

Scorpio is fascinated by power and control in all its forms. They don't like to compromise—it's all or nothing. Therefore they don't trust or respect anything that comes too easily. Be a bit of a challenge and keep them guessing. Maintain your own personal identity, in spite of Scorpio's desire to probe your innermost secrets.

Sex is especially important to those under this sign. They will demand fidelity from you though they may not plan to deliver it themselves, so communication on this level is critical. Explore Scorpio's fantasies together. Scorpio is a detective—watch your own flirtations—don't play with fire. This is a jealous and vengeful sign, so you'll live to regret it. Scorpios rarely flirt for the fun of it themselves. There is usually a strong motive behind their actions.

Scorpio has a fascination with the dark, mysterious side of life. If unhappy, they are capable of carrying on a secret affair. So try to emphasize the positive, constructive side of life with them. Don't fret if they need time alone to sort out problems. They may also prefer time alone with you to socializing with others, so plan romantic getaways together to a private beach or a secluded wilderness spot.

## The Sagittarius Lover

Be a mental and spiritual traveling companion. Sagittarius is a footloose adventurer whose ideas know no boundaries. So don't try to fence them in! Sagittarius resents restrictions of any kind. For a long relationship, be sure you are in harmony with their ideals and spiritual beliefs. They like to feel that their lives are constantly being elevated and taken to a higher level. Since down-to-earth matters often get put aside by Sagittarius schemes of things, get finances

under control (money matters upset more relationships with Sagittarius than any other problems), but try to avoid becoming the stern disciplinarian in this relationship (find a good accountant to do this chore).

Sagittarius is not generally a homebody (unless there are several homes). Be ready and willing to take off on the spur of the moment, or they'll go without you. Sports, outdoor activities, and physical fitness are important. Stay in shape with some of Sagittarius Jane Fonda's tapes. Dress with flair and style. It helps if you look especially good in sportswear. Sagittarius men like beautiful legs, so play up yours. And this is one of the great animal lovers, so try to get along with the dog, cat, or horse.

## The Capricorn Lover

These people are ambitious, even if they are the stay-at-home partner in your relationship. They will be extremely active, have a strong sense of responsibility to their partner, and take commitments seriously. However, they might look elsewhere if the relationship becomes too dutiful. They also need romance, fun, lightness, humor, and adventure!

Generation gaps are not unusual in Capricorn romances, where the older Capricorn partner works hard all through life and seeks pleasurable rewards with a young partner, or the young Capricorn gets a taste of luxury and instant status from an older lover. This is one sign that grows more interested in romance with age! Younger Capricorns often tend to put business way ahead of pleasure.

Capricorn is impressed by those who entertain well, have class, and can advance their status in life. Keep improving yourself and cultivate important people. Stay on the conservative side. Extravagant or frivolous loves don't last. Capricorn keeps an eye on the bottom line. Even the wildest Capricorns, such as Elvis Presley, Rod Stewart, and David Bowie, show a conservative streak in their personal lives. It's also important to demonstrate a strong sense of loyalty to your family, especially to older members. This reassures Capricorn, who'll be happy to grow old along with you!

## The Aquarius Lover

Aquarius is one of the most independent, least domestic signs. Finding time alone with this sign may be one of your greatest challenges. The are everybody's buddy, usually surrounded by people they collect, some of whom may be old lovers. However, it is unlikely that old passions will be rekindled if you become their best friend as well as lover, and if you get actively involved in other important aspects of their lives, such as the political or charitable causes they believe in.

Aquarius needs a supportive backup person who encourages them, but is not overpossessive when their natural charisma attracts admirers by the dozen. Take a leaf from Joanne Woodward, whose marriage to perennial Aquarius heartthrob Paul Newman has lasted more than thirty years. Encourage them to develop their original ideas. Don't rain on their parade if they decide suddenly to market their spaghetti sauce and donate the proceeds to their favorite charity, or drive racing cars. Share their goals and be their fan, or you'll never see them otherwise.

You may be called on to give them grounding where needed. Aquarius needs someone who can keep track of their projects. But always remember, it's basic friendship—with the tolerance and common ideals that implies—that will hold you together.

## The Pisces Lover

To keep a Pisces hooked, don't hold the string too tight! This is a sensitive, creative sign that may appear to need someone to manage life or point the direction out of their Neptune fog; but if you fall into that role, expect your Pisces to rebel against any strong-arm tactics. Pisces is more susceptible to a play for sympathy than a play for power. They are suckers for a sob story, the most empathetic sign of the zodiac. More than one Pisces has been seduced and held by someone who plays the underdog role.

They are great fantasists and extremely creative lovers, so use your imagination to add drama and spice to your time together. You can let your fantasies run wild with this

sign, and they'll go you one better! They enjoy variety in lovemaking, so try never to let it become routine.

Long-term relationships work best if you can bring Pisces down to earth and, at the same time, encourage their creative fantasies. Deter them from escapism into alcohol or substance abuse by helping them to get counseling, if needed. Pisces will stay with the lover who gives positive energy, self-confidence, and a safe harbor from the storms of life, as well as one who is a soul mate.

CHAPTER 15

# Is There Prosperity in Your Future?

There are big changes in the stars ahead, so projecting astrologically a few years down the line could point your career and investments in the most profitable direction.

For long-term trends, look to the outer planets, which cause major changes as they move into a different sign. Soon there will be a shift in the atmosphere as Pluto, the planet of transformation, moves into Capricorn in 2008 until 2024. (You'll notice a different kind of energy starting a few months in advance.) What's more, Jupiter, the planet of luck and expansion, also moves through Capricorn during 2008, accelerating changes and bringing luck to Capricorn, so expect many of that sign to surge into prominence. Bet on the sea goat (Capricorn's symbol) and areas associated with it. Capricorns should prepare to move into the limelight. ("It's about time," you Capricorns may well say!)

If you're headed for the fast track, set your sights on Capricorn fields, which will be going through radical changes. This will affect Capricorn-associated corporations, big business, government, institutions of all kinds, mining, land speculation, property owners and dealers, builders and building trades, contractors and engineers, civil service, providers of status products. Capricorn-influenced fields are known for function, structure, discipline, and order, so consider careers that have these qualities or can provide them to others.

## Everyone Old Is New

Want to cash in on a much-neglected market? Services and care for the aging should be booming with career opportu-

nities, thanks to our elder population explosion. Remember that the generation now entering the aging population was born with Pluto in Leo; it's the rock-and-roll generation, who will resist the idea of aging and retirement as long as possible.

This particular elder population will be highly visible and financially viable. They are big spenders who will be remaining much longer in the workforce. Those who do retire may begin second careers, so the workplace will be rethinking its relationship to grandmas and grandpas and changing to accommodate them. Since America has been a youth-oriented culture, expect a major transformation in advertising, retailing, fashion, housing, and health care.

Since the Pluto in Leo generation is one of the most image-conscious ever, anything that keeps these folks looking and feeling great is sure to succeed. Don't expect your grandma and grandpa to hang around the house. This is a curious, adventurous generation that will welcome opportunities to explore the globe that are especially tailored to their age group and interests.

## Cater to Horatio Alger

Capricorn is the Horatio Alger sign of rising through one's own volition and ambition. Self-improvement courses will be booming as we search for more fulfilling careers and try to keep up with new technology.

Do you enjoy helping others fulfill their potential? Career coaching—in fact, coaching in all aspects of life—is a hot field. In the corporate area, human resources is a much-touted area of job growth. You'll need skills in training and in helping other people find jobs. Get involved with helping people adapt to the times and retrain themselves for new careers. Leos, Sagittarius, Virgos, and Aquarius make excellent trainers and teachers. Aries are the supermotivators.

Education, especially high education, will be in for a whole new approach, as gray-haired students decide to complete their educations or simply enjoy expanding their knowledge. College towns will become hot retirement destinations, which

provide intellectual stimulation plus an elder-compatible atmosphere.

The demand for teachers will increase and provide a steady stream of jobs. Look into special education, private education of all kinds, and unusual approaches to teaching. The natural teaching signs—Virgo, Leo, Sagittarius, and Aquarius—are winners here.

Since the world has become a smaller place and the trend toward international involvement escalates, demand for language skills also increases. Americans may need to speak several languages including some once considered exotic for the average American, such as Chinese or Arabic. Language teachers, translators, and linguists, especially those with a Gemini emphasis in their charts, should find many opportunities.

## Waste Not, Want Not

Capricorn is an intensely practical sign that dislikes waste of any kind, so consider careers in recycling and waste management, antiques, renovation, preserving old buildings, land conservation, and teaching history.

Environment-related careers are hot options, since there will be so much cleaning up of toxic wastes, rebuilding after cataclysmic natural events, and redesigning of equipment. Engineers, attorneys, designers, bankers, and researchers should slant their career search in this direction. Taurus, Scorpio, Libra, Pisces, and Aquarius could make their fortune here.

## Keep Treasured Traditions Alive

It looks like a conservative time, when people will be concerned with traditional values. Hospitality businesses can capitalize on this trend by promoting the beloved holidays of all cultures, reviving the old customs and memories. Holiday vacations for the whole family to share, reunions, and celebrations could revitalize the resort and cruise business. Tourism that caters to the needs of the aging, but still adventurous, traveler should thrive.

## Head for the Hills

If you're thinking about a change of scene, consider relocating to a Capricorn-influenced place, which should have growth potential now. If you're adventurous, head for Central Europe, especially mountainous regions. The Balkans, Bosnia, Bulgaria, Lithuania, Macedonia, and Albania are Capricorn places. India, Belgium, Hesse and Constance in Germany, Mexico, and New Zealand are also on the Capricorn wavelength.

## Health Care for the Antiaging Population

Have you considered the health-care field? Careers in medical services are among the hottest prospects as the nation begins to reform its health-care systems. Physical therapists, nurses, physicians' assistants, and pharmacists, as well as health services administrators, will all be in demand to service the aging population. If you have strong Virgo, Scorpio, or Capricorn placements, which give you a flair for the health field and excellent organizational skills, you should consider this area. Compassionate signs such as Pisces and Cancer make excellent health caregivers.

Consider the Capricorn fields of knee surgery and therapy, bone and joint diseases, chiropractic care, dermatology. New techniques in self-enhancement, such as plastic surgery, dental work, and hair replacement, should also do well for this aging generation who'd love to look and feel forever young.

Therapists specializing in treatment of disabling conditions, optometrists, nursing home operators and managers, and home care for the aged should be thriving.

## The Talent Finder

Designers and manufacturers of clothing, furniture and equipment suited to the over-sixty consumer should also do

well. Look into this area if you have planets in Capricorn (ruler of old age), Pisces (creativity, compassion), Taurus and Cancer (associated with the home environment and of nurturing), and Aries (pioneering ventures).

Do you thrive on life in the fast lane? Sports and special events are high-visibility careers where salesmanship and flair count, so they're especially suited to fire signs Aries, Leo, and Sagittarius. Good communicators like Gemini and Libra do well in public relations in this market.

Capricorn-favored sports require great discipline and endurance and are luckiest when they take place in the mountains. Rock and mountain climbing, hiking, and skiing are specially favored.

There will be a continuing boom in fitness careers, with the emphasis on well-run health clubs, personal attention, and social atmosphere. As the population ages, there will be more emphasis on weight training and rehabilitation aimed at elder bodies. Virgos, Sagittarius, Leos, and Aries are specially suited to the high-energy demands of this field, while Libras, Geminis, and Pisces provide good communication, diplomacy, and compassion.

We'll be eating more consciously as America slims down (Capricorn is the sign of discipline). Diet-specific restaurants, vegetarian restaurants, diet consultants, and organic food farmers and gardeners should be expanding. We'll be especially concerned with the quality of our meat and seafood. This is a fertile area for Taurus, Virgo, Cancer, Pisces, and Leos with skills in working with agriculture, diet counseling, cooking, restaurant management, organizing farmers' markets, and managing health food stores.

## High-Tech Options

Though computer fields should continue to grow, the outsourcing of high-tech service jobs is also likely to continue. The good news is that there will still be a need for software designers, trainers, salespersons, and local repair staff, as computers have become an integral part of our lives. Aquarians are natural in all areas of computer work. Sagittarius and Geminis do well in teaching and sales, while

Capricorns excel in organization, Pisces in creative software design, and Cancers in applying high tech to industry.

Video-related careers can only get bigger in 2010 as Neptune, ruler of film, moves into Pisces, its strongest position. Video stores, cameras, and viewing equipment, new uses of video for education and entertainment, technical experts in production and performing—all should be booming. Pisces, Leo, Sagittarius, and Gemini should find plenty of opportunities in performance, sales, and marketing.

Take these tips from the stars and do your career planning with the planets!

CHAPTER 16

# Heath and Diet Makeovers from the Stars

Health spas, fitness resorts, gyms, yoga studios, and sports complexes are multiplying around the country. Vitamin stores and juice bars are opening up in malls. We're buying shelves of diet books. Yet we're still one of the fattest nations on the planet! This year, the stars say we'll have more discipline to make over our bad eating habits and resolve to become as healthy as possible. Astrology can clue you in to the tendencies that contribute to good or ill health (especially when it comes to controlling your appetite). Finding the right diet and health program and having the patience to stick with them over time could be your big challenge this year. So follow these sun-sign tips on how best to lose those extra pounds and make this your healthiest year ever.

## Aries Tips: Avoid the Quick Fix

Thanks to your hyperactive Mars-ruled lifestyle, you're sometimes too busy to bother with healthy meals in a calm atmosphere. You're more likely to grab carbohydrate-laden, calorie-packed fast foods for instant energy on the run. You need a regimen that gives you sustained energy, rather than a quick fix or a caffeine-fueled jump start. Aim for frequent small meals and carry healthy snacks with you to recharge your batteries. Protein and fruit smoothies in the morning might provide you with a quick, healthy head start to the day.

Aries is associated with the head, your most vulnerable area, which you should be especially careful to protect by wearing the appropriate headgear during risky activities and sports. Headaches warn you to slow down and take it easy for a while. If you've been stocking up on headache remedies, it might be time to consult a nutritionist for expert dietary advice.

Superbusy, impatient Aries tends to overschedule and stress out when others don't, won't, or can't keep up to your pace. Sports to the rescue! Swatting a ball, cheering on your favorite team, training for a marathon, or just running around the block can be the best remedies for whatever ails an Aries. Sports allow you to let off steam in an atmosphere of excitement and competition where you can feel the joy of winning. Your daring moves and Mars-powered energy should earn you a stellar spot on any team. If you're older, volunteer to coach local youngsters.

Martial arts of any kind appeal to your love of action. The slower, more flowing forms, such as tai chi, can be done throughout life. You don't have to be Jackie Chan or Russell Crowe to show your Aries flair for action heroics. Try racket sports (any sport that involves hitting or working with a swordlike object), fencing, tap dancing, or aerobics if martial arts don't give you a kick. However, remember to take time to check your equipment, warm up, and wait until you're properly conditioned before you jump to expert-level challenges.

Once you've found a sport you love, try not to push yourself too hard. Listen to your body when it tells you it's time to quit (never easy for Aries). Finally, know the difference between well-exercised, fatigued muscles and the pain that signals trouble.

## Taurus Tips: Downsize Portions

Taurus loves all kinds of food in large quantities—especially rich, creamy desserts and fried goodies. (Once you start eating rich food, you find it almost impossible to stop.) Deprivation in any form is not going to work for you, so find a diet that allows you healthy variations of the

foods you love most. Aim for smaller portions and fill up on skinny foods like salads. First, raid your refrigerator and eliminate any foods that are not on your diet. If it's there, you'll find it and eat it. The techniques for weight loss in Cher's diet books might inspire you.

Pleasure is the key to your exercise routine. You need an attractive place to work out, not a sweaty gym. Why not plan your workout to take place in one of the scenic areas of your town? Jogging or biking along a river or through a park, exploring the woodlands and seashore in your area with long nature hikes, or horseback riding along a scenic trail can make you look forward to exercising. Or plant an extensive garden that requires lots of active maintenance. If you live in an appropriate setting, get a dog that requires lots of exercise. Working with animals can also be a joy for Taurus.

Pay special attention to the Taurus area of the body: the neck. Yoga exercises, head rolls, the proper pillow, and a good masseur can make a big difference here. Though Taurus is a hardy sign with great stamina and endurance, you can become sluggish if you're overweight or if you have a thyroid problem. So, if you can barely drag yourself off the couch, be sure to check your thyroid. If you're not getting enough sleep, it could be due to tension in your neck. Try changing your pillow to one specially designed to support your neck.

Massage is one way to soothe the raging bull in you, especially if tension is lodging in your neck. Try shiatsu massage targeted to the acupressure points in the neck area. Neck massages are a sybaritic way to release tension and promote restful sleep.

## Gemini Tips: Make a Game of It

Gemini is an on-the-go sign that does not usually have a weight problem, as long as you keep moving. If life circumstances force you to be sedentary, however, you may eat out of boredom and watch the pounds pile on. Your active social life can also sabotage your weight with sumptuous party buffets and restaurant meals where you have to sam-

ple everything. Your challenge is to find a healthy eating system with enough variety so you won't get bored. Develop a strategy for eating out—at parties or restaurants—and fill up the buffet plates with salad or veggies before you sample the desserts. Sociable Geminis on a diet can benefit from group support in a system like Weight Watchers. Find a diet twin who'll support you and have fun losing weight together.

Gemini is associated with the nervous system, our body's lines of communications. If your nerves are on edge, you may be trying to do too many things at once, leaving no time for fun and laughter. When you overload your circuits, it's time to get together with friends and go out to parties. Investigate natural tension relievers, such as yoga or meditation. Doing things with your hands—playing the piano, typing, craftwork—is also helpful.

Gemini is also associated with the lungs, which are especially sensitive. If you smoke, consider quitting. Yoga, which incorporates deep breathing into physical exercise, brings oxygen into your lungs. Among its many benefits are the deep relaxation and tranquillity so needed by your sign.

Combine healthful activities with social get-togethers for fun and plenty of fringe benefits for everyone. Include friends in your exercise routines; join an exercise class or jogging club. Gemini excels at sports that require good timing and manual dexterity as well as communication with others, like tennis or golf. Those who jog may want to add hand weights or upper-body exercises, which will benefit the Gemini-ruled arms and hands. If you spend long hours at the computer, try an ergonomic keyboard for comfort and protection against carpal tunnel syndrome.

## Cancer Tips: Get the Emotional Support You Need

Dieting can be difficult for Cancers, who love good cuisine, find emotional solace with goodies, and fill up with comfort foods in tough times. There are sure to be conflicts in the Cancer who wants to be fashionably thin, but also to please

the family with Grandma's favorite dishes. Cancer food conflicts sometimes lead to eating disorders, as with Princess Diana. Remember that you must be nurtured emotionally as well as physically. A diet-therapy group might help you deal with issues surrounding food and give you the support you need to stick to a diet. Find nonfood ways to baby yourself, such as a visit to a spa, walks along the beach, or beauty treatments to help you feel good about yourself while you lose weight.

Get the family behind you when you diet. You'll never lose weight if they insist on eating caloric favorites in front of you. Challenge yourself to create diet-conscious variations of family recipes so the whole family can eat healthy.

Your natural water-sign element is also your best therapy. Sometimes just a walk by a pond or a brief stop by a fountain can do wonders to relieve emotional stress and tension. You will be more likely to stick to an exercise routine if it's in or near water. Pool aerobics, swimming, fishing, sailing, and all other all water sports provide ideal ways for you to stay fit.

Health-wise, Cancer is associated with the breasts. Have regular checkups, according to your age and family health history of breast-related illness, and be sure to wear the proper supportive bra. Cancer is also prone to digestive difficulties, especially gastric ulcers and eating disorders. When emotionally caused digestive problems from those stomach-knotting insecurities crop up, baby yourself with extra pampering. If you're feeling blue, a visit with loved ones, old friends, and family could provide the support you need. Plan special family activities that bring everyone close together.

## Leo Tips: The Downside of the Good Life

Leo's diet downfall might be your preference for the finer things in life, like dining on gourmet food at the best restaurants. And a Leo that is not getting the love and attention you need can easily turn to food for consolation. Give

yourself the royal treatment in nonfood ways and imagine how great you'll look in that sexy gold dress.

Like your lion namesake, Leos often tend to be carnivores, so a low-carbohydrate, high-protein diet might work best for you, such as the Perricone or Atkins diet. If you're having trouble getting started on your diet, give yourself a jump start with a spa vacation. Some extra pampering, plus expert advice, could see you through the first difficult week and get you on the road to healthy eating.

Leo is associated with the spine and heart, two important areas to guard throughout your life. Be sure you have a good mattress to support the vulnerable Leo spine. Learn some therapeutic exercises to strengthen and protect your back. Aerobic exercises that benefit the heart and lungs are also musts for Leo.

Ruled by the sun, you're one sign that usually loves to tan. However, considering the permanent damage sun exposure can cause, you may elect to remain porcelain pale like Madonna or to use a spray-on tanning product. Don't leave for the beach without a big hat, umbrella, and sunblock formulated for your skin type. Many makeup foundations now come with a sunblock added, a good idea for Leo ladies.

Leos are proud of your body and usually take excellent care of it. Like the archetypal Leo male, Arnold Schwarzenegger, you can summon up great discipline and determination to maintain your public image. To make your body worthy of the spotlight, consider a bodybuilding regimen in which you're supervised by a personal trainer. Be sure any exercise routine you choose emphasizes good posture. The way you carry yourself can make the most of your figure type and dramatically affect your energy level. Get that regal bearing!

## Virgo Tips: Find a Diet Coach

Since Virgo is associated with the digestive system, you can make quite an issue of food quality, preparation, and diet. Many of you will select a very detailed special diet to promote health, such as a macrobiotic diet. Potassium-rich veg-

etables are especially important, as is your relationship to whole grains. The mind-body connection to overweight has been emphasized by Virgo diet coach, Dr. Phil MacGraw. If you become overweight, it usually comes from coping with emotional or work-related stress. To counteract this tendency, add activitics to your life that promote peace of mind. Exercises that use mental as well as physical techniques could help you stay with your program.

As one of the most health-conscious signs in the zodiac, caring for the health of yourself and others is usually a high priority with Virgos. Many great doctors, nurses, and dieticians were born under Virgo, such as the noted heart surgeon Dr. Michael DeBakey.

You tend to troubleshoot your health, scheduling medical exams and appropriate diagnostic tests promptly. You have probably learned that running your life efficiently does much to eliminate health-robbing stress. It's a great comfort to know you've got a smooth health-maintenance routine in place to back you up.

Virgos benefit from exercises that stress the relationship of the mind and body, such as yoga or tai chi. Sports that require a certain technical skill to master can also challenge Virgo. The key factor in Virgo-appealing exercises is to offer self-improvement on several levels simultaneously, not just a boring or repetitive routine.

## Libra Tips: Resist Sweet Temptations

One of the most famous diet doctors, Dr. Robert Atkins, was a Libra. A well-spoken gentleman with a liking for sweets, he fit your sign's profile. At first, the low-carbohydrate diet he advocated was vilified by nutritional experts. In recent years, however, he has been vindicated, and the effectiveness of the Atkins diet proven. It could be the perfect diet for Libras who often put on too much weight from indulging in sweets. Because your sign rules the kidneys, it's no surprise that this diet advocates drinking plenty of water to cleanse the system as you reduce. Since you are one of the most social signs, you may entertain or be entertained often. Plan your food choices before you go

out, so you'll know exactly what to eat. Then you'll be more likely to resist sweet temptations. Dieting with your mate or a group of friends could provide the support you need and keep you on track when you go out to dinner.

Restoring and maintaining equilibrium is the Libra key to health. Balance in all things should be your mantra. If you have been working too hard or taking life too seriously, a dose of culture, art, or music or perhaps some social activity will balance your scales. Make time to entertain friends, be romantic with the one you love, and enjoy the artistic life of your city.

Since Libra is associated with the kidneys and lower back, watch these areas for misalignment or health problems. Consider yoga, spinal adjustments, or a detoxification program if your body is out of balance. Working out in a gym may be unappealing to aesthetic Libras. Since yours is the sign of relationships, you may enjoy exercising with a partner or with loved ones. Make morning walks or weekend hikes family affairs. Take a romantic bicycle tour, picnic in the autumn countryside. Libra is also the sign of grace, so any kind of dancing may appeal. Dancing combines art, music, romance, relaxation, graceful movement, social contact, and exercise.

Put more beauty in all areas of your life, and you'll be healthier and happier.

## Scorpio Tips: Diet for Self-Transformation

Scorpios never do anything halfway, so they need to be fully committed to their diets. Some Scorpios will go to great lengths to transform themselves, even resorting to extreme means like stomach stapling or gastric bypass, as Roseanne Barr did. You are gifted with amazing focus and discipline and can stick with any diet, once you have made up your mind. The trick is to eliminate self-destructive food habits. Finding a diet plan you can live with for long periods, such as the South Beach Diet, which worked for Hillary Clinton, will help you avoid the yo-yo diet syndrome.

Though Scorpio usually has a strong constitution that can literally rise from the ashes of extreme illness or misfortune, resist the temptation to take this for granted or sabotage your health with self-destructive habits. Try to curb excessive tendencies in any area of your life. Know when to quit and when to seek help; don't hesitate to ask for help when you need it.

Your sign is associated with regenerative and eliminative organs. Therefore, it follows that sexual activity can be a source of good or ill health for Scorpio. It is important to examine your attitudes about sex, to follow safe-sex practices, and to seek balance in sex, as in all other areas of your life.

It's no accident that Scorpio's month coincides with football season, which reminds us that sports are a very healthy way to defuse emotions. If you enjoy winter sports, be sure to prepare ahead of time for the ski slopes or the ice rinks. Be sure to warm up your muscles before you go all out. Water sports are a terrific outlet for Scorpio, so sign up for pool aerobics or competitive swimming and be sure to treat yourself to a vacation at a spectacular tropical beach resort. Somehow, just being near a saltwater environment can restore your equilibrium.

## Sagittarius Tips: Aim for Long-Range Benefits

Dieting is something Sagittarius does with great difficulty. There has to be more to it than just getting thin. Therefore, an eating plan that is part of a spiritually oriented lifestyle, such as vegetarianism, might have more appeal. Aim for long-range benefits by balancing a sane, practical eating plan with plenty of exercise. Beware of fad diets that promise instant results and come with a high-pressure sales pitch. Avoid gimmicks, pills, or anything instant; these solutions are especially tempting to impatient Sagittarius. Exercise is the greatest antidote to overeating for your sports-loving sign, so follow your guru (Jane Fonda), go for the burn, and work off those calories.

Good health for Sagittarius is often a matter of motivation. If you set a fitness goal, it will be much easier to stay motivated than if you exercise or diet haphazardly, so aim for the best you can be and then set a plan to achieve it. Once you've decided on a course of action, get going. Being on the move and physically active keeps you in the best of health, improves your circulation, and protects your arteries. Problems could come from injuries to the hip or thigh areas, as well as arterial problems, so protect yourself with the proper equipment for your sports activity and don't push yourself beyond your capacity.

Exercise is your greatest antidote to stress. Your sign loves working out in groups, so combine socializing with athletic activities and team sports. Touch football, biking, hikes, and long walks with your dog are fun as well as healthy. Let others know that you'd like a health-promoting birthday gift, such as sports equipment, a gym membership, or an exercise video. In your workouts, concentrate on Sagittarius-ruled areas—the hips, legs, and thighs.

If you're already in shape, try out Sagittarius sports such as downhill or cross-country skiing, Rollerblading, and basketball. Since you like to travel, plan an exercise routine that can be done anywhere. Isometric exercises, which use muscle resistance and can be done in a car or plane seat, are a good travel option. If you are always on the road, investigate equipment that fits easily in your suitcase, such as water-filled weights, home gym devices, elastic exercise bands. Locate hotels with well-equipped gyms or parks nearby where you can jog.

## Capricorn Tips: Disciplined Dieting

It was a Capricorn hostess and decorator, Lady Elsie de Wolfe Mendl, who introduced dieting to America, via the 1920s health guru Gayelord Hauser. Lady Mendl served very small portions of exquisitely prepared health food at her elegant dinner parties, a good tip for you who may need to downsize portions. One of the skinny signs, Capricorn has amazing self-discipline, a big help in maintaining weight loss. Exercise or active sports should help you keep

the pounds off without strenuous dieting. Food and mood are linked with Capricorn, so avoid eating to console or comfort yourself; instead, choose upbeat relaxed companions. Since you are likely to mix business with pleasure, plan your work-related lunches and dinners in advance so you won't be led astray by the dessert tray.

As a Capricorn, you naturally take good care of yourself, getting regular medical checkups and tending toward moderation in your lifestyle. You're one of the signs that ages well and remains physically active in your senior years. But Capricorn's fast-paced, action-packed life can be stressful, so here are some ways to unwind and put the spring back into your step.

Since Capricorn is associated with the bone structure, you need to watch for signs of osteoporosis and take preventive measures. Good posture and stretching exercises such as yoga are essential to remain flexible. You might practice yoga, as Christy Turlington does. Another way to counteract osteoporosis is by adding weight-bearing exercise to your routine. If your knees or joints are showing signs of arthritis, calcium supplements may be helpful. For those who enjoy strenuous sports, remember to protect your knees by doing special exercises to strengthen this area, and always warm up beforehand.

Capricorn's natural self-discipline is a big help in maintaining good health. Keep a steady, even pace for lasting results. Remember to balance workouts with pleasurable activities in your self-care program. Grim determination can be counterproductive, especially if one of your exercise goals is to relieve tension. Take up a sport for pure enjoyment, not necessarily to become a champion.

Since you probably spend much of your life in an office, check your working environment for hidden health saboteurs like poor air quality, bad lighting, and uncomfortable seating. Get an ergonomically designed chair to protect your back, or buy a specially designed back-support cushion if your chair is uncomfortable. If you work at a computer, adjust your keyboard and the height of the computer screen for ergonomic comfort.

Capricorn, the sign of Father Time, brings up the subject of aging. If sags and wrinkles are keeping you from looking as young as you feel, investigate plastic surgery to give you

a younger look and psychological lift. Teeth are also associated with your sign, a reminder to have regular dental cleanings and checkups.

## Aquarius Tips: The Diet Trendsetter

Aquarius is a sign of reaching out to others, a cue to make your diet program a social one. Sharing your diet with friends might keep you interested and prevent boredom. It worked for Oprah Winfrey, an Aquarius whose yo-yo weight gains and losses became media events. If you know you'll be going public for a party or wedding, you'll be motivated to look your best. The trick is to segue from dieting to an ongoing healthy lifestyle. Otherwise you'll be back up the scale again. Try to find a flexible plan that adapts to individual personalities rather than one that imposes a rigid diet structure. Keep a diet diary or online blog to help monitor yourself, a tip from Oprah.

Clean air is top priority for a health-wise air sign especially vulnerable to airborne allergies and viruses. The effects of air pollution might influence where you choose to live. If you life in a polluted environment, get an air purifier, ionizer, or humidifier. Aquarius tends to travel a lot (or may fly your own plane, as John Travolta and Lorenzo Lamas do). Protect yourself from infections that flourish in the enclosed environments of trains, buses, and planes.

Since Aquarius is associated with the circulatory system, you especially benefit from a therapeutic massage. Find your local day spa and schedule one of their relaxing hands-on treatments. New Age treatments are favored by experimental Aquarius, so consider alternative approaches to health and fitness. Perhaps the Ayurvedic approach from India or Chinese massage therapies might work for you. Calves and ankles are also Aquarius territory, which should be emphasized in your exercise program. Be sure your ankles are well supported. Be careful of sprains and strains, especially if you're a jogger.

You'll follow a fitness routine only if you can make your own rules and exercise at a convenient time, which could mean odd moments. If your schedule makes it difficult to

get to the gym or if you dislike the routine of regular exercise classes, videos might solve your problem. There is a vast selection of exercise videos to choose from. Exercising with friends could make staying fit more fun. Try several different kinds of exercise so you can vary your routine from yoga to kick-boxing when you get bored. Or set up a gym at home with portable home exercise equipment. (You're the type who will combine your treadmill sessions with a telephone conversation or TV news show.)

## Pisces Tips: The Addictive Eater

Pisces is a sign of no boundaries, one of the most difficult to discipline diet-wise. You can get hooked on a fattening food like French fries (or alcohol), a habit like coffee with lots of sugar and a roll, and easily gain weight. Your water-sign body may have a tendency to bloat, holding water weight at certain times, especially around the full moon. The key for you, as with so many others, is commitment and support. Don't try to go it alone. Get a partner, a doctor, a group, or one of the online diet-related sites to help. Since you're influenced by the atmosphere around you, choose to be with slim healthy friends and those who will support your efforts. Avoid those seemingly well-meaning diet saboteurs who say just one cookie won't do any harm. A seafood-based diet, like the Perricone diet, could be the right one for you. Your Pisces sisters—Queen Latifah, Liza Minnelli, Camryn Manheim, and Elizabeth Taylor—have slimmed down, and so can you!

Health-wise, supersensitive Pisces, associated with the lymphatic system, reacts strongly to environmental toxins and emotional stress. It's no accident that we often do spring cleaning during the Pisces months. Start your birthday off right by detoxing your system with a liquid diet or supervised fast. This may also help with water retention, a common Pisces problem. Lympathic drainage massage is especially relaxing and beneficial to Pisces.

The feet are Pisces territory. Consider how often you take your feet for granted and how miserable life can be when your feet hurt. Since our feet reflect and affect the

health of the entire body, devote some time to pampering them. Check your walking shoes or buy ones designed for your kind of exercise. Investigate custom-molded orthotic inserts if your arches are high. They could make a big difference in your comfort and performance.

Just as the sign of Pisces contains traces of all the previous signs, the soles of our feet contain nerve endings that connect with all other parts of our body. This is the theory behind reflexology, a therapeutic foot massage that treats all areas of the body by massaging the soles of the feet. For the sake of your feet, as well as your entire body, consider treating yourself to a session with a local practitioner of this technique.

Exercise is not a favorite Pisces activity, unless it is a creative activity like dance or ice-skating, or is related to your water element, such as water aerobics or swimming. A caring exercise instructor who gives you personal attention can also make a difference in your motivation. Walking regularly releases tension, gets you outdoors, and can be a way to socialize with friends away from the temptation of food and drink. Try doing local errands on foot, if you live in a city, or find a local park where you can take a daily hike. Invite someone you love or would like to get to know better to share this time with you, or get an adorable dog to accompany you.

CHAPTER 17

# Discover Your Taurus Personality

Did you know that your Taurus sun sign colors all areas of your life? What and whom you like, how you behave as a parent, your attitude toward your career—all have a strong Taurus influence. The more you know about the Taurus in you, the better you can use your personal solar power to help you make good decisions, from something as basic as what to wear today to deeper psychological issues, such as what compromises you might need to make in order to get along with a difficult boss or new lover. Your sun sign provides a time-honored guide to what's right for you, so why not turn to it when you're at a crossroads in your career, choosing a new hue for your walls, or deciding whether to pursue a romantic relationship. Let the following chapters empower you with the confidence that you're moving in harmony with your natural inclinations.

The basic characteristics of a Taurus are determined by blending several ingredients. First there's your Taurus element: earth. Earth signs are practical, down to earth, solid. Taurus functions in a fixed way; it is a builder, a sign of growth and abundance and of single-mindedness and stubbornness. Then there's your sign's polarity, which adds a feminine, receptive, yin dimension. Let's not forget your planetary ruler: Venus, the planet of love and beauty. Add your sign's location in the zodiac: in the second house of values, material possessions, what you own. Finally, stir in your symbol, the strong and solid bull.

This recipe influences everything we say about Taurus.

For example, you could easily deduce that a fixed earth sign with Venus as a ruler will love the sensual goodies of life. And that Taurus will be good with money, possessive, and a bit stubborn. But your individual astrological personality contains a blend of many other planets colored by the signs they occupy, plus factors such as the sign coming over the horizon at the exact moment of your birth.

However, the more Taurus planets in your horoscope, the more likely you'll follow your sun sign's prototype. On the other hand, if many planets are grouped together in a different sign, they will color your horoscope accordingly, sometimes making a low-key, mellow sun sign come on much stronger. So if the Taurus traits mentioned here don't describe you, there could be other factors flavoring your cosmic stew. (Look up your other planets in the tables in this book to find out what they might be!)

## The Taurus Man: The Comfort Lover

The Taurus man has a sharp eye for quality and value. You're interested in the tangible side of life, which can be fully experienced with all your senses. You'll work hard to provide yourself and your loved ones with material comforts. Born under a fixed, earth sign, you like solid, secure ground under your feet. Not for you is restless shifting from place to place (unless you have a strong Gemini influence in your horoscope). Taking frequent risks is not your cup of tea, either. Instead, each step is carefully considered before you make your move. Slow to commit and equally slow to let go, you are known for physical and emotional endurance, a tremendous asset in a business where you are required to be a judge of lasting value.

Endowed with stamina and persistence, you move steadily toward your goal, maintaining focus and control at all times. Like the strong, silent hero portrayed by Gary Cooper, rather than the swashbuckling extrovert on the fast track, you'll stick to your guns, rarely changing horses in midstream. Once you are committed, no one robs you eas-

ily of your rightful possessions or position. Taurus has so much patience that it takes a lot of pushing to make you angry. But one sure way of turning you into a raging bull is to threaten your well-established territory or your hard-won material security. You make a formidable enemy, and your sign has produced several of the world's fiercest dictators.

The average Taurus male is usually uncomplicated in wants and needs. What you see is what you get with Taurus. You are usually quite predictable and take life literally, preferring to think in terms of direct experience rather than abstract concepts. Not one for a Spartan lifestyle, Venus-ruled Taurus likes to enjoy the fruits of your labors to the fullest. You're susceptible to physical comfort, if not outright luxury: good food on your plate, the aroma of full-bloom roses or a simmering stew, the feel of beautiful fabrics. An atmosphere of plenty appeals to Taurus. Even the most pared-down Taurus lifestyle has comfort, sensual texture, carefully chosen objects, and an affectionate pet or two.

Because you love to be surrounded by comfort and beauty, you may overindulge in good food or accumulate collections of objects d'art. You'll devote much time and effort to making your beloved home as comforting and welcoming as possible. It may be very difficult to lure you away from your well-feathered nest. You prefer to entertain at home, remaining on secure familiar turf, where you can enjoy your treasures and pleasures to the fullest rather than venturing out to explore new territory.

## In a Relationship

The physical side of a relationship is high priority for the sensual Taurus man. You need to be touched, held, and hugged. You love to look at the beauty of the human form. Romantically, you'll tumble hard and fast for physical beauty, especially if combined with a voluptuous, well-sculpted body. The combination of sensuality and endurance makes Taurus one of the great lovers of the zodiac,

though your outward appearance is more wholesome and easygoing, like heartthrob George Clooney or movie heroes Jimmy Stewart, Bing Crosby, James Mason, and Gary Cooper.

Letting go of anything, whether it's a threadbare, once-beloved old sweater or your first love, is especially difficult for you. You can carry the torch for years after a romance has faded, sometimes staying in an unhappy or abusive relationship long after another sign would have departed. In the extreme, this becomes an obsession—Taurus never forgets, especially a broken promise.

Once you have established a loving, cozy, secure home base, you can be one of the most devoted husbands. You're happiest with a domestic, earth-mother woman who won't interfere in your equally comfortable work routines. Before committing yourself, however, you may experiment with different erotic adventures. Such is your fondness for beauty of all kinds that you could easily fall for a flirtatious charmer or a glamorous independent career woman.

Ultimately, though, you'd prefer having your wife nearby. A partner who is too self-sufficient will either send you off to greener pastures or make you see red. Since you have such a long memory for discomfort or grief, you may let grievances accumulate until you are pushed too far, then end the relationship with an explosion. However, when you do find a compatible mate, you can be the stable, secure, and sensual husband of most women's dreams.

## The Taurus Woman: Nature Girl

You are the earth mother of the zodiac, an unabashed, uninhibited sensualist who revels in beauty in all its earthly manifestations. An animal lover and green-thumbed gardener, you see divinity in nature and respond almost spiritually to physical beauty in all its forms. You feel a surge in your heart when you find a full-bloom rose, when an animal does something lovable or charming. Nature-loving Taurus takes an especially protective attitude toward the

environment and the welfare of animals (you're sure to have at last one beloved pet).

You're also conscious of what things cost, both in terms of talent and cold cash. No one can tell the "real thing" from the fake as well as you can. You never underestimate the worth of your own talent, either. It was Taurus supermodel Linda Evangelista who once proclaimed: "I never get out of bed for less than $10,000."

Another famous Taurus beauty was described: "She moves like a storm through life, and in the end, she gets just what she wants." A pronounced Taurus trait is stubbornness. When a Taurus woman sets her mind to something, there is no stopping her. With blinders on, you'll bulldoze ahead until you get what you want, disregarding public opinion or advice to the contrary. You'll patiently wait until your infallible instincts tell you the time is right to take action. Once on track, you won't be derailed by other options, no matter how tempting.

Taurus is slow to make changes. You'll find the particular style or image that works best for you and make it your own. Many Taurus women in show business remain memorable, with a style that others try to copy but few can imitate. Think of Audrey Hepburn, Carol Burnett, Barbra Streisand, Cher, Candace Bergen—each unique, memorable, and much imitated. While other stars fade, these talented Taurus go from strength to strength, improving with age as they build on their previous success.

One of your greatest gifts is your common sense. You're a realist who brings ideas down to earth. Though you may be less gifted in judging the complexities of other people, you do understand what really works. You drive a hard bargain, and you're the least likely of any sign to fall for a puffed-up sales pitch.

You'll hold people to their commitments, with little regard for those who change their minds or promise what they cannot deliver. Therefore, fire signs (Aries, Sagittarius, Leo) and air signs (Gemini, Libra, Aquarius) will present special difficulties for you. Their idea of commitment is always negotiable. Though you love their glamour and dash, you're not always willing to grant the flexibility these

signs demand, or to leave your comfortable abode to accompany them to more exciting places. (Many Taurus have "fear of flying," of losing control of their environment.) You'll also give short shrift to the playboy who changes his women frequently and to the loser who doesn't produce.

## In a Relationship

You rarely marry on a whim. Many of you give special consideration to a man's ability to provide the lifestyle of your dreams, or to create it with you. Because you dislike change or instability, you tend to stick with a marriage even after it has deteriorated. The most successful Taurus relationships are those where both partners have similar goals and a mutual agreement on the lifestyle they wish to achieve. You often make a particularly good partner for a sensitive, artistic man who appreciates the warm, stable, nurturing atmosphere you can provide.

You're usually a talented homemaker, though you may delegate some or most of the mundane chores to others. You prize your secure home turf and family life above all. Whether you stay rooted in the same place for decades or change homes on a whim, each nest will be beautifully and comfortably, if not luxuriously, appointed.

A wizard with money, you have a talent for budgeting, investing, and finding a bargain. You'll be a full-time mother, if necessary, devoting time and attention to your brood—though you may run a business on the side from your home.

# Taurus in the Family

## The Taurus Parent

Taurus takes to parenting naturally. You provide the ideal atmosphere and qualities to nurture a growing child, as you love to nurture all living things. Taurus is an especially effective parent for young children, who benefit most from

your calm, patient qualities. You provide a secure foundation of love, and a stable family atmosphere.

Your heart goes out to children who are growing up in difficult circumstances, and you can be a tireless charity worker on their behalf. A good example was Taurus Audrey Hepburn, who traveled the world on behalf of UNESCO, even though ill herself. Cher's work with disfigured children also comes to mind.

You thoroughly enjoy the early childhood stages, when your demonstrative, affectionate nature seems designed to give the child a sense of security. Later, as the child grows more independent, it may be difficult for you to let go. You may find it especially difficult to deal with the rebellious teenager who has a stubborn streak to match yours. Indeed, many children of Taurus remain in the family nest into adulthood. A Taurus mom is a tough act to follow, as many young wives have discovered! And there is no one as protective of his children throughout their lives as a Taurus dad.

The song "There's No Place Like Home" was surely written by a Taurus. Images of Mother baking chocolate-chip cookies in the kitchen and Daddy comfortably lodged in his favorite chair with a big dog lounging at his feet are Taurus stereotypes. Though few Taurus can manage the Norman Rockwell fantasy in today's world, this ideal is close to Taurus hearts. Rare is the Taurus who doesn't long for a place in the country with swings on the trees, fragrant rose bushes, and a well stocked kitchen.

## The Taurus Stepparent

Your steady, calm nature can be reassuring to stepchildren longing for a stable atmosphere. Patiently, you'll wait for the children to become accustomed to the new family structure. When they do, you'll be warm and affectionate. However, when you must assert your disciplinary authority, do so with calm control. Understand that youngsters with strong wills may resent your position.

Stepchildren will teach you to develop flexibility, and can

expand your horizons if given the chance. Be open to an extended family situation that may not follow the traditional rules. Children will appreciate your allowing them time alone with their biological parent to share mutual interests and strengthen bonds.

## The Taurus Grandparent

In spirit, Taurus grandparents are picture-book elders of a Norman Rockwell painting, even if they look young and glamorous. By this time, you've established a warm, comfortable home and are content to gather all the family round. The Taurus grandma is the archetypal matriarch with a large brood to nurture, whether they are your own or other children in need. Chances are, your extended family will include all the relatives of your in-laws.

Yours will be the home where all the family gathers for holiday feasts, the garden of prizewinning flowers and fresh vegetables, and the special recipes no one else can quite duplicate. You'll be concerned about the children's future and may provide a trust fund or nest egg to finance their education. As the years go by, you'll strengthen family ties by planning celebrations, sending thoughtful notes, and making frequent phone calls. Your grandchildren will remember gratefully how you taught them the true meaning of family traditions by providing them with a strong sense of their own roots.

CHAPTER 18

# Taurus Stellar Style: The Fashion Trends, Home Decor, Colors, and Getaways That Suit Taurus Best

Whether you're ready for an extreme makeover or simply want to update your wardrobe, look to your sun sign for the trends and colors that will harmonize with your Taurus personality.

## Taurus Chic

A fixed earth sign, Taurus is not one for fads or fashion trends. You're known for a unique, unforgettable style that remains consistent over the years. You know what you like and ignore the rest of the pack. You tend to evolve into your own look, be it dramatic (Cher), softly feminine (Andie MacDowell), high fashion (Audrey Hepburn), or classic (Renee Zellweger and Penelope Cruz). There is always an element of sensuality to the way you dress, regardless of whether you're voluptuous or slender. Luxurious fabrics and sensuous textures are a Taurus trademark. Many Taurus like body-revealing looks, such as those favored by Cate Blanchett and Uma Thurman.

Sensual Taurus, one of the best colorists in the zodiac, is sure to have strong opinions about what you do and do not like. The colors of the countryside in the springtime

are sure to be favorites, and they look good on you. Usually you prefer pastels and quiet calm shades. Emerald green, the color of your birthstone, is also second nature to Taurus.

Taurus women have especially lovely necks and throats, emphasized with beautiful necklaces, as Barbra Streisand does (you probably have an impressive jewelry collection), and off-the-shoulder styles. Like Kimora Lee Simmons, model and designer of the Baby Phat collection, you may be a shopper who accumulates overstuffed closets crammed with clothes and accessories. Some of these you regard as clothing investments to be retained for years. Your best strategy is to stick to simple shapes in luxurious fabrics. Avoid anything fussy, especially if you've overindulged your Taurus appetite for good food.

Donatella Versace, a Taurus designer with a sexy edge, has posed her models in sumptuous mansions and clothes that glorify—and expose—the body beautiful. Valentino has dressed socialites and movie stars who appreciate the way his designs play up natural elegance and femininity. Jean Paul Gaultier shows the sexy side of Taurus in his avante-garde clothes for rock stars like Madonna. Michelle Pfeiffer, Janet Jackson, Cate Blanchett, and Uma Thurman are classic Taurus beauties whose looks should inspire you to make the most of your own.

Aim to be distinctively and consistently you. Create your own styles. Don't latch on to a look for the sake of being fashionable. Finally, be sure to play up your femininity with a signature perfume, like Audrey Hepburn, Cher, and Candace Bergen did.

## Time for a Home Makeover? Bring Taurus into Every Room!

You're the original earth mother or nature girl. Chances are you've got a jungle of green plants in your city window, or a beautiful garden in the backyard. So take a leaf or a

flower from nature, and you'll be right on target when planning your home. The luxurious look of English or French country houses or the comfortable warmth of a cozy farmhouse suits you well. If you must live in the city, try to live near a park, use floral prints (or gutsy earthy colors), and fill your windows with plants (even indoor trees) to bring nature indoors, especially if you are looking out on a brick wall. Flowers spilling from antique containers are another wonderful Taurus touch. Your furniture should be roomy and comfortable, upholstered in a feel-good fabric.

You're one of the great collectors of the zodiac; you do it for both pleasure and investment. Perhaps you'll accumulate a trove of pottery or delicate porcelain, artworks, sculpture, records, jewelry, and antiques. Be sure there are enough shelves to display your treasures beautifully. All those bargains you've scored on eBay may take up a lot of room, however. Use your Taurus creativity to devise some decorative storage solutions, ones that will protect your finds, yet make them accessible. Antique chests and armoires can be filled to capacity with your latest acquisitions.

Since you love good food and entertain at home, you'll want a large, well-equipped kitchen. The Taurus kitchen is usually the family gathering place, so you may want to combine it with a family room or use an open plan in order to socialize with your family while you cook.

Your animal companions should be considered also, with spaces to roam and places to roost. Provide an indoor carpeted cat tree for your feline friends and some comfortable dog beds for Rover.

## The Taurus Sound Track

One of the most musical signs, you respond to rich, sensual sounds of all kinds, especially vocal music, because Taurus is associated with the voice. Perhaps you have a well-tuned piano or guitar for at-home musical entertainment. Family sing-alongs are a Taurus specialty. Since you

are sensitive to the slightest distortion in tone, invest in an excellent sound system. You may collect the great vocalists like Barbra Streisand, Cher, Willie Nelson, and Ella Fitzgerald. Or rock to Janet Jackson, Stevie Wonder, and David Byrne. Taurus songwriters like Burt Bacharach and Irving Berlin created sensuous sounds that glorify the human voice.

## Taurus Away from Home

If turf-loving Taurus travels, it's usually for the following reasons: gourmet food, fantastic bargain shopping, or luxurious pampering. Sometimes, you just have to get away from it all, so look for a home away from home when you travel. A comfortable bed-and-breakfast or a familiar hotel with a good restaurant where the owners know your preferences would be best. A luxurious cruise ship on which you can travel without a constant change of rooms or a pampering spa with spectacular views of fragrant gardens will soothe you when you are away from familiar turf. Or rent your own romantic castle somewhere like Tuscany or Provence, with a pastoral landscape and a town famous for its cuisine.

When you pack, be sure to include a few comfort items, such as a fragrant candle to take away the stale smell of hotel rooms, a favorite scarf to drape over a lamp, some framed photos of loved ones, your own special scented bath oils and shower gels, and some delicious little snacks. You might even want to bring a small travel-size coffee press with your special coffee blend. A touch of luxury when you travel can make a world of difference, especially after a long day of sightseeing or shopping. For evenings on the road, a DVD you've been longing to see could buffer any feelings of homesickness. Don't forget your favorite bathrobe, and pamper yourself with breakfast in bed.

You'll need an extra bag—or two—for all the goodies you accumulate on shopping trips to the local markets. Invest in featherweight ballistic nylon suitcases and totebags

that fold up in their own little cases, perfect for stashing your cache of souvenirs. Always carry an extra shopping bag with you. You never know when or where a bargain will appear!

CHAPTER 19

# Your Taurus Career Finder

## What Does Taurus Bring to the Table?

What makes some Taurus more successful than others? Taurus has a special combination of talents and abilities that make you stand out. By discovering and developing your special sun-sign strengths, you'll not only be likely to find a career you truly enjoy, but you'll be able to channel your efforts to areas where you'll be most successful.

Taurus is a long-term survivor in the working world, with more endurance and persistence than any other sign. You need a career with staying power, and work best when you stick to one career direction. In the riskier professions, you often succeed because you simply hang in there the longest, weathering the storms. The downside is that you may vegetate in a job that has no challenge, because you value the steady income. Taurus does not like change, especially sudden changes, so look for an initial job that offers strong growth potential. A company that promotes steadily upward from within would be ideal.

## Where to Find Opportunity

Since Taurus is the sign of buying, appraising, and accumulating, you thrive in careers such as retailing, trading of any

sort, auctions, dealing in art or collectibles, banking, or real estate. You might do very well in the new online auction field, especially if you have access to antiques or collectibles. Your love of nature could lead you into farming, landscape gardening, horticulture, or animal breeding. Taurus is a natural builder, so consider architecture, construction, or engineering. Your sensual side could gravitate to careers in music, culinary arts, fashion, photography, jewelry design, or the fragrance industry.

## The Taurus Leader

If you have dreams of running a business that will bring financial and personal satisfaction, some inspiration from those who achieved phenomenal success could help you make those dreams a reality. Every sign has representatives of billionaires who have followed certain proven wealth-building secrets that you can apply in your own life. Taurus is a natural empire builder who goes into business for long-term gains. Yours is the sign of staying power that rarely switches careers. To find a field you like and develop a career slowly and steadily is the Taurus style. William Randolph Hearst, who founded a newspaper empire, and Hollywood's Aaron Spelling, who developed TV series like *Dynasty,* are good examples.

When you're supervising others, you like total control of your turf, which can make you a steady and wise leader, a benevolent dictator, or a tyrant. Though you can be demanding, you are usually even-tempered and patient, and you value loyalty.

You like the last word on each aspect of your business, rarely changing your mind once you have made a decision. Though you might be very nurturing of underlings, you may hesitate to give them the independence they need to grow by trial and error. You tend to promote from within, working with people you have known for some time, with the goal of building a solid structure for your organization. You'll value that structure rather than flashy ideas or flash-

in-the-pan products. Try to be more flexible and open to new ideas.

## The Taurus Team Player

Once you are comfortable in a steady job, you tend to settle in for the long term and rise steadily through the ranks. You are oriented toward seeing concrete results rather than speculating; therefore, you may not be the most ambitious employee, especially when rising to the top involves taking many risks. But as a valued member of the team, you're the one who can be counted on to ride out storms, handle crises with common sense, negotiate cleverly, and come through in a pinch.

## Promote Yourself!

You're in the driver's seat. It's up to you to decide how to best utilize your Taurus gifts in order to bring you the highest return on the investment of your time and energy. Pick a company with potential that promotes from within. Then play up your best Taurus attributes.

- Loyalty
- Thoroughness
- Financial savvy
- Patience and perseverance
- Reliability
- Steadiness
- Evaluation and appraisal skills
- Practicality
- Negotiation skills

CHAPTER 20

# Let Taurus Celebrities Teach You About Your Sun Sign

It's a fun to find out who else was born under Taurus, especially if it's one of your favorite celebrities. Someone in the public eye who was born on or near your birthday is sure to have many of the traits you do. You may even have a Taurus twin born the same day and year. Notice how your famous sign mates used their Taurus qualities for better or for worse, how they rose from obscurity to fame (and vice versa), what helped or hindered their success, and even how they dress to play up their Taurus star quality. Could this work for you as well?

You have a host of fabulous Taurus celebrities to inspire you. The over-the-top lifestyles of Kimora Lee Simmons, Dennis Rodman, and Cher for high visibility. The ultrafeminine beauty of Michelle Pfeiffer, Penelope Cruz, and Uma Thurman for looks that thrill. The Taurus sense of humor is exemplified by Jerry Seinfeld, Jay Leno, Carol Burnett, and Bea Arthur. The mellow Taurus man: George Clooney, David Beckham, Jack Nicholson—the sexiest in the zodiac. If you're a tabloid fan, how do your sun-sign mates show their Taurus traits as they cope with scandal and reinvent themselves?

If there's someone who intrigues you, go deeper into his life by finding his other planets in the tables in this book. You'll learn more about him as you apply the effects of Venus (turn-ons), Mars (temper), Saturn (fear factor), and Jupiter (luck) to sun-sign traits. You'll be amazed at how the total planetary picture lights up when you have a living example to refer to.

If you've caught the astrology bug, you can move on to analyze the charts of current newsmakers and match your astrology skills with the experts. Of the many celebrity sites on the Internet, the most accurate source of famous birthdays is www.astrodatabank.com, which has charts of world events and headline makers, plus the observations of amateur and professional astrologers. Try it!

## Taurus Celebrities

Ryan O'Neal (4/20/41)
Jessica Lange (4/20/49)
Luther Vandross (4/20/51)
Carmen Electra (4/20/72)
Anthony Quinn (4/21/15)
Queen Elizabeth II (4/21/26)
Charles Grodin (4/21/35)
Patti Lupone (4/21/49)
Tony Danza (4/21/51)
Andie MacDowell (4/21/58)
Aaron Spelling (4/22/28)
Jack Nicholson (4/22/37)
Peter Frampton (4/22/50)
Lee Majors (4/23/39)
Sandra Dee (4/23/42)
Michael Moore (4/23/54)
Valerie Bertinelli (4/23/60)
Melina Kanadaredes (4/23/67)
Renee Zellweger (4/23/69)
Shirley MacLaine (4/24/34)
Barbra Streisand (4/24/42)
Eric Bogosian (4/24/53)
Al Pacino (4/25/39)
Talia Shire (4/25/46)
Hank Azaria (4/25/64)
Carol Burnett (4/26/33)
Coretta Scott King (4/27/27)
Anouk Aimee (4/27/34)

Sheena Easton (4/27/59)
Saddam Hussein (4/28/37)
Ann-Margret (4/28/41)
Jay Leno (4/28/50)
Penelope Cruz (4/28/74)
William Randolph Hearst (4/29/1863)
Duke Ellington (4/29/1899)
Jerry Seinfeld (4/29/55)
Daniel Day-Lewis (4/29/57)
Michelle Pfeiffer (4/29/57)
Carnie Wilson (4/29/68)
Andre Agassi (4/29/70)
Uma Thurman (4/29/70)
Cloris Leachman (4/30/30)
Willie Nelson (4/30/33)
Jill Clayburgh (4/30/44)
Kirsten Dunst (4/30/82)
Pierre Teilhard de Chardin (5/1/1881)
Kate Smith (5/1/1909)
Satyajit Ray (5/1/21)
Bing Crosby (5/2/1904)
Earl Blackwell (5/2/13)
Bianca Jagger (5/2/45)
Christine Baranski (5/2/52)
Jon Bon Jovi (5/2/62)
David Beckham (5/2/75)
Doug Henning (5/3/47)
Wynonna (5/3/64)
Kimora Lee Simmons (5/3/75)
Audrey Hepburn (5/4/29)
Pia Zadora (5/4/55)
Randy Travis (5/4/59)
Ann B. Davis (5/5/20)
Tammy Wynette (5/5/42)
Rudolph Valentino (5/6/1895)
George Clooney (5/6/61)
Robert Browning (5/7/1812)
Darren McGavin (5/7/22)
Rick Nelson (5/8/40)
Melissa Gilbert (5/8/64)

Enrique Iglesias (5/8/75)
Candace Bergen (5/9/46)
Billy Joel (5/9/49)
Bono (5/10/60)
Linda Evangelista (5/10/65)
Martha Graham (5/11/1894)
Valentino (5/11/32)
Louis Farrakhan (5/11/33)
Natasha Richardson (5/11/63)
Katharine Hepburn (5/12/1907)
Gabriel Byrne (5/12/50)
Tom Snyder (5/12/36)
Stephen Baldwin (5/12/66)
Bea Arthur (5/13/26)
Peter Gabriel (5/13/50)
Dennis Rodman (5/13/61)
Cate Blanchett (5/13/69)
David Byrne (5/14/52)
Jasper Johns (5/15/30)
Chazz Palminteri (5/15/51)
Muktananda (5/16/08)
Liberace (5/15/19)
Pierce Brosnan (5/16/52)
Tori Spelling (5/16/73)
Perry Como (5/18/12)
Margot Fonteyn (5/18/19)
Janet Jackson (5/18/66)
David Hartman (5/19/35)
Nora Ephron (5/19/41)
Adela Rogers St. Johns (5/20/1894)
Cher (5/20/46)

CHAPTER 21

# The Taurus Power of Attraction: Your Chemistry with Every Other Sign

Understanding how your sun sign works as part of a couple can help you make wise decisions about your most important relationships: romantic, business, or friendship.

Traditional astrological wisdom holds that signs of the same element (for Taurus, that means other earth signs: Capricorn and Virgo) are naturally compatible. So are signs that are in complementary elements, such as earth signs with water signs. In these relationships, communication flows easily and you'll feel most comfortable with each other.

But do you want comfort at certain times of your life? What happens when you meet someone, sparks fly, and an irresistible magnetic pull draws you together, or when disagreements and challenges fuel intrigue, mystery, and passion? (Think of the sexy verbal sparring in Jane Austen's novel *Pride and Prejudice.*) Even though it may end sadly, you'll never forget or regret that passionate encounter. Indeed, many lasting marriages happen between incompatible sun signs, while some ideally matched couples fizzle after a few years.

Once you understand how your partner's sun sign is likely to view yours and what each of you wants from a relationship, you'll be in a much better position to judge whether this combination has happiness potential. Will there be chemistry or challenges where you'll both need to compromise . . . and are you willing to make them?

The following celebrity couples can help you visualize

each Taurus combination. Notice that some are legendary couples, others showed promise but broke up after a few years, and still others existed only in the fantasy world of film or television (but still captured our imagination).

## Taurus/Aries

### GOOD CHEMISTRY:

Aries gets slow-moving Taurus up and at 'em, waving a red flag before the bull. Taurus is excited and ready to charge. Aries gets direction, follow-through, and solid backup support, as well as a warm, loving sensual companion who is devoted and loyal.

### COMPROMISES:

Adapting to each other's pace calls for compromise, as Aries learns that you cannot be pushed, and you learn that Aries wants everything now. You could lock horns over short-term versus long-term goals. You'll prefer comfortable, luxurious surroundings, while Aries happily sacrifices comfort for adventure. Separate vacations might be the only solution.

### SIGN MATES:

Taurus Katharine Hepburn and Aries Spencer Tracy

## Taurus/Taurus

### GOOD CHEMISTRY:

Loyalty and emotions run deep with these sign mates. Here is the cozy, familiar, comfortable kind of love, spiced by strong sensuality. In this solid, secure relationship, you could be so contented, you never leave home!

COMPROMISES:

Disagreements, if they occur, can be devastating. You two lock horns and never let go. Or there's a permanent stand-off. The other possibility is you'll bore, rather than gore, each other to death, or look for stimulation elsewhere.

SIGN MATES:

Tauruses Carmen Electra and Dennis Rodman

## Taurus/Gemini

GOOD CHEMISTRY:

Next-door signs may be best friends as well as lovers. In this case, Gemini gets you out of the house and into the social scene, adding laughter to love. Taurus has a soothing, stabilizing quality that can make nervous Gemini bloom.

COMPROMISES:

Homebody Taurus usually loves one-on-one relationships, while social Gemini loves to flirt with a crowd. Gemini needs to curb their roving eyes and bodies. Infidelity can be serious business with Taurus. The balance scales between freedom and license swing and sway here.

SIGN MATES:

Taurus Andre Agassi and Gemini Steffi Graf
Taurus Queen Elizabeth II and Gemini Prince Phillip

## Taurus/Cancer

GOOD CHEMISTRY:

In theory, this should be one of the best combinations. Taurus can't ever get too much affection, which Cancer

happily provides. And Taurus protects Cancer from the cold world with solid, secure assets. Both are home loving, emotional, and sensual.

### COMPROMISES:

Cancer dark moods plus Taurus stubbornness could create some muddy moments. Both partners should look for constructive ways to let off steam rather than brood and sulk over grievances.

### SIGN MATES:

Taurus Barbra Streisand and Cancer James Brolin

## Taurus/Leo

### GOOD CHEMISTRY:

Leo passion meets Taurus sensuality, and there's a volcanic physical attraction as you test each other's strength. Both lovers of beauty and comfort, you also have high ideals, fidelity, good food, and music going for you. Taurus money management could provide Leo with a royal lifestyle. The Leo confidence makes Taurus bloom.

### COMPROMISES:

Tensions between these two fixed signs are inevitable. The Leo extravagance and your Taurus possessiveness could be bones of contention. Leo plays dangerous games here, such as denying affection or sex. Focus on building emotional security and avoiding no-win emotional showdowns.

### SIGN MATES:

Taurus Bianca Jagger and Leo Mick Jagger

# Taurus/Virgo

**GOOD CHEMISTRY:**

Taurus admires the Virgo analytical mind, while Virgo admires Taurus concentration and goal orientation. Virgo feels secure with predictable Taurus. You enjoy taking care of each other. Relaxed, soothing Taurus brings out Virgo sensuality. Virgo brings the world of ideas home to Taurus.

**COMPROMISES:**

Virgo nagging can cause Taurus self-doubt, which can show up in bullheaded stubbornness. The Taurus slow pace and ideal of deep-rooted comfort could feel like constraint to Virgo, who needs the stimulation of diversity and lively communication.

**SIGN MATES:**

Taurus Audrey Hepburn and Virgo Mel Ferrer

# Taurus/Libra

**GOOD CHEMISTRY:**

Both Venus-ruled signs, who are turned on by beauty and luxury, you are happy to indulge each other. Libra brings intellectual sparkle, style, and social savvy to Taurus. Taurus gives Libra financial stability and adoration. And Libra profits from your strong Taurus sense of direction and decisiveness.

**COMPROMISES:**

Taurus is possessive and enjoys staying at home. Libra loves social life and flirting. Curb your jealousy, Taurus, because Libra flirtations are rarely serious, only part of the social game. Libra can be extravagant, while Taurus sticks

to a budget and loves to watch money pile up in the bank—another cause for resentment.

### SIGN MATES:

Taurus Evita and Libra Juan Peron
Taurus Kimora Lee Simmons and Libra Russell Simmons

## Taurus/Scorpio

### GOOD CHEMISTRY:

Many marriages happen when these opposites attract. Taurus has a calming effect on the Scorpio innate paranoia. And Taurus responds to Scorpio intensity and fascinating air of mystery. Together, these signs have the perfect complement of sensuality and sexuality.

### COMPROMISES:

Problems of control are inevitable when you both want to run the show. Avoid long and bitter battles or silent standoffs by drawing territorial lines from the start. Then stick to them!

### SIGN MATES:

Taurus Jessica Lange and Scorpio Sam Shepard
Taurus Penelope Cruz and Scorpio Matthew McConaughey

## Taurus/Sagittarius

### GOOD CHEMISTRY:

Sagittarius energizes Taurus and gets this sign to take calculated risks and dare to think big. Taurus provides the solid support and steady income that can make Sagittarius ideas

happen. Sagittarius will be challenged to produce. Taurus to stretch and grow.

**COMPROMISES:**

You are very different types who are not especially sympathetic to each other's needs. Taurus believes in hard work, Sagittarius in luck and seizing the moment of opportunity. Sagittarius is a rolling stone; Taurus is a quiet meadow. Sagittarius appreciates freedom; Taurus appreciates substance.

**SIGN MATES:**

Taurus Kirsten Dunst and Sagittarius Jake Gyllenhaal

## Taurus/Capricorn

**GOOD CHEMISTRY:**

Your similar traditional values can make communication easy. This is a combination that works well on all levels. You find it easy to set goals, to organize and support each other. There are earthy passion and instinctive understanding.

**COMPROMISES:**

There may be too much earth here. The relationship can become too dutiful, practical, and unromantic. You both need to expand your horizons occasionally, and may look for stimulation elsewhere. Taurus may resent the Capricorn devotion to career, since home and family are top priority.

**SIGN MATES:**

Taurus Jack Nicholson and Capricorn Diane Keaton
Taurus Katharine Hepburn and Capricorn Howard Hughes

# Taurus/Aquarius

**GOOD CHEMISTRY:**

This is an uncomfortable, but stimulating, partnership between the conventional Taurus and the rule-breaking Aquarius. Taurus takes care of the practical, while Aquarius provides the inspiration and social involvement that shakes Taurus out of a rut.

**COMPROMISES:**

Resolution of conflicts can wear this one out. Taurus is predictable. Aquarius is unpredictable. Taurus loves privacy. Aquarius is a people person. Taurus wants to settle down. Aquarius needs space. Taurus is possessive. Aquarius is detached.

**SIGN MATES:**

Taurus Cher and Aquarius Sonny Bono

# Taurus/Pisces

**GOOD CHEMISTRY:**

This could be your dream lover. You both love the good things in life and can indulge each other sensually and sexually. Your Taurus focus adds stability and direction to Pisces, while Pisces creativity is lovingly encouraged by Taurus.

**COMPROMISES:**

Taurus wants Pisces to produce, not just dream, and will try to corral the slippery fish into steady employment. Not a good idea! Pisces can't be bossed or caged, and will swim off, leaving Taurus with the dotted line unsigned!

**SIGN MATES:**

Costars Taurus Audrey Hepburn and Pisces Rex Harrison
Ballet stars Taurus Margot Fonteyn and Pisces Rudolf Nureyev

CHAPTER 22

# Astrological Overview for Taurus in 2007

Welcome to 2007, Taurus!

Overall, it looks like a very good year for you. Your ruler, Venus, begins the year in Capricorn and your solar ninth house. Even though it's there for only two days, you can expect a nice surprise related to publishing or higher education. On January 3, it moves into Aquarius and your solar tenth house, a bonus for your career.

Since Venus also governs romance and the arts, let's look at some dates for both areas. From March 17 to April 10, Venus will be in your sign. This transit heightens your sexuality and sex appeal and generally smoothes out any rough edges in your personal life. Another excellent time for romance falls between July 14 and November 8, when Venus is in Virgo and forms a harmonious angle to your sun. However, Venus will be retrograde between July 27 and September 8, so romance may not run quite as smoothly then. Friends you haven't seen for a while and former lovers could enter your life again during that time. This period also favors creative work and all things you do for enjoyment.

If you're planning to move this year, there could be delays until early September, when Saturn moves out of your solar fourth house. Ironically, though, the first four months of the year will be excellent for obtaining loans and mortgages. You may also develop an interest in metaphysics or deepen your interest by taking workshops and seminars.

On September 2, Saturn moves into Virgo and your solar

fifth house. This transit, which takes about two and a half years, should provide structure.

The best periods to apply for and obtain mortgages and loans occur from the beginning of the year to April 4, when Jupiter in your solar eighth house is moving direct, and from August 6 to December 17. On December 18, Jupiter moves into Capricorn. For the next year, your worldview will expand. New opportunities should come to you related to foreign travel, higher education, and publishing.

Your most physically active periods fall between June 24 and August 6, when Mars is in your sign. This period also favors sexual relationships.

The best time for any kind of communications falls between April 27 and May 10, when Mercury is in your sign. Other good times are from August 19 to September 4 and from December 20 to the end of the year.

There are four eclipse dates to watch for this year. Two of them involve Virgo; two involve Pisces. Lunar eclipses tend to bring up emotional issues related to the sign and house in which they fall, and solar eclipses tend to reveal something that has been hidden. On March 3, the lunar eclipse in Virgo could bring up an emotional issue related to your creativity, your children, or a romance. Two weeks later, on March 18, the solar eclipse in Pisces brings to light something that has been hidden in terms of friendships and your wishes and dreams.

On August 28, there's a lunar eclipse in Pisces. This eclipse hits your solar eleventh house, impacting friendship. Some shift may occur in your goals and aspirations. On September 11, the solar eclipse is in Virgo, so something related to creativity, children, and romance that has been hidden from you will be revealed.

Every year, Mercury turns retrograde three times, and during these periods, it's easy to be misunderstood, travel plans often go awry, and computers and other appliances act up. It's also a good idea not to negotiate or sign contracts. The times to watch for are:

*February 13—March 7*—Mercury retrograde in Pisces (your eleventh house). This retrograde period affects your

friendships, goals, and aspirations. It's a good time to review and reevaluate issues in those areas.

*June 15—July 9*—Mercury retrograde in Cancer (your third house). Miscommunication issues could surface with siblings and neighbors. Travel plans may change.

*October 11—November 1*—Mercury retrograde in Scorpio (your seventh house). Be clear and concise in your communications with a partner or spouse!

CHAPTER 23

# Eighteen Months of Day-by-Day Predictions—July 2006 to December 2007

***Moon sign times are calculated for Eastern Standard Time and Eastern Daylight Time. Please adjust for your local time zone.***

## JULY 2006

***Saturday, July 1 (Moon in Virgo)*** This is probably a long weekend for you, so kick back and have some fun. Be as detailed as you want about what you do to have fun, but just make sure that you enjoy yourself!

***Sunday, July 2 (Moon in Virgo to Libra 1:07 p.m.)*** By this afternoon, you're in a fine mood, perhaps even a romantic one. Someone you meet through friends is a romantic possibility. The chemistry is there. Go for it!

***Monday, July 3 (Moon in Libra)*** Is it possible that the new romantic interest in your life is a coworker? If so, don't let the relationship distract you from your responsibilities. Keep things low-key.

***Tuesday, July 4 (Moon in Libra)*** Today marks the beginning of the second Mercury retrograde of the year. Mercury turns retrograde in Leo, in your fourth house. This retrograde period impacts your home life for the next two

weeks. Miscommunication with family members is likely. Have patience. Remain flexible.

***Wednesday, July 5 (Moon in Libra to Scorpio 1:14 a.m.)*** As the moon moves into Scorpio, easy answers satisfy you even less than usual. You're determined to get to the bottom line about a relationship. By tomorrow, you probably do it!

***Thursday, July 6 (Moon in Scorpio)*** Jupiter turns direct in Scorpio, in your seventh house. This is great news for your personal and professional partnerships. The expansion in this area of your life will pick up again and become nothing short of remarkable.

***Friday, July 7 (Moon in Scorpio to Sagittarius 10:14 a.m.)*** As the moon moves into your eighth house, you have a much clearer picture of power issues in your life—who has the power, who wields it. Something that is hidden comes to light.

***Saturday, July 8 (Moon in Sagittarius)*** Make sure your insurance premiums and quarterly taxes are paid up. Trust that the universe will do its part if you do yours. It's called faith.

***Sunday, July 9 (Moon in Sagittarius to Capricorn 3:25 p.m.)*** You're able to use your worldview and spiritual beliefs in a concrete, specific way. It could involve publishing, travel, politics, or religion. It's time to start living by your own wisdom.

***Monday, July 10 (Moon in Capricorn)*** A trip overseas results in expanded revenue for your company. If you're employed by someone else, you take part in a project that helps expand the company to overseas markets. Either way, you win.

***Tuesday, July 11 (Moon in Capricorn to Aquarius 5:46 p.m.)*** Yes, it's hot outside, and you don't feel very

much like traveling. But any professional responsibilities you perform today benefit you in the long run. The higher-ups take notice.

***Wednesday, July 12 (Moon in Aquarius)*** Your network of friends and acquaintances plays into your affair. Romance is in the offing—perhaps with a colleague or even the boss? Any relationship that begins under this transit may run into problems down the road.

***Thursday, July 13 (Moon in Aquarius to Pisces 7:00 p.m.)*** As the moon enters your eleventh house, your idealism leaps into stark relief. What can you do to make the world a better place for everyone? Ultimately, what will your legacy be? These are the kinds of questions you try to answer today.

***Friday, July 14 (Moon in Pisces)*** You do a lot of inner work related to your dreams and hopes. If you feel you aren't making the progress that you think you should in some area of your life, look to the areas where you feel you're successful. Build on that success.

***Saturday, July 15 (Moon in Pisces to Aries 8:39 p.m.)*** Your passions are deep today. Any relationship that begins under this transit is sure to trigger sexual fireworks. Even if it doesn't last, you'll remember this affair.

***Sunday, July 16 (Moon in Aries)*** Restlessness and solitude—those are the hallmarks of the day. And that's fine. You need some time alone to recharge your batteries. Head into the woods. Go hiking. Do something physical.

***Monday, July 17 (Moon in Aries to Taurus 11:45 p.m.)*** The moon is in your sign again—don't you feel great? Take on whatever you want. You'll succeed at it.

***Tuesday, July 18 (Moon in Taurus)*** Venus moves into Cancer and your third house for a three-week stay. A romance is possible with someone who lives in your area or

even in your neighborhood. It could be someone you meet through a sister or female friend.

***Wednesday, July 19 (Moon in Taurus)*** Even if you're a bit more stubborn than usual, you don't feel any angst about it. In fact, you feel pretty good about life in general. Remember this feeling. It comes around more often than you realize.

***Thursday, July 20 (Moon in Taurus to Gemini 4:39 a.m.)*** The Gemini moon loves variety and change; the Taurus sun doesn't like either one. But you need to change something in your finances; today is a good day to figure out what it is.

***Friday, July 21 (Moon in Gemini)*** You're mentally restless and your thoughts keep coming back to money. Come up with some new ideas about how to increase your income. Then apply that Taurus persistence and make it happen!

***Saturday, July 22 (Moon in Gemini to Cancer 11:29 a.m.)*** Mars moves into Virgo and remains there for about six weeks. This transit is excellent for creative work. It gives you the energy to accomplish what you need to. It also makes you something of a perfectionist.

***Sunday, July 23 (Moon in Cancer)*** You may be insecure about your ability to say what you think and feel. Instead of talking about it, keep your thoughts to yourself for the day and do all the talking you want tomorrow evening.

***Monday, July 24 (Moon in Cancer to Leo 8:25 p.m.)*** You may experience moments of unease and not be able to pinpoint the reason. Just try to go with the flow, and by this evening, the mood will be gone.

***Tuesday, July 25 (Moon in Leo)*** You're feeling flamboyant, maybe even flashy. Dress the way you feel. A special someone takes notice.

***Wednesday, July 26 (Moon in Leo)*** You spruce up your house with plants. These plants are boldly colored, lush, and green; they transport you. In fact, anyone who walks into your house reacts the same way.

***Thursday, July 27 (Moon in Leo to Virgo 7:37 a.m.)*** The moon joins Mars in your fifth house. Any romance that begins now is founded on a mutual pleasure or interest. Perhaps you and your new love are involved in a creative project together.

***Friday, July 28 (Moon in Virgo)*** Mercury finally turns direct again in Leo, ending a period of mix-ups and tension at home. Start making plans for your family's summer vacation! Get everyone's input on where to go.

***Saturday, July 29 (Moon in Virgo to Libra 8:28 p.m.)*** Finish up your home-improvement projects so tomorrow you can play. A new romantic interest may pitch in to help.

***Sunday, July 30 (Moon in Libra)*** It's a good day to get out and about and have some fun. Yes, your mind may be on work and everything you have to do tomorrow. But for today, make every moment count.

***Monday, July 31 (Moon in Libra)*** You and a coworker come up with an idea to add some artistic spice and pleasure to your daily routine. Other coworkers hear about it, and suddenly, everyone is in on it. Not a bad way to end the month!

***Tuesday, August 1 (Moon in Libra to Scorpio 9:08 a.m.)*** You and your partner are in the same place today—in the mood for romance and sex. Is it possible to knock off early from work to head out for a romantic dinner? Of course it's possible.

***Wednesday, August 2 (Moon in Scorpio)*** Someone may rub you the wrong way. Resist the impulse to lash out—or to get even. Take the situation in stride.

***Thursday, August 3 (Moon in Scorpio to Sagittarius 7:14 p.m.)*** An issue surfaces concerning your spouse's income or property that you own together. Look for the big picture and don't lose your cool. By tomorrow, everything is clear.

***Friday, August 4 (Moon in Sagittarius)*** You're restless to travel and may need to take stock of your jointly held finances before you buy any tickets. If your insurance and tax bills are paid up, maybe it's time to treat yourself to a slice of paradise, wherever that may be for you.

***Saturday, August 5 (Moon in Sagittarius)*** Your mother or some other female in your life may need your support and assistance. You are glad to help out and do so with patience and grace.

***Sunday, August 6 (Moon in Sagittarius to Capricorn 1:20 a.m.)*** When the moon forms a harmonious angle to your sun, you feel nearly as good as you do when the moon is in your sun sign. Your health is remarkably good, and you are diligent about maintaining it. Your thoughts today, though, may turn to the spiritual side of your life as well.

***Monday, August 7 (Moon in Capricorn)*** Taurus has the patience to meditate. Today that may be just what you need. Remain centered and pay attention to your breathing. Don't let others upset you, or you may regret it.

***Tuesday, August 8 (Moon in Capricorn to Aquarius 3:48 a.m.)*** You wake this morning with a hundred ideas racing through your head. Seize one and follow it. Chances are it leads you to make some innovative decisions regarding your career.

***Wednesday, August 9 (Moon in Aquarius)*** How much risk are you willing to take, Taurus? That's the central question, and it relates to your career. Maybe it's time to change careers. Consider the possibilities.

***Thursday, August 10 (Moon in Aquarius to Pisces 4:11 a.m.)*** With Mercury direct in Leo, your home is a hub of activity. If the activity gets to be too much, you can always steal away by yourself for an hour. Let your intuition guide you.

***Friday, August 11 (Moon in Pisces)*** Public speaking, promotion, and publicity are all good activities. Anything you do before the public will be well received.

***Saturday, August 12 (Moon in Pisces to Aries 4:23 a.m.)*** Now you have Venus joining Mercury and Saturn in your fourth house. Your love life is sure to heat up; creative projects unfold smoothly. Women prove helpful.

***Sunday, August 13 (Moon in Aries)*** You may withdraw from the chaos today. You feel a need to be alone or to work in solitude. You can be the power behind the scenes in someone else's life.

***Monday, August 14 (Moon in Aries to Taurus 6:01 a.m.)*** Celebrate! The moon is in your sign again. Your sex appeal and general charisma go way up. Someone who has been watching you from a distance becomes bold.

***Tuesday, August 15 (Moon in Taurus)*** You're in the mood for romance, and the stars are on your side! Plan a special dinner with your lover. As a Taurus, you probably cook well, so make it a gourmet evening.

***Wednesday, August 16 (Moon in Taurus to Gemini 10:08 a.m.)*** It's time to apply your considerable willpower to your financial situation. Decide what level of income would be comfortable for you and then pour your willpower into attracting opportunities that pay that figure.

***Thursday, August 17 (Moon in Gemini)*** A Libra or an Aquarius plays into your life. This person has ideas about financial planning that will benefit you. Listen. Gather more information. Then decide.

***Friday, August 18 (Moon in Gemini to Cancer 5:04 p.m.)*** The moon in Cancer forms a harmonious angle to your sun. Your mind is more intuitive; you're able to spot synchronicities as they happen. Follow them. Synchronicities are the voice of the universe, pointing you in a particular direction.

***Saturday, August 19 (Moon in Cancer)*** You have more contact than usual with your siblings or other relatives. You're nostalgic for the past and may get out the digital camera and start recording the events in your own life. Writing in a journal may be another option for exploring your mood.

***Sunday, August 20 (Moon in Cancer)*** You feel a need to get near a body of water, so you drive to a lake or even to the ocean. Even a river will do. You associate water with renewal.

***Monday, August 21 (Moon in Cancer to Leo 2:34 a.m.)*** A stray animal finds its way into your life. Ask yourself what this type of animal means to you and what its possible message for you might be. Look for the metaphors.

***Tuesday, August 22 (Moon in Leo)*** Yesterday's stray animal is now your pet. Your kids are thrilled. And actually, you're pretty thrilled about it too.

***Wednesday, August 23 (Moon in Leo to Virgo 2:08 p.m.)*** Romance, sex, pleasure, fun, creativity, your kids, gambling, speculation—all of these areas could play into your life. Pick one area to explore when you get up this morning and observe the details. Record them. Become a witness to your own life patterns.

***Thursday, August 24 (Moon in Virgo)*** Your novel or screenplay suddenly makes sense. You're connecting the dots, understanding how one piece fits into another.

***Friday, August 25 (Moon in Virgo)*** Your muse is working overtime, feeding you exactly what you need to finish what you're doing. And you, in turn, may be feeding information or inspiration to someone else. You may be that person's mentor.

***Saturday, August 26 (Moon in Virgo to Libra 3:01 a.m.)*** Get your hair cut. Go to the gym. Take a yoga class. Go shopping. Do something for yourself today.

***Sunday, August 27 (Moon in Libra)*** Mercury moves into Virgo and your fifth house today. If you're a writer, you're in for a wonderful two weeks. Mercury in this sign forces you to pay attention to the small details that make up good writing.

***Monday, August 28 (Moon in Libra to Scorpio 3:56 p.m.)*** Detective, sleuth, researcher—all of these hats fit today and relate to a contract that you're negotiating. Consult with your partner. Decide on a strategy.

***Tuesday, August 29 (Moon in Scorpio)*** Sometimes in relationships, there are mountains to climb and plunging valleys to negotiate. So move through the day with your usual patience. That's about the best you can do.

***Wednesday, August 30 (Moon in Scorpio)*** You and your significant other have a heart-to-heart talk. It opens up intuitive connections between you that may not have

existed before. This is what you've been after all along: the deeper stuff, the heart of it all.

***Thursday, August 31 (Moon in Scorpio to Sagittarius 3:00 a.m.)*** Big pictures aren't always easy to see. But once you see them, it's difficult to go back to the way things were before. That's okay. It may be time to release relationships that no longer work.

## SEPTEMBER 2006

***Friday, September 1 (Moon in Sagittarius)*** Jury duty. Is it really as bad as they say? Approach it with an open mind and a willingness to learn something new.

***Saturday, September 2 (Moon in Sagittarius to Capricorn 10:35 a.m.)*** It's already apparent this is going to be a busy month. So lay the groundwork for the future. Make the minutes count.

***Sunday, September 3 (Moon in Capricorn)*** You attend a seminar on spiritual topics that have a big impact on how you see yourself and your role in the world. You may realize it's time to integrate your spirituality into the rest of your life. You're up to the challenge, Taurus.

***Monday, September 4 (Moon in Capricorn to Aquarius 2:15 p.m.)*** Pluto turns direct in Sagittarius, in your eighth house. The effects of this movement are subtle, but you'll find that anything concerning joint resources moves smoothly.

***Tuesday, September 5 (Moon in Aquarius)*** Time to put on a smile and network. Socialize. Make an effort to draw people into your court. This pays off for you professionally in the long run.

***Wednesday, September 6 (Moon in Aquarius to Pisces 2:57 p.m.)*** Venus moves into Virgo, a wonderful transit that

enhances your creativity. It also bodes well for a romance that begins on the basis of nothing more than pure pleasure. Even if this relationship develops into something more—and it probably will—enjoy it for what it is right now.

***Thursday, September 7 (Moon in Pisces)*** Mars moves into Libra, in your sixth house. This transit energizes your daily routine and may get you more involved with coworkers. You seek balance in your work life and hope to find some sort of artistic venue that makes things . . . well, more interesting!

***Friday, September 8 (Moon in Pisces to Aries 2:24 p.m.)*** By this afternoon, you're ready to head out into the wilds. Go camping and bring your dog along as your companion. You need the solitude.

***Saturday, September 9 (Moon in Aries)*** You're short-tempered, but ideas are whizzing through you at the speed of light. Keep a recorder handy while you drive and a notepad with you the rest of the time. Don't let these ideas get away from you.

***Sunday, September 10 (Moon in Aries to Taurus 2:31 p.m.)*** As the moon moves into Taurus this afternoon, your mood improves immeasurably. Someone close to you challenges something you believe or that you value. You defend the value with grace.

***Monday, September 11 (Moon in Taurus)*** You find an answer you need online or in a book. A Libra or a Sagittarius plays a role in your life. That role could include a flirtation or the beginning of a romance.

***Tuesday, September 12 (Moon in Taurus to Gemini 5:00 p.m.)*** Mercury moves into Libra and into your sixth house. This transit signals activity that is out of the ordinary in your daily routine. You have more communication than

usual with coworkers. Ideas are flying, and the boss likes them!

***Wednesday, September 13 (Moon in Gemini)*** You've got the right stuff! Your mind and your communication skills are sharp, and your charisma is working in your favor.

***Thursday, September 14 (Moon in Gemini to Cancer 10:54 p.m.)*** Your mother or another female relative may need your support and help. Enlist the aid of your neighbors to accomplish a neighborhood cleanup. You'll get to know people you've lived close to for years.

***Friday, September 15 (Moon in Cancer)*** You're checking out other neighborhoods, hoping to find something that suits you. You may find, though, that the grass isn't always greener. Perhaps the best route to go is to refurbish the house where you live.

***Saturday, September 16 (Moon in Cancer)*** The past has a strange pull on you today. You're remembering childhood days and how you felt then. Honor these memories in some way—then release them.

***Sunday, September 17 (Moon in Cancer to Leo 8:15 a.m.)*** You're feeling somewhat protective about your family and personal space. Try not to smother anyone. Relish your time with your loved ones.

***Monday, September 18 (Moon in Leo)*** The moon joins Saturn in your fourth house. You could feel somewhat restricted or confined. Or perhaps your responsibilities are getting to be a bit too burdensome. Maybe it's time to delegate.

***Tuesday, September 19 (Moon in Leo to Virgo 8:07 p.m.)*** You're psyched for working on your creative projects. You're able to fine-tune your project, and by the end of the day, you love what you've done.

***Wednesday, September 20 (Moon in Virgo)*** If you have a health concern, it's a minor problem. Perhaps an adjustment in your diet or nutrition is in order. Seek advice from an alternative-health practitioner.

***Thursday, September 21 (Moon in Virgo)*** You get help or advice from a woman who works in a creative field. She gives you tips about the business that prove to be invaluable.

***Friday, September 22 (Moon in Virgo to Libra 9:07 a.m.)*** You have a disagreement with a coworker that upsets you. But after thinking about what happened, you realize the coworker is right. You admit this to the person, and all is well again.

***Saturday, September 23 (Moon in Libra)*** You feel wonderful. You and a friend visit a local museum or art gallery and soak up some culture. This evening is a good time for romance. Be prepared!

***Sunday, September 24 (Moon in Libra to Scorpio 9:55 p.m.)*** Intense emotions highlight your day. These emotions center around a personal relationship that has had a few bumps and scrapes lately. Get to the bottom of it before things escalate beyond anyone's control.

***Monday, September 25 (Moon in Scorpio)*** Your sex life heats up. If you're a woman and you've been hoping to get pregnant, this could be the night! The moon is sharing your seventh house with Jupiter. An auspicious combination.

***Tuesday, September 26 (Moon in Scorpio)*** You do some detective work on the job. Something you've lost is found. Research pays off.

***Wednesday, September 27 (Moon in Scorpio to Sagittarius 9:17 a.m.)*** As the moon moves into your ninth house, your perceptions broaden. Your spiritual beliefs come into

play. Are you all talk? Or do you practice what you preach?

***Thursday, September 28 (Moon in Sagittarius)*** You have an overseas visitor, an old friend you haven't seen in a long time. This person whets your hunger for travel; this evening, you start searching the Internet for travel deals.

***Friday, September 29 (Moon in Sagittarius to Capricorn 6:02 p.m.)*** If you haven't been called for jury duty yet, today you may get a notice. Don't groan. Look at it as a learning experience.

***Saturday, September 30 (Moon in Capricorn)*** As Venus moves into Libra, a romance with a coworker gets off the ground. During the next two weeks, you'll have stars in your eyes and your heart will be filled to overflowing.

## OCTOBER 2006

***Sunday, October 1 (Moon in Capricorn to Aquarius 11:25 p.m.)*** The month begins with Mercury moving into Scorpio and your seventh house. This transit favors contracts and honest communication with your spouse or partner. Research you do pays off down the line.

***Monday, October 2 (Moon in Aquarius)*** The moon joins Neptune in your tenth house. This transit favors dealings with the public. If you network and do promotion, you or your company or product will be well received.

***Tuesday, October 3 (Moon in Aquarius)*** You may be reassessing certain facets of your career path. A slight adjustment in your thinking may be necessary. But with the moon in visionary Aquarius, you should do just fine!

***Wednesday, October 4 (Moon in Aquarius to Pisces 1:34 a.m.)*** Get out there, and do some publicity for your

company or your product. Network with friends. This evening, you attend a group gathering.

***Thursday, October 5 (Moon in Pisces)*** As the moon joins Uranus in Pisces, your intuition deepens considerably. You have a startling insight into the motives of a friend. Will the friendship survive the revelation?

***Friday, October 6 (Moon in Pisces to Aries 1:33 a.m.)*** With the nip of fall in the air, you head out by yourself to explore the woods or a town where you've never been. You prefer to go alone. Go recharge your batteries, Taurus!

***Saturday, October 7 (Moon in Aries)*** Try not to hold your anger in today. If you're annoyed, express it. If you have something on your mind, say it. A Sagittarius comes to you with some fascinating ideas.

***Sunday, October 8 (Moon in Aries to Taurus 1:05 a.m.)*** The moon goes into your sign, Taurus. Celebrate! You're feeling good about everything, and all that good feeling attracts someone you've been interested in for a long time.

***Monday, October 9 (Moon in Taurus)*** How can you make your life more harmonious? That's the central question of the day; by the end of the day, you have your answer.

***Tuesday, October 10 (Moon in Taurus to Gemini 2:06 a.m.)*** You're looking for investments that will turn a fast profit. Do your research and cull your facts, and you may change your mind and settle for something with long-term security.

***Wednesday, October 11 (Moon in Gemini)*** You spend way too much time running around and doing errands that may not be related to anything that interests you. Time to pause, take a deep breath, and reevaluate how you spend your time.

***Thursday, October 12 (Moon in Gemini to Cancer 6:21 a.m.)*** Once upon a time when you were much younger, you were happy! So what happened? You delve into your early childhood for an answer. A relative or neighbor helps you figure things out.

***Friday, October 13 (Moon in Cancer)*** You look at real estate as a potential investment. Or you may see a home that you would like to buy. Gather your facts and don't move hastily.

***Saturday, October 14 (Moon in Cancer to Leo 2:38 p.m.)*** As the moon joins Saturn in your fourth house, you feel emotionally stifled. Remember that the feeling will pass. Get out and do something that brings you emotional satisfaction.

***Sunday, October 15 (Moon in Leo)*** You get involved in a home-renovation project that thrills you. You're beautifying the outside of your house and the property as well. The value of your home just went way up!

***Monday, October 16 (Moon in Leo)*** One of your children has a problem at school that needs to be addressed. Listen with an open heart.

***Tuesday, October 17 (Moon in Leo to Virgo 2:16 a.m.)*** It's your day to dive into creative projects. You're especially attentive to all the details that make up the larger picture. It pays off.

***Wednesday, October 18 (Moon in Virgo)*** Keep your dentist or doctor appointment. These appointments are not for anything serious. You may sign up for a yoga class.

***Thursday, October 19 (Moon in Virgo to Libra 3:20 p.m.)*** You're feeling quite amorous; your attention is focused on a coworker. When this person responds to your overtures, you get bold and make a date.

***Friday, October 20 (Moon in Libra)*** Get your hair cut. Buy some new clothes or even a new pair of shoes. Make yourself feel attractive.

***Saturday, October 21 (Moon in Libra)*** You and a friend or coworker visit a museum or art gallery or attend a concert. The event stimulates your mutual creativity and a possible collaboration is born.

***Sunday, October 22 (Moon in Libra to Scorpio 3:55 a.m.)*** Your emotions are a powerful force. When you bring the full power of what you feel against a challenge, you resolve it quickly and cleanly.

***Monday, October 23 (Moon in Scorpio)*** Mars moves into Scorpio, the sign that it rules. This transits heats up your sex life, and your partnerships in general become emotional powerhouses. Resist the urge to get even with someone who has hurt you.

***Tuesday, October 24 (Moon in Scorpio to Sagittarius 2:54 p.m.)*** Now you're in for it! Venus joins the moon and Mars in your seventh house, a powerful combination that spells romance, love, great sex, and a lucky break with contracts. By this afternoon, the moon has moved into another sign, but your morning is sure to be hopping!

***Wednesday, October 25 (Moon in Sagittarius)*** With your physical and sexual energy in a state of heightened awareness, you're able to see the larger picture of the resources you share with other people. If you don't like what you see, then take steps to change it.

***Thursday, October 26 (Moon in Sagittarius to Capricorn 11:48 p.m.)*** As the moon moves into your ninth house, you may decide to take an adult-education course in something that interests you. Or you may sign up for a seminar on spirituality.

***Friday, October 27 (Moon in Capricorn)*** You have a lot of options today. But is your new strategy sound? Can you make it work in the real world?

***Saturday, October 28 (Moon in Capricorn)*** Mercury turns retrograde in Scorpio. This is the last Mercury retrograde of the year. By now, you know what to do and not do. This movement could result in miscommunication with your spouse or significant other, so be clear and concise when you speak.

***Sunday, October 29—Daylight Saving Time Ends (Moon in Capricorn to Aquarius 5:17 a.m.)*** The moon moves into your tenth house, putting you more in front of the public. Network. Touch base with your e-mail group. A Gemini plays a role.

***Monday, October 30 (Moon in Aquarius)*** You have some cutting-edge ideas that you should implement in your career or business. Take the risk. You won't regret it.

***Tuesday, October 31 (Moon in Aquarius to Pisces 9:11 a.m.)*** Happy Halloween! What a great day for a moon in Pisces, a sign that involves fantasy and intuition. Put on your costume and trick or treat with your kids, Taurus.

## NOVEMBER 2006

***Wednesday, November 1 (Moon in Pisces)*** It's the perfect day for networking with friends and acquaintances. This afternoon, you may attend one of your group meetings with fellow writers, bridge players, or actors.

***Thursday, November 2 (Moon in Pisces to Aries 10:47 a.m.)*** You're able to use your energy to achieve whatever you tackle. You should go to the gym to burn off some of that energy. Nurture your patience. You may need a lot of it.

***Friday, November 3 (Moon in Aries)*** Your creative drive is powerful. Indulge it. The results will surprise you! A Sagittarius figures into the picture and provides a broader perspective.

***Saturday, November 4 (Moon in Aries to Taurus 11:05 a.m.)*** The moon goes into your sign before noon, and you feel the difference. Your mood goes from grumpy to great! You attract a Capricorn or another Taurus and suddenly have a date tonight!

***Sunday, November 5 (Moon in Taurus)*** A local gallery holds treasures that intrigue you. You may have an impulse to buy something expensive. Just be sure the check has cleared!

***Monday, November 6 (Moon in Taurus to Gemini 11:47 a.m.)*** Hold off on investments until after November 17, when Mercury will be moving direct again. Look, do your research, and gather your facts, but don't buy!

***Tuesday, November 7 (Moon in Gemini)*** Someone questions your values. You rise to your own defense with admirable aplomb and win over a potential adversary with your convincing argument.

***Wednesday, November 8 (Moon in Gemini to Cancer 2:46 p.m.)*** Make an appointment with a Realtor to show you the house that has captured your attention. Assess the surrounding neighborhoods and nearby schools. Is this a place you would love living in?

***Thursday, November 9 (Moon in Cancer)*** Don't make an offer on that house until after November 17! Some things must be taken on faith, and this time, you must believe that the trust is working on your behalf. The house will still be available after November 17.

***Friday, November 10 (Moon in Cancer to Leo 9:35 p.m.)*** Your home is a hub of activity. The phones are

ringing and people are dropping by—it all disrupts your schedule. But perhaps that's as it should be. You need to give yourself a break, Taurus.

***Saturday, November 11 (Moon in Leo)*** You throw a party tonight. Good friends bring other friends, and pretty soon, you're working the room, making new contacts. It pays off by the end of the year.

***Sunday, November 12 (Moon in Leo)*** Your partner or significant other gives you a beautiful gift. You go out tonight looking flashy and gorgeous. A nice feeling, isn't it?

***Monday, November 13 (Moon in Leo to Virgo 8:20 a.m.)*** If one of your kids doesn't want to go to school today, don't push the idea. Even kids need to recharge their batteries from time to time.

***Tuesday, November 14 (Moon in Virgo)*** Your novel or screenplay is finished. Now read it over with an eye for details. Small corrections may be needed. After Mercury turns direct on November 17, send it off to your agent or editor.

***Wednesday, November 15 (Moon in Virgo to Libra 9:15 p.m.)*** Your business partnerships are expanding and you're putting in a lot of overtime. But the beauty is that you're loving it. This is truly your pleasure.

***Thursday, November 16 (Moon in Libra)*** You and a coworker get together after work to dive into a collaborative project. It's creative and artistic and you're having so much fun with it the time gets away from you.

***Friday, November 17 (Moon in Libra)*** Venus moves into Sagittarius and your eighth house. Between now and December 11, romance is possible with someone you meet at a seminar or at work. An Aries or a Gemini plays into the picture. Mercury turns direct today! Celebrate.

***Saturday, November 18 (Moon in Libra to Scorpio 9:48 a.m.)*** Any bumps you've been experiencing with your partner should start smoothing out. You're in a romantic mood, your partner loves it.

***Sunday, November 19 (Moon in Scorpio)*** Uranus turns direct in Pisces. This movement releases energy that has been internalized these last several months. New friends enter your life; your insights between now and the end of the year are fresh.

***Monday, November 20 (Moon in Scorpio to Sagittarius 8:16 p.m.)*** The moon joins Venus in your eighth house. A romance or affair could begin with a foreign-born individual or with someone who works in publishing, higher education, or the law.

***Tuesday, November 21 (Moon in Sagittarius)*** You have the broader perspective on things like taxes and insurance. Be sure your payments are up-to-date. You and a partner may look at a piece of property for investment purposes.

***Wednesday, November 22 (Moon in Sagittarius)*** You may want to try meditation as a means to obtain information from your higher self. Five or ten minutes a day will benefit you enormously. If you're traveling, do some yoga postures so you don't get stiff.

***Thursday, November 23 (Moon in Sagittarius to Capricorn 4:26 a.m.)*** Jupiter moves into Sagittarius, the sign that it rules, and remains there for about a year. This brings enormous changes and expansion into resources you share with others or that they share with you.

***Friday, November 24 (Moon in Capricorn)*** You're in the groove, Taurus. With the moon in Capricorn, it's now much easier to bring your dreams to fruition. A Virgo helps you do this.

***Saturday, November 25 (Moon in Capricorn to Aquarius 10:41 a.m.)*** A Gemini, a Libra, or both are supportive of your professional goals. They are consummate networkers and connect you with some powerful people.

***Sunday, November 26 (Moon in Aquarius)*** You're playing a game of chance and risk. It pays off, much to everyone else's surprise. But deep down, you always sensed you would be the winner.

***Monday, November 27 (Moon in Aquarius to Pisces 3:21 p.m.)*** Your ability to fantasize and imagine are powerful. A dream provides information or inspiration that you need. Another Pisces could figure prominently in the day's affairs.

***Tuesday, November 28 (Moon in Pisces)*** As the holidays approach, you're meeting more people, making new contacts. Be sure to tell them about your company or product. Don't be shy!

***Wednesday, November 29 (Moon in Pisces to Aries 6:30 p.m.)*** Sit back and chill out. You need a rest, Taurus. Turn on the TV or grab that novel you've been wanting to read. Spend the day indulging yourself.

***Thursday, November 30 (Moon in Aries)*** Your need for solitude may continue. As long as your partner understands the need, everything is fine. You'd better be clear about your intentions.

•

## DECEMBER 2006

***Friday, December 1 (Moon in Aries to Taurus 8:27 p.m.)*** The moon goes into your sign this evening. Your sex appeal goes through the roof. This is a great way to head into the last month of the year.

***Saturday, December 2 (Moon in Taurus)*** You attract someone who has interested you for a long time. The flirtation or romance takes off.

***Sunday, December 3 (Moon in Taurus to Gemini 10:06 p.m.)*** Books and communication play into your affairs. You and a friend head out to a café to meet with friends.

***Monday, December 4 (Moon in Gemini)*** Invest today. Mercury is direct now; it's a good time to negotiate contracts.

***Tuesday, December 5 (Moon in Gemini)*** Mars moves into Sagittarius, joining Jupiter in your eighth house. This energizes your jointly held resources. Apply for a mortgage or a loan. You'll get it. Saturn turns retrograde in Leo, creating tension at home.

***Wednesday, December 6 (Moon in Gemini to Cancer 1:02 a.m.)*** Something comes to light in your relationship with a sister, a brother, or another relative. It's nothing terrible, but it deepens your understanding of that person.

***Thursday, December 7 (Moon in Cancer)*** You find the right house. You and your spouse or partner discuss it and make an offer. Try to be flexible, however. Your first offer may not be accepted.

***Friday, December 8 (Moon in Cancer to Leo 6:53 a.m.)*** Mercury moves into Sagittarius, joining Jupiter and Venus in your eighth house. News arrives concerning taxes or insurance. A check is in the mail.

***Saturday, December 9 (Moon in Leo)*** You're in a flamboyant, upbeat mood. Your mood spreads to other people, and as a result, you attract the attention of a special someone.

***Sunday, December 10 (Moon in Leo to Virgo 4:32 p.m.)*** Details, details—they fly at you from everywhere

today. Your car could be in need of some minor repairs, your creative project might need fine-tuning, or your kids may come for advice.

***Monday, December 11 (Moon in Virgo)*** Venus moves into Capricorn. Romance with a foreigner could be on the horizon between now and the end of the year. If you travel overseas, you meet someone special, and the trip is fruitful and productive.

***Tuesday, December 12 (Moon in Virgo)*** Plan your day so that it revolves around whatever brings you pleasure. Take advantage of every moment.

***Wednesday, December 13 (Moon in Virgo to Libra 5:01 a.m.)*** A Capricorn or a Gemini invites you to a party. Through the contacts you make, a new job offer could come up. Now you'll have to make a decision.

***Thursday, December 14 (Moon in Libra)*** You're able to see all sides of a given work issue and act as mediator for several people with whom you work. Your boss notices your negotiation skills.

***Friday, December 15 (Moon in Libra to Scorpio 5:43 p.m.)*** Intense and powerful emotions rule the evening. You and your partner go out Christmas shopping and disagree on an item you want to buy. You buy it anyway.

***Saturday, December 16 (Moon in Scorpio)*** Yesterday's disagreement morphs into today's passions. With tensions rising because of the approaching holidays, you find refuge with each other.

***Sunday, December 17 (Moon in Scorpio)*** You do your research and dig for answers. By the end of the day, you have the answers you need. Now you're ready to negotiate a contract.

***Monday, December 18 (Moon in Scorpio to Sagittarius 4:10 a.m.)*** The moon in your eighth house brings experiences and reactions to taxes, insurance, and inheritances. You visit your attorney and get your papers in order.

***Tuesday, December 19 (Moon in Sagittarius)*** Christmas is just days away, and you're panicking because you haven't found the right gift for your in-laws. You hit the mall this evening and find one in the nick of time.

***Wednesday, December 20 (Moon in Sagittarius to Capricorn 11:39 a.m.)*** The exotic and the foreign capture your interest today. It may start with a travel brochure that you see. Is a trip in order for the holidays?

***Thursday, December 21 (Moon in Capricorn)*** A Virgo and Cancer figure prominently in your life today. One of them may be an unexpected visitor. The visit adds to your holiday stress until you make a conscious decision just to go with the flow.

***Friday, December 22 (Moon in Capricorn to Aquarius 4:49 p.m.)*** Everyone is in a generous mood. This generosity translates into professional advantages for you. Network and socialize. Put your ideas down on paper.

***Saturday, December 23 (Moon in Aquarius)*** Your boss is impressed with your proposal. Now you have to wait to the end of the year, but the hard work is done and the payoff comes early next year.

***Sunday, December 24 (Moon in Aquarius to Pisces 8:44 p.m.)*** Your family and friends are with you tonight to celebrate Christmas Eve. Everyone's heart is open and receptive. You're creating memories for your kids.

***Monday, December 25 (Moon in Pisces)*** Merry Christmas! A new family pet could be under the Christmas tree. Gather information on how to take care of your new pet. It's time for the kids to learn responsibility.

***Tuesday, December 26 (Moon in Pisces)*** You may be rethinking your goals. Start drawing them up now so that you're ready on New Year's Eve to state your resolutions.

***Wednesday, December 27 (Moon in Pisces to Aries 12:05 a.m.)*** Mercury moves into Capricorn and your ninth house. Your thoughts really turn to the foreign and exotic today. Tahiti, anyone?

***Thursday, December 28 (Moon in Aries)*** Take the day off and relax. You've earned it. But for you, relaxing could mean a hike in the woods, rock climbing, or some other physical activity. Whatever it is, go do it, Taurus.

***Friday, December 29 (Moon in Aries to Taurus 3:09 a.m.)*** What a great way to end the year, with the moon in your sign right before New Year's Eve. Enjoy the way this transit makes you feel. Then learn to conjure the feeling when you don't have it. That's part of the magic of living!

***Saturday, December 30 (Moon in Taurus)*** You and a Virgo hit it off. You take in the sights, eat in new restaurants, and generally get to know each other. You like what you see.

***Sunday, December 31 (Moon in Taurus to Gemini 6:17 a.m.)*** Celebrate the coming new year with friends who share your passion and interests. Promise yourself that you'll live up to your resolutions for next year.

HAPPY NEW YEAR!

***Monday, January 1 (Moon in Gemini)*** With the moon in your second house of finances and possessions, you identify closely with what's yours, and that includes your values. Take care of paying what you owe and collecting what's yours. But avoid major purchases.

***Tuesday, January 2 (Moon in Gemini to Cancer 10:15 a.m.)*** You start out the day feeling versatile and changeable. You have a tendency to spread yourself too thin or to diversify too much. You're writing memos or making lots of calls. By late morning, you change perspectives, and your thoughts turn toward the home front.

***Wednesday, January 3 (Moon in Cancer)*** With Venus moving into your tenth house, you could be in line for a raise or public recognition of your efforts. A romantic liaison is possible with a peer or boss! Watch your step. When the fascination wears off, things could turn ugly.

***Thursday, January 4 (Moon in Cancer to Leo 4:15 p.m.)*** Go with the flow. Gather information, but don't make any absolute decisions until tomorrow. You could be exploring the unknown, a mystery of some sort. See things as they are, not how you'd like them to be.

***Friday, January 5 (Moon in Leo)*** With the moon in Leo, you feel gregarious. You're more impulsive than usual. Creativity is highlighted. You balance your usual Taurus stability with a flair for drama.

***Saturday, January 6 (Moon in Leo)*** The moon is in your fourth house. Stay home to handle repairs and catch up on household chores. Retreat to a private place for relaxation and meditation. You could have dealings with a parent.

***Sunday, January 7 (Moon in Leo to Virgo 1:19 a.m.)*** Get out and meet new people; have new experi-

ences. A flirtation could turn serious. Avoid people with negative attitudes. Think positive. Get a fresh start.

*Monday, January 8 (Moon in Virgo)* With the moon in Virgo, you're doubly grounded. But your usual plodding persistence and determination are anchored with a sense of detail and a need for perfection and order. If you get anything done, it'll be just right.

*Tuesday, January 9 (Moon in Virgo to Libra 1:15 p.m.)* Your imagination is keen. Your curiosity and intuition are highlighted. Your positive attitude pays off as your optimism spreads and you gain new support. Take time to listen to others. Have some fun and recharge your battery. Tomorrow could be trying.

*Wednesday, January 10 (Moon in Libra)* With the moon in your sixth house, you may feel stressed on the job. It might be difficult to express your feelings. Don't act like a martyr. Keep your resolutions about exercise, and help others wherever you can.

*Thursday, January 11 (Moon in Libra)* The pressure is off, and romance is in the air. Your focus is on a relationship, possibly a new romance. Nurture it. Take time to go to a concert, a museum, or an art gallery. Your personal grace and magnetic appeal are emphasized. You may have a new creative project on your mind.

*Friday, January 12 (Moon in Libra to Scorpio 2:08 a.m.)* It's all about service. Be understanding and avoid conflict. Try to make people happy today. Cheer up someone who's not feeling well. Be generous and tolerant of others. But avoid scattering your energies, and know when to back off.

*Saturday, January 13 (Moon in Scorpio)* With the moon in your seventh house, you may be dealing with partnerships and contracts, possibly a marriage. Whether business or personal, keep the focus on relationships, but be

aware that any conflicts could be more emotional than usual. Women play a prominent role.

***Sunday, January 14 (Moon in Scorpio to Sagittarius 1:12 p.m.)*** Be bold and courageous. It's a power day for you. Play it your way, but open your mind to a new approach that could bring in considerable financial rewards. Someone in a powerful position is watching you.

***Monday, January 15 (Moon in Sagittarius)*** With Mercury in your tenth house, communications related to your profession are good. A short business trip might be in order in the near future. You also may want to move ahead on plans for a long-distance trip, possibly to a foreign country. Look beyond the immediate.

***Tuesday, January 16 (Moon in Sagittarius to Capricorn 8:50 p.m.)*** With Mars in your ninth house, long-distance travel is on the horizon. Beware of accidents in travel. There could be a sexual affair overseas or with someone involved in publishing or higher education. You have a spiritual affinity with this person.

***Wednesday, January 17 (Moon in Capricorn)*** Don't make waves. There's some waiting involved for matters to develop, especially related to a partnership. Don't rush or show resentment. Avoid taking on a major job, although there may be pressure to do so.

***Thursday, January 18 (Moon in Capricorn)*** With the moon in Capricorn, you're double grounded. Your normal sense of determination and stability is coupled with structure, self-discipline, and ambition. No one will say that you're acting flighty or lazy!

***Friday, January 19 (Moon in Capricorn to Aquarius 1:16 a.m.)*** Yesterday's energies follow you. Your organizational skills are highlighted. You're building foundations, but control your impulses to spend too much. Take a close look at budgets. Persevere, as you always do!

***Saturday, January 20 (Moon in Aquarius)*** Your prestige gets a boost. You're in the public eye. You're warm and considerate with fellow workers, but don't blur the boundaries between your professional and personal lives.

***Sunday, January 21 (Moon in Aquarius to Pisces 3:49 a.m.)*** Be diplomatic, especially if you're in the company of in-laws or extended family members. You may encounter emotional outbursts and people making unfair demands. Be supportive, do a good deed, but know when to say enough.

***Monday, January 22 (Moon in Pisces)*** The moon is in your eleventh house. Join together with people of like minds. You have deeper contact than usual with those people. While you're naturally persistent and determined, you need to review your goals from time to time. Make sure your goals are an expression of who you really are.

***Tuesday, January 23 (Moon in Pisces to Aries 5:53 a.m.)*** Open your mind to a new approach that could bring in big bucks! Make sure that you appear successful, even if you don't feel that way. Be aware that fear of failure might attract tangible experiences. Business discussions go well for you.

***Wednesday, January 24 (Moon in Aries)*** With the moon in Aries, it's a great day to combine your native sense of stability and commitment with a willingness to pursue new ideas and launch a new project. Avoid any reckless actions or becoming impatient with others.

***Thursday, January 25 (Moon in Aries to Taurus 8:29 a.m.)*** You're at the top of your cycle. Be independent and creative. Don't be discouraged by naysayers. Call on your native Taurus persistence and determination. Don't follow others. Stress your originality.

***Friday, January 26 (Moon in Taurus)*** The moon is in your sign. You're in the public view. Your feelings and

thoughts are aligned. You're vital and getting recharged for the month ahead. Relations with the opposite sex go well.

***Saturday, January 27 (Moon in Taurus to Gemini 12:10 p.m.)*** With Venus in your eleventh house, group work as well as public speaking goes smoothly and successfully. Your friends come to your aid. They facilitate you in achieving your wishes and dreams. There could be romance through a friend.

***Sunday, January 28 (Moon in Gemini)*** With the moon in your second house, you feel best when you're surrounded by familiar objects or by people who share your values. Combined with your native Taurus energy, you identify emotionally with all that you possess and value. You may find a lost object, and you'll be particularly pleased with the discovery.

***Monday, January 29 (Moon in Gemini to Cancer 5:17 p.m.)*** Take a risk or find a new perspective. You can overcome obstacles with ease. In matters of romance, you may find that variety is the spice of life. Think freedom, move beyond restrictions, and get ready for change.

***Tuesday, January 30 (Moon in Cancer)*** The moon is in your third house. Write, particularly in a journal, where you can explore your deepest feelings. Your thinking may be unduly influenced by matters of the past. Female relatives may play a role. Watch for an invitation for a social gathering. By all means, make plans to attend as long as it's not tomorrow.

***Wednesday, January 31 (Moon in Cancer)*** With the moon in Cancer, you'll feel best staying home this evening and attending to matters related to your family, home, and personal environment. You're sensitive to the feelings of others, especially those of loved ones. Tend to their needs. Do something with your partner and children.

***Thursday, February 1 (Moon in Cancer to Leo 12:15 a.m.)*** The moon is in your fourth house, which relates to home and the foundations of who you are. You may feel emotionally possessive. Spend time at home with loved ones. Avoid buying real estate unless you feel intuitively certain.

***Friday, February 2 (Moon in Leo)*** With Mercury moving into your eleventh house, you can focus on your wishes and dreams and expect rapid movement. Your contact with friends pays off. You communicate well with a group, especially with those of like mind. Examine your overall goals, make sure they express who you really are, and make an effort to communicate them to others.

***Saturday, February 3 (Moon in Leo to Virgo 9:34 a.m.)*** A mystery awaits you, and that could mean a journey into the unknown. Go with the flow and maintain your emotional balance. Revealing hidden knowledge may be essential for your success. Avoid self-deception.

***Sunday, February 4 (Moon in Virgo)*** Your energy flows with less resistance. You're feeling physically vital and in harmony with yourself and those around you. Be emotionally honest. It's a good day for creative exploration. You have the ability to tap deeply into the unconscious.

***Monday, February 5 (Moon in Virgo to Libra 9:15 p.m.)*** Finish whatever you started. Complete old projects, and make room for the new. Plan a long trip. Look beyond the immediate. Visualize for the future. Set goals and then get to work.

***Tuesday, February 6 (Moon in Libra)*** As a Taurus, you're usually health conscious. However, don't let your stubborn side turn into self-denial, especially related to health needs. Keep your resolutions about exercise and

diet. It's important to keep your emotional and mental states in balance.

***Wednesday, February 7 (Moon in Libra)*** The energy from yesterday flows forward. Personal health matters may occupy your attention. You may feel somewhat emotionally repressed. Others may nag. But don't act like a martyr. Things will look better tomorrow.

***Thursday, February 8 (Moon in Libra to Scorpio 10:10 a.m.)*** You feel more optimistic. Your vitality is stronger than in recent days, and you express yourself well. Follow your intuition. Be happy, positive, upbeat.

***Friday, February 9 (Moon in Scorpio)*** With the moon in your seventh house, it's a good day to focus on relationships, either business or personal. You probably feel energetic and want to accomplish a great deal. Make sure that you develop harmony between your professional and private lives, or you could find difficulty achieving whatever you set out to do.

***Saturday, February 10 (Moon in Scorpio to Sagittarius 10:02 p.m.)*** Get ready for change. Approach the day with an unconventional mind-set. Get a new point of view. Release any restrictions that bind you. Key words for the day are change, variety, and freedom.

***Sunday, February 11 (Moon in Sagittarius)*** The moon is in your eighth house. Your experiences are more intense than usual. Concerns about a project or belongings that you share with someone could arise. Avoid being overpossessive. You may attract the attention of powerful people related to whatever you're pursuing. Metaphysics could be involved.

***Monday, February 12 (Moon in Sagittarius)*** Your native Taurus sense of stability and commitment could be challenged by restlessness as ideas or plans arise that could involve long-distance travel. Remember that your stable

and determined nature will travel with you wherever you go!

***Tuesday, February 13 (Moon in Sagittarius to Capricorn 6:43 a.m.)*** Mercury goes retrograde and stays that way until March 7. Communications can be difficult during this period. There could be disruption of plans, especially with groups. If you sign any contracts, make sure you read the fine print.

***Wednesday, February 14 (Moon in Capricorn)*** With the moon in your ninth house, you may feel a need to escape from your usual routine. That could mean taking a workshop or attending a seminar. It could also favor plans for a foreign journey. Your interests could turn to philosophy and worldviews.

***Thursday, February 15 (Moon in Capricorn to Aquarius 11:36 a.m.)*** You're at the top of your cycle. Don't be afraid to turn in a new direction. Make room for a new love! Creative people play a role.

***Friday, February 16 (Moon in Aquarius)*** The moon is in your tenth house of profession and career. Avoid any emotional displays in public. Don't allow your stubborn side to show. Group activities are highlighted. Make sure that you make yourself understood. Play your hunches and give others a hand.

***Saturday, February 17 (Moon in Aquarius to Pisces 1:31 p.m.)*** Ease up on your routines. Relax and enjoy yourself. Spend time with a favorite hobby. Remember a special anniversary or birthday, or just attend to family matters.

***Sunday, February 18 (Moon in Pisces)*** You can combine your native sense of stability and commitment with flights of imagination. Compassion and deep spirituality are highlighted. You seek universal knowledge and explore eternal truths.

***Monday, February 19 (Moon in Pisces to Aries 2:07 p.m.)*** In spite of your grounded Taurus attributes, you tend to be versatile and changeable. You diversify and expand, but be careful not to overdo it. Your curiosity leads you in new directions, and you should promote your new ideas.

***Tuesday, February 20 (Moon in Aries)*** With the moon in your twelfth house, work behind the scenes. Otherwise, you may encounter volatile emotions. Keep your feelings secret, especially if you are initiating something new. Relations with the opposite sex may be difficult. Remember Mercury is retrograde!

***Wednesday, February 21 (Moon in Aries to Taurus 3:04 p.m.)*** With Venus and the moon in your twelfth house, it's a passionate time. A secret romance could be unfolding. Alternately, you may want to go off by yourself for physical activity. Or an exploration of the unconscious or past lives would be fruitful.

***Thursday, February 22 (Moon in Taurus)*** With the moon in your first house, you get your battery recharged for the month ahead. Health-related or physical activity may take precedence. You feel well balanced. You're sensitive to others' feelings, so relations with the opposite sex go well.

***Friday, February 23 (Moon in Taurus to Gemini 5:42 p.m.)*** Finish up whatever you've been working on, and don't start anything new. Use the day for reflection, expansion, and concluding projects. Promote yourself or your product. Strive for universal appeal. You're particularly attractive to the opposite sex.

***Saturday, February 24 (Moon in Gemini)*** With the moon in your second house, you identify emotionally with all that you value. You may need to adapt to new situations regarding finances. Put off any big purchases for a few days.

Make room in your schedule to socialize with friends this evening.

***Sunday, February 25 (Moon in Gemini to Cancer 10:48 p.m.)*** Mars moves into your tenth house, which means there's new energy in your professional life. Powerful people take note. Be aware that strong emotions related to a coworker could lead to romance—for better or worse.

***Monday, February 26 (Moon in Cancer)*** The moon is in your third house. You may be involved with a social gathering with relatives and neighbors. Be aware that you need to keep conscious control of your emotions when communicating with others. A female relative could be involved.

***Tuesday, February 27 (Moon in Cancer)*** You may be involved in nurturing activities related to friends or pets. The Cancer moon tends to soften your rigidity. You're also protective of family and neighborhood. It's a good time for writing, because the Cancer moon allows you to express your emotions.

***Wednesday, February 28 (Moon in Cancer to Leo 6:30 a.m.)*** Drama and passion are highlighted. You step to center stage. You're feeling majestic. You might dress in bold colors or wear extravagant jewelry. The focus is on showmanship, advertising, and publicizing yourself or your product.

## MARCH 2007

***Thursday, March 1 (Moon in Leo)*** With the moon in your fourth house, you're dealing with the foundations of who you are. You might encounter some challenge to the structure of your daily life. Hidden tensions may arise, and you may feel ill at ease with yourself. Take time to retreat to a private place. It's a good day to meditate.

***Friday, March 2 (Moon in Leo to Virgo 4:32 p.m.)*** Things may not be as they seem. Use your intuition and delve into whatever it is that you can't see clearly. Knowledge is essential to success. Get a broad view of the situation, possibly with the help of an ally, and avoid self-deception.

***Saturday, March 3 (Moon in Virgo)*** The moon is in your fifth house, and there's a lunar eclipse. Emotional issues related to creativity or children could surface. Be yourself. You may feel possessive of a loved one and protective and nurturing with your children or a pet.

***Sunday, March 4 (Moon in Virgo)*** With the moon in another earth sign, you feel well grounded, but more picky than usual. In whatever you're doing, you seek perfection, and you want everything in order. You're more concerned than normal about details. Assist someone in need of help.

***Monday, March 5 (Moon in Virgo to Libra 4:26 a.m.)*** You're at the top of your cycle. Stress your individuality. Take a leadership role. It's a fresh start. Don't follow others; avoid naysayers. Stress originality and express your opinions dynamically.

***Tuesday, March 6 (Moon in Libra)*** You're working to balance your mental and emotional sides. But you may feel somewhat repressed emotionally. Tend to health matters, but help someone in need or visit someone who would appreciate your company.

***Wednesday, March 7 (Moon in Libra to Scorpio 5:18 p.m.)*** Mercury goes direct. Your communications with others will go smoothly. You get your point across. Misunderstandings are resolved. Forgive and forget.

***Thursday, March 8 (Moon in Scorpio)*** Scorpio is your polar opposite, Taurus, and you can draw on the intuition of Scorpio, while remaining your grounded self. You can

also draw on the passion of the water sign while balancing it with your native sensuality.

***Friday, March 9 (Moon in Scorpio)*** With the moon in your seventh house, it's all about partnerships, either personal or business-related. Be aware that any conflict will be more emotional than usual. Make sure that others don't manipulate your feelings.

***Saturday, March 10 (Moon in Scorpio to Sagittarius 5:38 a.m.)*** Diplomacy wins the way. At home, you may need to make some adjustment that could relate to duties, schedules, or plans. If you've been lax in attending to home responsibilities, make an extra effort to help out.

***Sunday, March 11—Daylight Saving Time Begins (Moon in Sagittarius)*** With the moon in your eighth house, you could explore metaphysical matters. Look to the bigger picture; seek knowledge and wisdom. Your experiences could be more intense than usual.

***Monday, March 12 (Moon in Sagittarius to Capricorn 4:35 p.m.)*** It's your power day. Play it your way. Business discussions go well, but open your mind to a new approach. Be courageous. It's a goal-oriented day, especially in the late afternoon.

***Tuesday, March 13 (Moon in Capricorn)*** With the moon in another earth sign, you're well grounded. But don't let your interest in security and stability blind you if a higher goal or purpose arises. You're ready to move into a position of power and authority.

***Wednesday, March 14 (Moon in Capricorn to Aquarius 10:53 p.m.)*** You're at the top of your cycle again. Take advantage of it. Get a fresh start. Trust your hunches, stress originality, and avoid people with closed minds.

***Thursday, March 15 (Moon in Aquarius)*** The moon is in your tenth house of profession and career. You may be

feeling an elevation in prestige. With your business activities highlighted, your life is more public than usual. Make sure that you avoid any emotional displays in public.

***Friday, March 16 (Moon in Aquarius)*** Group activities are highlighted. You're more responsive to the needs and moods of others. You feel a warmth toward your coworkers. Play your hunches, look beyond the immediate, and dance to your own tune, while helping others.

***Saturday, March 17 (Moon in Aquarius to Pisces 1:31 a.m.)*** Venus moves into Taurus. Your love life picks up! You're in the right place at the right time. It's a day for good luck. You easily overcome obstacles. The emphasis is on quality. Get ready for new and better things coming your way.

***Sunday, March 18 (Moon in Pisces)*** There's a solar eclipse in Pisces, your eleventh house. Some issue concerning friends comes to the surface. It could involve your dreams and goals. Make sure that your goals express who you really are. Revise, if necessary. Make use of your imagination. Follow any artistic urges.

***Monday, March 19 (Moon in Pisces to Aries 1:42 a.m.)*** It's all about service. Do a good deed for someone. Visit with someone who's ill or just feeling down. Be understanding to the needs of others. But take care not to scatter your energies.

***Tuesday, March 20 (Moon in Aries)*** You may feel like pulling back. If so, withdraw and revitalize yourself. By working behind the scenes, you can make a breakthrough, especially if you quietly initiate a new project. It could have some mystical or spiritual aspects to it.

***Wednesday, March 21 (Moon in Aries to Taurus 1:16 a.m.)*** Expect a financial coup. Unexpected money may arrive. You could feel as if you've just won the lottery! Be courageous and know that powerful people are watching.

*Thursday, March 22 (Moon in Taurus)*    With the moon in your sun sign, you get recharged for the month ahead. You're more appealing to the public, and your visibility may be elevated. You feel as strong as a bull. Relations with the opposite sex go well.

*Friday, March 23 (Moon in Taurus to Gemini 2:07 a.m.)*    Yesterday's powerful energy continues as you explore your creative options. Don't be afraid to turn in a new direction. Express your opinions dynamically. In romance, a flirtation could turn serious.

*Saturday, March 24 (Moon in Gemini)*    The moon is in your second house of finances, possessions, and values. Take care of payments and collect what's owed you. You identify closely with your possessions. If you've lost something of value recently, you'll find it. Keep your values intact. Don't let others lead you astray.

*Sunday, March 25 (Moon in Gemini to Cancer 5:49 a.m.)*    You may realize that your spiritual values are more important than material goods. Those values may be expressed through the unity of your family or of a small group. It's a good day to relax and to be happy, positive, and upbeat.

*Monday, March 26 (Moon in Cancer)*    With the moon in your third house, you write from a deep place. It's an especially good day for writing in a journal. When communicating with others—especially relatives—keep conscious control of your emotions. Your thinking may be unduly influenced by matters from the past.

*Tuesday, March 27 (Moon in Cancer to Leo 1:05 p.m.)*    Think freedom, change, and variety. Be versatile and changeable. Promote your new ideas. People take note of your writing and communications skills. Experiment and change your perspective.

*Wednesday, March 28 (Moon in Leo)* The moon moves into your fourth house. Look inward and consider where you stand. How can you improve your situation so that you will lead a happier, more fulfilling life? Is there a bad habit, one that annoys others, that you can break? If so, do it!

*Thursday, March 29 (Moon in Leo to Virgo 11:28 p.m.)* Is there a mystery that haunts you, possibly something that you don't understand? If so, investigate the matter. Dig deep for information. As you pursue the matter, make sure that you avoid self-deception. Keep any secrets entrusted to you to yourself.

*Friday, March 30 (Moon in Virgo)* Tend to health matters. Watch your diet. Exercise. Stick close to home, if possible. Tend to details. Clean up the house, literally or symbolically. Be a perfectionist.

*Saturday, March 31 (Moon in Virgo)* The moon is in your fifth house of creativity, love, and children. You'll have great emotional depth in a relationship. Be yourself. You may have more involvement with children or pets. Follow a creative pursuit.

## APRIL 2007

*Sunday, April 1 (Moon in Virgo to Libra 11:45 a.m.)* Spirituality is emphasized. You look at the big picture. Try to see things as they are, not as you wish them to be. Express your desires in order to avoid confusion and conflicts.

*Monday, April 2 (Moon in Libra)* Romance and relationship issues are highlighted. Try to seek harmony and peace. Avoid conflict. Your personal grace and magnetism are emphasized. You feel a physical attraction toward someone who finds you sexy.

*Tuesday, April 3 (Moon in Libra)* Strive for broad appeal. Look beyond the immediate. Let go of preconceived

notions. Wrap up any unfinished projects. Don't start anything new. Take time for reflection, and imagine how you can expand your boundaries.

***Wednesday, April 4 (Moon in Libra to Scorpio 12:37 a.m.)*** The moon is in your seventh house. The focus falls on personal relationships, business partnerships, marriage, and contracts. Any conflicts will be more emotional than usual. It's difficult to maintain a detached and objective point of view. Don't let others manipulate your feelings.

***Thursday, April 5 (Moon in Scorpio)*** Jupiter goes retrograde in your eighth house. As a result, you may have a few bumps along the way if you're applying for a mortgage or loan. There could be hassles related to taxes, insurance, investments, or anything that you share with someone else. It's nothing major.

***Friday, April 6 (Moon in Scorpio to Sagittarius 12:57 p.m.)*** Mars moves into your eleventh house. That helps stimulate friendships, networking, or parties. It's a great day for public speaking. Your wishes and dreams are energized.

***Saturday, April 7 (Moon in Sagittarius)*** You escape the daily routine through your sense of humor. Step away from the ordinary and look to the big picture. There could be long-distance travel coming up. It's a good day for fiction writing.

***Sunday, April 8 (Moon in Sagittarius to Capricorn 11:36 p.m.)*** The emphasis is on freedom of thought and actions. Approach the day with an unconventional mind-set. Release old structures; find a new point of view. Or maybe you need a change of scenery.

***Monday, April 9 (Moon in Capricorn)*** With the moon in your ninth house, you could be involved with someone born in a foreign land. Alternately, you might be planning

the structure of a getaway to a foreign country. Gain new knowledge through a workshop or seminar.

***Tuesday, April 10 (Moon in Capricorn)*** With Mercury in your twelfth house, it's a good day for writing projects or research. You'll feel best if you withdraw and keep your opinions to yourself. You may think that others will hold what you say against you. You can get in touch with your hidden side.

***Wednesday, April 11 (Moon in Capricorn to Aquarius 7:23 a.m.)*** Venus moves into your second house. It's a good day for money! Checks arrive. You get a break and possibly a raise or promotion. It's a good day for making money from the arts.

***Thursday, April 12 (Moon in Aquarius)*** You work well with a group, and at the same time, your individuality is highlighted. You should see some movement in your professional life. You're more in the public view. Your prestige is elevated.

***Friday, April 13 (Moon in Aquarius to Pisces 11:39 a.m.)*** You're at the top of your cycle. Your sense of individuality is further enhanced after events yesterday. Be independent and creative. Take a leadership role. Express your opinions. Make room for a new love!

***Saturday, April 14 (Moon in Pisces)*** With the moon moving into your eleventh house, you gain deeper contact with friends. Combine your native Taurus sensuality with compassion. Your social consciousness is awakened. Pay attention to synchronicities. Remember your dreams tonight.

***Sunday, April 15 (Moon in Pisces to Aries 12:47 p.m.)*** Spiritual values are highlighted. Your day features social activities. Use your charm, wit, and your natural ability to express yourself. Remain flexible and optimistic. Your popularity is on the rise.

*Monday, April 16 (Moon in Aries)* It's a great time to start a new project, but volatile emotions may dog you. Relations with the opposite sex could be difficult. Avoid getting impatient or annoyed with others. It's better to withdraw and work behind the scenes.

*Tuesday, April 17 (Moon in Aries to Taurus 12:12 p.m.)* Get ready for change. Be versatile and willing to take a risk, but don't diversify too much. Promote your new ideas, and look for the possibility of a long-term commitment. People take note of your writing or communications skills.

*Wednesday, April 18 (Moon in Taurus)* With the moon in your first house, your emotional self comes to the forefront. You're particularly sensitive to what other people say to you or about you. You may feel happy one moment, then sad the next. But overall, your feelings and thoughts are aligned, and you attract new energy to recharge yourself for the month ahead.

*Thursday, April 19 (Moon in Taurus to Gemini 11:52 a.m.)* Saturn goes direct. That means that you may delve into a mystery and explore the unknown. Go with the flow. You have the energy available to build new structures in your life.

*Friday, April 20 (Moon in Gemini)* The moon is in your second house. It's a good day for new money to arrive. Your financial picture improves. You identify closely with your possessions, which makes you feel at ease. Put off any major new purchases for a few days.

*Saturday, April 21 (Moon in Gemini to Cancer 1:51 p.m.)* It's all about beginnings and endings, with the emphasis on the latter. Use the day for reflection, expansion, and completing projects. Accept whatever comes your way. It's all part of the cycle.

*Sunday, April 22 (Moon in Cancer)* The moon moves into your third house. You write from a deep place. Your verbal communications and opinions might evoke strong emotions, especially from a female relative. Keep conscious control when you speak.

*Monday, April 23 (Moon in Cancer to Leo 7:39 p.m.)* Partnership is highlighted. Be supportive and patient with others. You may hear about a proposal for marriage involving a family member. Don't make waves or show resentment. Consider your motivation and your position.

*Tuesday, April 24 (Moon in Leo)* The moon is in your fourth house of home and the foundation of who you are. Spend time at home with family, but find time to retreat to a private place for meditation. Your ability to recall your dreams is enhanced. Look for a message from your dreaming self.

*Wednesday, April 25 (Moon in Leo)* Your native stability, sensuality, and determination are combined with the flair of Leo. A romance makes you feel as if you're royalty. Everything about it is majestic. Passions are high. Dress boldly, be adventurous, advertise, and promote yourself.

*Thursday, April 26 (Moon in Leo to Virgo 5:25 a.m.)* Freedom of thought and action is highlighted. Read, write, and learn. You're curious and open to new ideas. Take a seminar or workshop, if possible. Get ready for change. You can overcome any obstacles with ease.

*Friday, April 27 (Moon in Virgo)* With Mercury moving into your first house, your mind is now in sync with your emotions. It's a good day for any kind of mental work, especially communicating and networking with others.

*Saturday, April 28 (Moon in Virgo to Libra 5:46 p.m.)* A mysterious matter is highlighted. Explore and investigate. Get to the root of the mystery. Make sure that

you don't reveal your source of information, especially if you've promised to keep it secret.

***Sunday, April 29 (Moon in Libra)*** Romance is highlighted. Go out with your honey to a concert, the theater, an art gallery, or a museum. Your sensuality plays a role. Wear your jewelry. You sparkle!

***Monday, April 30 (Moon in Libra)*** Play the role of mediator. You keep everything in balance and attend to details as you seek harmony and peace. Your personal grace and magnetism pay off as you help others. But don't be a martyr in order to achieve harmony.

## MAY 2007

***Tuesday, May 1 (Moon in Libra to Scorpio 6:42 a.m.)*** Look for a financial coup. Business discussions go well. Open your mind to a new approach that could bring in big money. It's your chance to expand and gain recognition, power, and even fame.

***Wednesday, May 2 (Moon in Scorpio)*** With the moon in your seventh house, the polar opposite of Taurus, your intuition is heightened. Intense emotional experiences are likely. Control issues might surface. You may feel like going to extremes. It's best to forgive and forget.

***Thursday, May 3 (Moon in Scorpio to Sagittarius 6:48 p.m.)*** You're at the top of your cycle again. You get a fresh start and a chance to take a leadership role. Be independent and creative. Get out and meet new people. Your ambition is highlighted as well as your native Taurus persistence.

***Friday, May 4 (Moon in Sagittarius)*** You may feel as if your self-expression is stifled in some way. If it's due to a relationship, think twice about what you get from the

partnership and whether it's time to end it. A Leo or a Sagittarius plays a vital role.

***Saturday, May 5 (Moon in Sagittarius)*** For the next two weeks, your thoughts may be on a long-distance trip that you're planning. If you're a writer, this is an excellent time to finish a manuscript. Don't start anything new until the moon moves into your sign.

***Sunday, May 6 (Moon in Sagittarius to Capricorn 5:21 a.m.)*** Your sex appeal is powerful. You feel so self-confident that you may get a bit cocky concerning what you can realistically accomplish. Tend to the details, but don't forget to have some fun!

***Monday, May 7 (Moon in Capricorn)*** You're well grounded with the moon moving into another earth sign. Your native sense of persistence and determination is combined with a new awareness of structure and self-discipline. Your ambition drives you, but that may mean more responsibility and a heavier work load.

***Tuesday, May 8 (Moon in Capricorn to Aquarius 1:48 p.m.)*** With Venus moving into your third house, it's a good day for working on a writing project. Later, you get together with friends, relatives, and neighbors. Friendships with the opposite sex are also enhanced.

***Wednesday, May 9 (Moon in Aquarius)*** Look beyond the immediate. Play your hunches. Your native sensuality is combined with a strong sense of individuality. Dance to your own tune; follow your heart. Stay persistent and determined.

***Thursday, May 10 (Moon in Aquarius to Pisces 7:32 p.m.)*** Play it your way. Look for a chance for fame or at least recognition. You gain power and prestige. Business dealings go well. If ever there's a day to win the lottery, it's today!

***Friday, May 11 (Moon in Pisces)*** With Mercury in your second house, yesterday's energies are enhanced. Look for an investment windfall. You would profit by attending an investment club meeting. You could earn money from public speaking.

***Saturday, May 12 (Moon in Pisces to Aries 10:20 p.m.)*** You shine today. It's a new beginning. You move into a leadership role. Your individuality, independence, and creativity are enhanced. Trust your hunches. You could make room for a new love.

***Sunday, May 13 (Moon in Aries)*** The moon enters your twelfth house, which deals with the personal unconscious and anything hidden. Pursue a mystical or spiritual discipline. Write down your dreams, and see if there's a message for you. Unconscious attitudes may surface as you attempt to initiate something new; you may feel like withdrawing and working behind the scenes. Progress is made, but in secret.

***Monday, May 14 (Moon in Aries to Taurus 10:50 p.m.)*** Your attitude determines everything. Be happy, positive, and upbeat. Diversify either your friendships or your business dealings. Insist on all the information before you act. Spend time with your family, or those close to you.

***Tuesday, May 15 (Moon in Taurus)*** With Mars moving into your first house, you're physically and mentally recharged for the month ahead. Your feelings and thoughts are aligned. Nothing can stop you! If you're not careful, you could be accident prone.

***Wednesday, May 16 (Moon in Taurus to Gemini 10:35 p.m.)*** You can expand even further on yesterday's high-powered energy. But you may need a change of scenery. You could be considering a move. It's a good day to take a risk and get a new point of view. Your physical desires are strong. Think before you act!

*Thursday, May 17 (Moon in Gemini)* With the moon in the second house of finances and possession, check on your investments. You could reap a windfall. Watch your spending. Put off big purchases for another few days. Enjoy your home environment and everything that you possess.

*Friday, May 18 (Moon in Gemini to Cancer 11:39 p.m.)* Something mysterious comes to your attention. It could involve family or friends. Gather information, but don't make any absolute decisions until tomorrow. Knowledge is essential for understanding. Discuss and defend your beliefs, express your desires, but avoid self-deception.

*Saturday, May 19 (Moon in Cancer)* You may attend a social gathering. Get out and enjoy the spring weather. Your neighbors, siblings, or other relatives are involved in your day. Stay in control of your emotions when you communicate with others.

*Sunday, May 20 (Moon in Cancer)* Your home and personal environment take priority. You may feel moody off and on, and you're particularly sensitive to the moods of others. Try to do something with your children and spouse or significant other.

*Monday, May 21 (Moon in Cancer to Leo 3:57 a.m.)* You're starting off the week on the right foot. You get a fresh start. Be independent; take the lead in a new project. Your individuality is emphasized. Refuse to let naysayers discourage you. In romance, a flirtation could turn serious.

*Tuesday, May 22 (Moon in Leo)* You feel impulsive, passionate, and ready to step to center stage. Romance and love are highlighted. Break the ice. Let the other person know what you think. Dress in bold colors; do something different with your hair and wardrobe.

*Wednesday, May 23 (Moon in Leo to Virgo 12:27 p.m.)* Make use of your natural ability to express your-

self. Your vitality is highlighted. Avoid any native stubbornness. Be imaginative, charming, and witty. Remain flexible.

***Thursday, May 24 (Moon in Virgo)*** With Neptune going retrograde in your tenth house until October 31, examine your spiritual beliefs and attempt to incorporate them into your profession. How can you be more compassionate and in line with eternal truths?

***Friday, May 25 (Moon in Virgo)*** Freedom of thought and action is emphasized. Be versatile and open to change. Take a risk. You can overcome obstacles with ease. Release old structures and make way for a new point of view.

***Saturday, May 26 (Moon in Virgo to Libra 12:17 a.m.)*** You try to keep everything in balance regarding health matters, daily work, and your efforts to help others. You can't do everything. Don't turn yourself into a martyr for the cause. Pay attention to your health; remember to exercise.

***Sunday, May 27 (Moon in Libra)*** Romance and relationships are highlighted. Go to a concert, the theater, a museum, or an art show. Seek harmony and peace with your mate. Your sensuality plays a role. You keep everyone in balance. Your personal grace and physical appearance are pleasing to others.

***Monday, May 28 (Moon in Libra to Scorpio 1:12 p.m.)*** With Mercury moving into your third house, communications with others speed up, possibly through a series of e-mails. You get your message across with lightning speed. You could reach many people quickly by attending a social gathering.

***Tuesday, May 29 (Moon in Scorpio)*** Your sex life picks up, but there could be some resentment. You need to work hard to create harmony between your personal and professional lives. Your physical vitality is high and you

want to move ahead, but you'll be blocked if you don't resolve these conflicts.

***Wednesday, May 30 (Moon in Scorpio)*** With the moon in your seventh house, partnerships, marriages, and contracts are highlighted. Deal with the issues related to personal and business relationships. As with yesterday, you must find harmony between your personal and business lives in order to achieve your goals. Confrontations with the opposite sex are likely.

***Thursday, May 31 (Moon in Scorpio to Sagittarius 1:07 a.m.)*** You can't get away from it. It's about partnerships again! You need to be supportive and patient, even if your partner nags. Cooperation is highlighted. Be kind and understanding. Don't rush or show resentment. Use your intuition to get you through the day.

## JUNE 2007

***Friday, June 1 (Moon in Sagittarius)*** There could be some tension related to taxes, insurance, or investments. It probably involves something that you share with another person, such as a spouse. Whatever is happening can affect your feelings about your belongings. It's best to back off and not claim sole possession of something you share.

***Saturday, June 2 (Moon in Sagittarius to Capricorn 11:10 a.m.)*** You're at the top of your cycle, a perfect time for taking a leadership role and moving beyond any recent conflict. Use your individuality and imagination. Creative people will be attracted to you. Don't be put off by the naysayers. Let your intuition guide you.

***Sunday, June 3 (Moon in Capricorn)*** You need to get away from the usual routine in order to advance your new ideas. You may be feeling restless and looking for a change in scenery. You might attend a workshop or seminar. Alternately, you could plan an extended journey to a foreign land.

***Monday, June 4 (Moon in Capricorn to Aquarius 7:16 p.m.)*** Social events are on the horizon. Be optimistic; your attitude is everything. Be positive and upbeat. Spread your good news. Relax and chat with others.

***Tuesday, June 5 (Moon in Aquarius)*** Venus moves into your fourth house of the home and real estate. It's a good day for love and romance at home. You might redecorate a home office or spend money on other home improvements. An influx of money makes life more comfortable. Enjoy!

***Wednesday, June 6 (Moon in Aquarius)*** Group activities or a social event is highlighted. Look beyond the immediate as you use your energy to persevere under current conditions. Stress your individuality. Your wishes and dreams are coming true. Dance to your own tune.

***Thursday, June 7 (Moon in Aquarius to Pisces 1:25 a.m.)*** Diplomacy wins your way. Try focusing on making people happy, especially those who might be surprised by your acts of kindness. Be understanding, generous, and tolerant. Visit someone who is ill or in need of cheering up.

***Friday, June 8 (Moon in Pisces)*** Pay attention to your dreams. How do they relate to your ambitions and goals? Work with a group of like-minded people. Your contact with friends goes deeper than usual. You work out any difficulties you've had with someone.

***Saturday, June 9 (Moon in Pisces to Aries 5:27 a.m.)*** You have a chance to expand and gain recognition. It's your day for fame and power. Open your mind to new approaches that could bring in big bucks. Be courageous.

***Sunday, June 10 (Moon in Aries)*** The moon moves into your twelfth house. Withdraw and work behind the scenes. You can finish projects and plan for new ones. Whatever you're working on, you may feel like keeping it

to yourself, rather than allowing others to analyze and criticize.

***Monday, June 11 (Moon in Aries to Taurus 7:30 a.m.)*** Take the lead on a new project. It's a fresh start. Get out and meet new people; have new experiences. Express your opinions dynamically.

***Tuesday, June 12 (Moon in Taurus)*** The energy generated yesterday flows strongly. With the moon in your first house, you get recharged for the month ahead. You feel physically vital and appealing to the public. Relations with the opposite sex go well. Your thoughts and feelings are aligned.

***Wednesday, June 13 (Moon in Taurus to Gemini 8:24 a.m.)*** It's a number 3 day. Your charm, wit and vitality work well for you today. Expect an invitation from a friend or loved one. Your attitude determines everything so stay positive and upbeat.

***Thursday, June 14 (Moon in Gemini)*** The moon is in your second house, making it a good day to make money through investments. You feel best when you're surrounded by familiar objects. It's not the objects themselves that attract you, but your emotions and memories from events related to them.

***Friday, June 15 (Moon in Gemini to Cancer 9:46 a.m.)*** Mercury goes retrograde and remains that way until July 9. Work behind the scenes as much as possible for the next three weeks. Revise, review, and reevaluate your creative activities. Communications can be confusing. Allow yourself plenty of time for arriving at appointments. Put off signing contracts, if possible, or examine all the details closely.

***Saturday, June 16 (Moon in Cancer)*** Don't be too stubborn when it comes to dealing with family members and domestic matters. Even though you may feel moody,

do something with your mate and children. It's a good day for the beach and a swim.

***Sunday, June 17 (Moon in Cancer to Leo 1:25 p.m.)*** You could be exploring the unknown, investigating some sort of mystery. Keep any secrets entrusted to you. Things may not be as they look. Gather information, but don't make any absolute decisions. Maintain your emotional balance.

***Monday, June 18 (Moon in Leo)*** You could encounter some challenges to the structure of your daily life. Buried tensions may come to the surface. If so, make good use of the situation and clear the air. Be bold and forthright. Let others know exactly what you think. But don't let your stubbornness get in the way.

***Tuesday, June 19 (Moon in Leo to Virgo 8:46 p.m.)*** Use your native persistence and determination to finish what you've started. It's a good day for endings and mentally preparing for new beginnings. Reflect on where you want to go. Accept whatever comes your way, but look beyond the immediate.

***Wednesday, June 20 (Moon in Virgo)*** Your energy flows smoothly. Your life seems easier. You get along well with others, and you're in a creative mood. Be your sensual self. You'll find greater emotional depth in your love life. Children and animals may play a role.

***Thursday, June 21 (Moon in Virgo)*** Your determination and stability combine with Virgo's pursuit of perfection and order. You're well grounded, but make sure that you attend to health matters. Remember to exercise and watch your diet.

***Friday, June 22 (Moon in Virgo to Libra 7:44 a.m.)*** Social activities are highlighted. Ease up on your routines. Relax and enjoy yourself. Your wit and charm are appreci-

ated. Your popularity is on the rise. Spread your good news. Have fun! You deserve it.

***Saturday, June 23 (Moon in Libra)*** Uranus goes retrograde in your eleventh house until November 24. That means you may experience sudden upsets in friendships. You may be rethinking your goals and dreams, also your spiritual beliefs. You could encounter occasional technological setbacks. If your computer isn't protected from viruses, take steps to make it so.

***Sunday, June 24 (Moon in Libra to Scorpio 8:27 p.m.)*** Mars moves into your first house. You're feeling physically vital. Relations with the first house go well. You may want to get out to walk in nature, attend to your garden, or listen to music.

***Monday, June 25 (Moon in Scorpio)*** With the moon moving into Scorpio, your polar opposite sign, you can expect intense emotional experiences and heightened sexuality. You feel passionate about something or someone. There's a secret involved, and you seek answers.

***Tuesday, June 26 (Moon in Scorpio)*** The moon moves into your seventh house of partnerships, marriage, and contracts. Some control issues arise. It may be difficult to maintain a detached and objective view. Be careful that others don't manipulate your feelings.

***Wednesday, June 27 (Moon in Scorpio to Sagittarius 8:25 a.m.)*** Play it your way! Make sure that you appear successful, even if you don't feel that way. Look for a financial windfall.

***Thursday, June 28 (Moon in Sagittarius)*** Your sense of humor helps you through the day. You're feeling expansive. You could be planning a long trip. You're looking at the big picture. It could deal with publishing or the law. Don't limit yourself. Think prosperity and abundance.

***Friday, June 29 (Moon in Sagittarius to Capricorn 6:06 p.m.)*** You're at the top of your cycle. It's a day for exploration and discovery. Don't be afraid to turn in a new direction. Trust your hunches; your intuition is highlighted. Creative people play a role.

***Saturday, June 30 (Moon in Capricorn)*** Your persistence and determination are coupled with a sense of self-discipline, structure, and ambition. You're well grounded and ready to take on new responsibilities. Don't forget to follow a regular exercise routine.

## JULY 2007

***Sunday, July 1 (Moon in Capricorn)*** With the moon moving into your ninth house, you feel a need to get away from the usual routine. Your interest in certain ideas may lead you to take a seminar or workshop on a subject of significance to you. A foreign country or a foreigner may play a role in your plans.

***Monday, July 2 (Moon in Capricorn to Aquarius 1:25 a.m.)*** Don't make waves. Be supportive and patient. The spotlight is on cooperative efforts. Partnerships and marriage are key. Consider the direction you and your partner are headed.

***Tuesday, July 3 (Moon in Aquarius)*** A social event can help you in your profession or career. Look beyond the immediate. Dance to your own tune; follow your heart. In romance, don't blur the boundaries between your professional and personal lives.

***Wednesday, July 4 (Moon in Aquarius to Pisces 6:53 a.m.)*** Your organizational skills are highlighted. Use your energy to persevere. Don't get sloppy. You're building foundations. Be methodical and thorough. Emphasize quality in whatever you're doing.

***Thursday, July 5 (Moon in Pisces)*** Your imagination plays a role. Follow your hunches; watch for synchronicities. See if you can remember your dreams from last night. What are they telling you? Tonight you can program a dream. Make a request before going to bed.

***Friday, July 6 (Moon in Pisces to Aries 10:57 a.m.)*** The emphasis is on service to others. Be diplomatic; try to make people happy, especially those who aren't expecting it. Help out wherever you can. Be understanding, but don't scatter your energies.

***Saturday, July 7 (Moon in Aries)*** Get started on something new. You'll do best if you work behind the scenes. The less said about your plans the better. You communicate your deepest feelings to another person.

***Sunday, July 8 (Moon in Aries to Taurus 1:54 p.m.)*** Play it your way. You have a chance to expand, to gain recognition, power, and even fame. But you need to open your mind to a new approach. If you do, it could bring in big bucks!

***Monday, July 9 (Moon in Taurus)*** Mercury goes direct. That means communications improve. Things that were confused come into focus. Everything that has happened in the last three weeks starts to make sense. At the very least, it's behind you, and you're ready to move ahead.

***Tuesday, July 10 (Moon in Taurus to Gemini 4:10 p.m.)*** You get a fresh start. Trust your hunches; your originality is highlighted. Be independent and creative. Stress your individuality; don't follow others. In romance, a flirtation could turn more serious.

***Wednesday, July 11 (Moon in Gemini)*** With the moon in your second house, check your investments. You may find that they are paying off. Your values play a key role. With any new investments, put your money in a place where it will support your values.

***Thursday, July 12 (Moon in Gemini to Cancer 6:40 p.m.)*** Ease up on your routines. Have some fun in preparation for tomorrow, when you'll need discipline and focus. Spend time on a hobby or conversation with friends. Get your battery recharged.

***Friday, July 13 (Moon in Cancer)*** Control your impulses. Fulfill your obligations. You're building foundations for the future. Whatever you communicate, whether it's verbal or written, tends to be heartfelt and meaningful. Make sure you stay in control of your emotions.

***Saturday, July 14 (Moon in Cancer to Leo 10:44 p.m.)*** Venus moves into your fifth house. It's a great day for romance, fun, and creative activities. You tend to be nurturing and protective toward your children. If you don't have kids, love your pets!

***Sunday, July 15 (Moon in Leo)*** The moon moves into your fourth house. Another good day for staying close to home with family, maybe doing some repairs or maintenance to your house or yourself! Retreat to a private place. Quiet your mind—breathe, meditate, relax.

***Monday, July 16 (Moon in Leo)*** Strut your stuff. Center stage is all yours. Be bold and courageous. Advertise and publicize yourself or your pet project. Dress for the part. Be extravagant. Wear more jewelry than usual. Showmanship is the order of the day.

***Tuesday, July 17 (Moon in Leo to Virgo 5:40 a.m.)*** Business discussions go well. You could pull off a financial coup. Focus on a power play. Here's your chance to expand and gain more recognition.

***Wednesday, July 18 (Moon in Virgo)*** Tend to health matters. Exercise and watch your diet. Stop fretting. Tend to all the details on whatever you're pursuing. Dig deep for information. Seek perfection and order. On the home front, take time to tidy up the place.

***Thursday, July 19 (Moon in Virgo to Libra 3:54 p.m.)*** You're at the top of your cycle. Stress originality. Take the initiative to start something new; don't be afraid to turn in a different direction. Get out and meet new people; have new experiences.

***Friday, July 20 (Moon in Libra)*** The moon moves into your sixth house; you might feel emotionally down from yesterday's high energy. Help others wherever possible, but avoid acting like a martyr. Pay attention to the details of whatever you're pursuing.

***Saturday, July 21 (Moon in Libra)*** Romance is highlighted. The Libra moon in your sign embellishes your native sensuality. Your personal grace and magnetism are emphasized. Your physical attractiveness draws attention. Wear jewelry and some of your finest things. Go out to a concert, a movie, or the theater.

***Sunday, July 22 (Moon in Libra to Scorpio 4:19 a.m.)*** It's an excellent day to clean out the old. It could be a closet, an attic, or a garage. It could be symbolic of yourself! Try not to let your native stubbornness get in your way. You're building a foundation for the future.

***Monday, July 23 (Moon in Scorpio)*** With the moon moving into your seventh house, the focus is on your personal and business relationships. You can expect any conflicts to be more emotional than usual. It's difficult to maintain a sense of detachment. If you avoid being stubborn, you can minimize any confrontations.

***Tuesday, July 24 (Moon in Scorpio to Sagittarius 4:31 p.m.)*** It's all about service to others. Be tolerant and generous. Be diplomatic and understanding, even if you encounter difficult people. An adjustment in your domestic life may be necessary.

***Wednesday, July 25 (Moon in Sagittarius)*** Your energy keeps you driving ahead. You're persistent and determined.

But from time to time, you need to get away so you can grasp the bigger picture. Today is one of those days. Go for it!

***Thursday, July 26 (Moon in Sagittarius)*** The moon is in your eighth house, indicating that your experiences could be intense. That's especially true regarding the things that you share with others. You may be dealing with taxes, insurance, and investments. You may attract the interest of powerful people.

***Friday, July 27 (Moon in Sagittarius to Capricorn 2:23 a.m.)*** With Venus going retrograde in your fifth house, you need to guard your emotions, or you could be misunderstood. Any efforts to make quick money through speculation may backfire. Sexual encounters purely for pleasure probably won't develop into lasting relationships.

***Saturday, July 28 (Moon in Capricorn)*** The moon moves into your ninth house, emphasizing higher education and long-distance travel. Take a workshop or seminar. Step back and view the big picture. A foreign person may be involved. Alternately, plan a journey to a foreign country.

***Sunday, July 29 (Moon in Capricorn to Aquarius 9:14 a.m.)*** Cooperation and partnerships are emphasized. You may be dealing with business partnerships and proposals. In romance, it could mean a new relationship develops. Help comes through friends, loved ones, or through a partner.

***Monday, July 30 (Moon in Aquarius)*** Group activities are highlighted. Your visionary abilities come to the forefront. Your wishes and dreams are coming true. You work well with others, and at the same time, you manage to successfully pursue your own objectives.

***Tuesday, July 31 (Moon in Aquarius to Pisces 1:41 p.m.)*** Tear down in order to rebuild. Be methodical and

thorough. You're building a creative base. In romance, you may feel somewhat inhibited in showing affection.

## AUGUST 2007

***Wednesday, August 1 (Moon in Pisces)*** The moon moves into your eleventh house. Group activities and friends play a key role. Your contact with friends is deeper than usual, and they help you achieve your wishes and dreams.

***Thursday, August 2 (Moon in Pisces to Aries 4:43 p.m.)*** Play your hunches, but make sure you have all the information to make an informed decision. Listen to others. Be generous with your time. Remain optimistic and positive. Expect an invitation from a friend or a loved one.

***Friday, August 3 (Moon in Aries)*** The moon's in your twelfth house, and that means that it's a good day for deep contemplation. Take time to retreat to a private space and consider where you are headed. If you're developing a new project, it's best to keep it to yourself.

***Saturday, August 4 (Moon in Aries to Taurus 7:16 p.m.)*** With the moon moving into your fourth house, it's a favorable situation for creative people who work at home. You might host a gathering of writers. Intellectual activities are highlighted. Expect a lot of e-mail and phone calls. Alternately, your attention may turn to activities with your children.

***Sunday, August 5 (Moon in Taurus)*** The moon rises in your first house—a good sign! You can count on gaining new energy that will carry you through the dog days of August. Your vitality is enhanced; your relations with the opposite sex work well. Stay positive. Your feelings and thoughts are aligned.

***Monday, August 6 (Moon in Taurus to Gemini 8:02 p.m.)*** Jupiter goes direct in your eighth house, which means you attract money and opportunities through other people's resources. It's a good time to get a mortgage or an equity loan or more credit. Your financial base grows, but be aware that you'll also have a tendency to spend more.

***Tuesday, August 7 (Moon in Gemini)*** Mars powers its way into your second house. Its presence stimulates new financial strength and activity related to finances. It could mean that you'll be working two jobs or long hours, enabling your earning capacity to go up.

***Wednesday, August 8 (Moon in Gemini)*** Your native tendency to persevere in a determined manner to reach your goal mixes with the air sign Gemini. So you get your message across. It's also a good day to write, revise, and publicize.

***Thursday, August 9 (Moon in Gemini to Cancer 1:37 a.m.)*** You're at the top of your cycle and ready to roll. You get a fresh start and a chance to do it your way. Take the lead and don't follow others. In romance, make room for a new love.

***Friday, August 10 (Moon in Cancer)*** The moon moves into your third house of communications, relatives, and the everyday world. Your thinking may be unduly influenced by the past. A visit by a relative could come into play in your day. You communicate with others in your neighborhood and make your opinions known.

***Saturday, August 11 (Moon in Cancer to Leo 6:42 a.m.)*** Ease up on your routines; relax and enjoy a social outing. Use your charm and wit; remain flexible. Spread your good news. Your attitude determines everything.

***Sunday, August 12 (Moon in Leo)*** The moon shifts to your fourth house. You're ready to take bold steps to make

changes in your home. Your plans for redecorating your home environment could get extravagant. Take the needed steps, but make sure that you don't overdo it. You feel emotionally possessive with your mate and children.

***Monday, August 13 (Moon in Leo to Virgo 2:04 p.m.)*** Freedom of thought and action is at the heart of your day. Release old structures; get a new point of view. Look for a potential for long-term commitment. Your native sense of stability balances the urges for change and variety.

***Tuesday, August 14 (Moon in Virgo)*** Your earth energy multiplies with the moon in Virgo. You attend to all the details, seeking order around you. Does that mean it's time to clean the house or your room? Others will appreciate your help.

***Wednesday, August 15 (Moon in Virgo)*** Something mysterious or secretive is going on, and you have a chance to get to the bottom of it. By acting, you may avoid self-deception. See things as they are, not how you'd like them to be. Knowledge is essential to success.

***Thursday, August 16 (Moon in Virgo to Libra 12:05 a.m.)*** The moon in your sixth house deals with daily work, health, and service. Help others, but don't act like a martyr. Take care of your own health. Remember to exercise and watch your diet. In romance, you may feel as if you aren't able to express your feelings.

***Friday, August 17 (Moon in Libra)*** As you persist with your goals, you may find a need to keep everyone in balance around you. Make sure that your effort to harmonize your environment doesn't throw you off balance! Take time this evening to get out and attend a concert or go to a movie.

***Saturday, August 18 (Moon in Libra to Scorpio 12:14 p.m.)*** You're at the top of your cycle. Push ahead with

your own ideas. Creative people will play a role. Take the initiative and find a new direction. Don't be discouraged by naysayers who may be jealous of your originality and ambition.

***Sunday, August 19 (Moon in Scorpio)*** Mercury moves into your fifth house. That's great for any kind of writing project. Your creativity is enhanced. Your mind also may turn to romance. You may be taking a short trip for pleasure. You may also have more dealing than usual with kids.

***Monday, August 20 (Moon in Scorpio)*** It's a great day for writing, speaking in public, or acting. Try not to scatter your energy. Work toward a definite goal. Be confident that you can accomplish whatever you set out to achieve.

***Tuesday, August 21 (Moon in Scorpio to Sagittarius 12:45 p.m.)*** The moon enters your eighth house. Your experiences may be more intense than usual, especially if you're dealing with possessions that are shared with someone. Issues related to taxes, insurance, investments, or publishing might come up. Don't be stubborn, Taurus.

***Wednesday, August 22 (Moon in Sagittarius)*** Use your sense of humor. Look for the big picture to complement your efforts to maintain your stability. A matter related to the law, courts, or the justice system may come up, possibly related to jury duty.

***Thursday, August 23 (Moon in Sagittarius to Capricorn 11:20 a.m.)*** The theme is service. Be diplomatic with others, even those who might nag. At home, take care of an issue that needs resolving. Avoid any stubbornness. Be understanding and do a good deed for someone.

***Friday, August 24 (Moon in Capricorn)*** You find the structure you need to accomplish your goals. You feel a great sense of self-discipline and ambition. You're well grounded and determined to move ahead.

***Saturday, August 25 (Moon in Capricorn to Aquarius 6:35 p.m.)*** The energy from yesterday expands. You have a chance to gain recognition, power, and even fame. Open your mind to a new approach that will bring in big bucks. Expect a financial coup.

***Sunday, August 26 (Moon in Aquarius)*** Break old paradigms. Seek a new path. You have the energy of a visionary and the determination to follow up. Look beyond the immediate and stress your individuality.

***Monday, August 27 (Moon in Aquarius to Pisces 10:35 p.m.)*** You're at the top of your cycle. You're ready to put to use the energy of the past two days. You get a fresh start. Be independent and creative. Follow your heart; express your opinions dynamically.

***Tuesday, August 28 (Moon in Pisces)*** After the recent high energy you've been experiencing, you're ready to retreat and look inward. Compassion and deep spirituality play a part. You seek eternal truths and universal knowledge. Pay attention to synchronicities and to your dreams.

***Wednesday, August 29 (Moon in Pisces)*** Use your keen imagination. Your charm and your wit win the way for you. Ease up on your routines. Spread your good news and remain happy and upbeat. Make time to listen to others.

***Thursday, August 30 (Moon in Pisces to Aries 12:25 a.m.)*** With the moon in your twelfth house, work behind the scenes. You may feel like keeping your feelings secret, even if it's to your advantage to express them. Contact a close friend and communicate your deepest feelings.

***Friday, August 31 (Moon in Aries)*** The Aries moon combines with your energy to give you an opportunity to launch a new idea or set off on a new adventure. Your power of persuasion is strong, but be aware that your emotions may be volatile. Avoid any reckless behavior and maintain your patience.

***Saturday, September 1 (Moon in Aries to Taurus 1:36 a.m.)*** You're engaging to others whether it's your written word, your speaking ability, or your talent to act. Avoid scattering your energies. Work toward a definite goal. Your attitude determines everything.

***Sunday, September 2 (Moon in Taurus)*** Saturn enters your fifth house. There could be delays in romance. You might fall for an older person. Your kids might need structure. You need to order your priorities and find the right structure for your creative voice.

***Monday, September 3 (Moon in Taurus to Gemini 3:31 a.m.)*** Freedom of thought and action is highlighted. Seek diversity, variety, or maybe a change of scenery. You might even consider relocating. It's a day to take risks and find a new perspective.

***Tuesday, September 4 (Moon in Gemini)*** The moon moves into your second house. Money matters look positive, but it's a good idea to put off any big purchases for a few days. Consider investing in something that supports your values. Take care of payments and collections.

***Wednesday, September 5 (Moon in Gemini to Cancer 7:09 a.m.)*** Mercury moves into your sixth house. You want to be just and fair to everyone around you, especially coworkers. You may be doing more communicating with coworkers so everyone understands what needs to be accomplished.

***Thursday, September 6 (Moon in Cancer)*** Tend to matters at home. Beautify your surroundings in some way, even if there's some expense involved. You may be feeling somewhat moody, and you're sensitive to the moods of others. If possible, go for a swim.

***Friday, September 7 (Moon in Cancer to Leo 1:00 p.m.)*** Pluto goes direct, releasing energy that you can use to transform your life in a positive way. Finish up projects and get ready for a new beginning. Use the day for reflection and plans for expansion.

***Saturday, September 8 (Moon in Leo)*** Venus goes direct, which means that it's an ideal time for pursuing a romance and matters dealing with the arts. Get started or continue to refurbish or redecorate your home.

***Sunday, September 9 (Moon in Leo to Virgo 9:11 p.m.)*** It's all about partnerships and cooperation. Don't make waves. Relax, don't rush, and show your appreciation for others. Help comes through friends, loved ones, or a business partner.

***Monday, September 10 (Moon in Virgo)*** The moon moves into your fifth house of creativity, love, and children. You may be possessive of loved ones. You're involved with the creative facet of your life through work, education, or a hobby. Contact with children and animals could play an important role.

***Tuesday, September 11 (Moon in Virgo)*** With the moon in another earth sign, pay attention to your health. Start exercising if you're not doing so. Watch your diet. Stick close to home. Focus on details, and dig deep for information. Put the Virgo tendency toward perfectionism to good use by tidying the house.

***Wednesday, September 12 (Moon in Virgo to Libra 7:32 a.m.)*** Release old structures and get a new point of view. Approach the day with an unconventional mind-set. Get ready for change. Experiment; take a risk. You can overcome obstacles with ease.

***Thursday, September 13 (Moon in Libra)*** The moon moves into your sixth house, which affects your emotions. You may be feeling somewhat repressed in your daily work.

Attend to details, but avoid acting like a martyr. Focus on your health. Take time to exercise.

***Friday, September 14 (Moon in Libra to Scorpio 7:37 p.m.)*** There's an inkling of mystery surrounding events; you may take a journey into the unknown. Go with the flow, and maintain your emotional balance as you seek answers. Avoid confusion and conflicts. Express your desires, but avoid self-deception.

***Saturday, September 15 (Moon in Scorpio)*** Control issues surface, along with intense emotional experiences. You may be following up on secret meetings held yesterday. Investigate and be aware of possible deception. Be careful not to go to extremes.

***Sunday, September 16 (Moon in Scorpio)*** You may be involved in discussions concerning philosophy, theology, or psychology. You may have a difficult time maintaining your objectivity. Forgive and forget, but be careful not to let others manipulate your feelings.

***Monday, September 17 (Moon in Scorpio to Sagittarius 8:21 a.m.)*** You're at the top of your cycle. Initiate a new project and take a leadership role. Creative people are attracted to you, especially if you emphasize originality. Explore and discover. Trust your hunches. You're on a creative roll.

***Tuesday, September 18 (Moon in Sagittarius)*** With the moon in your eighth house, you may need to attend to matters related to joint finances. Your experiences related to a joint venture are more intense than normal. You could draw powerful people into your life. A matter related to metaphysics, possibly past lives, catches your interest.

***Wednesday, September 19 (Moon in Sagittarius to Capricorn 7:52 p.m.)*** Your intuition is highlighted. Stay optimistic. Your attitude determines everything. Be happy and

enthusiastic when you tell others your good news. Make sure you take the time to listen to their news.

***Thursday, September 20 (Moon in Capricorn)*** The moon is in your ninth house, which means that higher education and the higher mind as well as long-distance travel are emphasized. You need to get away from your usual routine. Take a seminar or workshop; plan a trip. A foreign person may play a role, or you may consider a foreign destination for your next journey.

***Friday, September 21 (Moon in Capricorn)*** With the moon in another earth sign, you are doubly grounded. Even if you're feeling restless, you persevere while you take advantage of the structure and self-discipline of Capricorn. Set your goals and follow through.

***Saturday, September 22 (Moon in Capricorn to Aquarius 4:18 a.m.)*** You help out someone in need. Focus on making the people around you happy. Your stability is appreciated. Be understanding of others, but avoid scattering your energies. Leave time for music in your busy day.

***Sunday, September 23 (Moon in Aquarius)*** Your sense of prophecy is heightened. Group activities are highlighted. Look beyond the immediate. Play your hunches. Help others where you can, but leave time to dance to your own tune.

***Monday, September 24 (Moon in Aquarius 8:56 a.m.)*** Business discussions go well. Focus on a power play. Look for a financial coup. Your courage against the odds could result in recognition, even fame.

***Tuesday, September 25 (Moon in Pisces)*** Use your imagination. Look for clues in your dreams. Your ideas are ripe. Be compassionate. Follow your spiritual values. Seek universal knowledge and eternal truths.

***Wednesday, September 26 (Moon in Pisces to Aries 10:23 a.m.)*** Be independent and creative. You get a fresh start. Your ambition and persistence pay off, Taurus. Stress your individuality and trust your hunches.

***Thursday, September 27 (Moon in Aries)*** Mercury moves into your seventh house of partnerships and marriage. It's a good time to sign contracts and launch new ideas, particularly joint ventures. You communicate well with both personal and business relationships.

***Friday, September 28 (Moon in Aries to Taurus 10:18 a.m.)*** Mars moves into your third house. Your emotions are fired up, and you charge ahead in your daily work life. You communicate well with this new energy. Take time to write in a journal or a deeply personal letter to a close friend.

***Saturday, September 29 (Moon in Taurus)*** The moon remains in your first house, and you're revitalized for the month ahead. You're feeling physically vital and appealing to the public. You're attuned to others, and your relations with the opposite sex go well.

***Sunday, September 30 (Moon in Taurus to Gemini 10:35 a.m.)*** Your physical desires are strong. You're willing to take a risk. Change, variety, and freedom from restrictions are key to your day. You communicate your thoughts and feelings well; you're versatile and changeable.

## OCTOBER 2007

***Monday, October 1 (Moon in Gemini)*** With the moon in your second house, watch your spending. Put off any major purchases for another day. You may feel an urge to go to extremes, especially regarding someone who owes you something. In this case, you may need to forgive and forget.

***Tuesday, October 2 (Moon in Gemini to Cancer 12:58 p.m.)*** Variety is the spice of life. Get ready for change. Get a new perspective. Take a seminar or workshop. Read, write, and learn. Experiment. Have an unconventional mind-set.

***Wednesday, October 3 (Moon in Cancer)*** With the moon in your third house, you could be involved in a beautification program in your neighborhood. On the racier side, you might have an affair with someone in the neighborhood. Communications and writing go well. You get a break from a woman, possibly a relative. You might receive an invitation for a social gathering coming up this weekend.

***Thursday, October 4 (Moon in Cancer to Leo 6:28 p.m.)*** Discuss and defend your beliefs. Make sure you see things as they are, not as you wish them to be. Avoid self-deception. Maintain your emotional balance. Go with the flow.

***Friday, October 5 (Moon in Leo)*** The moon is in your fourth house of the home and your foundations. Tend to loved ones. Stay close to home or retreat to a private place. Tend to details, such as beautifying your home. Love and nurture those around you. Meditate and find your balance.

***Saturday, October 6 (Moon in Leo)*** You may feel possessive of loved ones. Your natural sensuality is sparked by passion. You openly display your affection. You may feel as if you're playing a part in a romantic comedy. Be impulsive and honest. You're at center stage.

***Sunday, October 7 (Moon in Leo to Virgo 3:04 a.m.)*** You're at the top of your cycle. Get out and meet new people; have new experiences. Explore, discover, and create something new. In romance, make room for a new love.

***Monday, October 8 (Moon in Virgo)*** Venus moves into your fifth house, which definitely warms things up. There's

a lot of romance and good sex in the picture. If you're a parent, you'll have smooth relations with your children.

***Tuesday, October 9 (Moon in Virgo to Libra 1:58 p.m.)*** Ease up on your routines. Relax and enjoy yourself. Recharge your batteries. Listen to others. Enjoy leisurely conversations. You may be feeling close to your family or a small group.

***Wednesday, October 10 (Moon in Libra)*** The moon moves into your sixth house, the house of daily work, health, and service. Approach things intuitively in the workplace. Pay attention to your health. If you help others, they'll appreciate it and reciprocate.

***Thursday, October 11 (Moon in Libra)*** Mercury goes retrograde and stays that way until November 1. You can expect some confusion and misunderstanding related to communications, travel, appliances, or machinery. Double-check your arrangements. Keep your receipts. Try to put off making major decisions or signing a crucial document.

***Friday, October 12 (Moon in Libra to Scorpio 2:14 a.m.)*** Service to others is the key to your day. Help others where you can, and things will go smoothly. Do a good deed for someone or visit a friend who's feeling ill. Be understanding, generous, and tolerant. Music might play a role.

***Saturday, October 13 (Moon in Scorpio)*** Your sense of stability and determination could be jolted by an intense emotional experience. Be aware of possible deception, secret meetings, things happening behind closed doors. Use your intuition as you investigate what's going on.

***Sunday, October 14 (Moon in Scorpio to Sagittarius 2:58 p.m.)*** Play it your way. You have a chance to expand your role and to gain recognition, fame, and power. But you need to open your mind to a new approach that could bring in big bucks.

*Monday, October 15 (Moon in Sagittarius)* Make use of your sense of humor, especially if you're dealing with a matter related to the law, courts, or legal matters. Watch for a publishing opportunity or a chance to get away on a long journey. What's the big picture?

*Tuesday, October 16 (Moon in Sagittarius)* Any involvement or pursuit of matters dealing with metaphysics could attract the attention of powerful people. It could be an interest that you share with another person, possibly a spouse. Your experiences could be intense.

*Wednesday, October 17 (Moon in Sagittarius to Capricorn 3:04 a.m.)* Cooperation and partnership are highlighted. Don't make waves, even if other people are annoying you. Be kind and understanding. Show your appreciation of others. You may do some soul searching regarding a relationship.

*Thursday, October 18 (Moon in Capricorn)* With the moon in your ninth house, you expand your vision. You could deal with matters related to the academic world. Education, worldviews, and foreign places or foreign people might play a role.

*Friday, October 19 (Moon in Capricorn to Aquarius 12:52 p.m.)* Your organizational skills and willingness to persevere come into play. Be methodical and thorough, which should be no problem for you. Emphasize quality. You may need to tear down in order to rebuild.

*Saturday, October 20 (Moon in Aquarius)* The moon is in your tenth house of profession and career. A matter involving your reputation or ambitions may come up. A discussion with a boss could bring an issue to a head. Avoid blurring the boundaries between your professional and personal life.

*Sunday, October 21 (Moon in Aquarius to Pisces 7:03 p.m.)* Focus on making the people around you happy,

especially those who don't expect that from you. Be understanding of others, but avoid scattering your energies. Leave time for music in your busy day.

***Monday, October 22 (Moon in Pisces)*** With the moon in your eleventh house, friends play an important role. Your associations with groups and friends are enhanced. Opportunities may arise in unexpected ways; things will improve as a result. Examine your goals; make sure that they are an expression of who you are.

***Tuesday, October 23 (Moon in Pisces to Aries 9:25 p.m.)*** Business discussions go well, especially if you're courageous and stand up for what you believe, even if it isn't popular. You're being watched by people in power, and it could pay off in a big way.

***Wednesday, October 24 (Moon in Aries)*** With the moon in your twelfth house, you feel a need to withdraw and turn inward. Your tendency is to keep your feelings secret, even if you need to speak your mind. You may prefer to confide your deepest thoughts to a good friend.

***Thursday, October 25 (Moon in Aries to Taurus 9:08 p.m.)*** Individuality is stressed. Take the initiative to start a new project; don't be afraid to turn in a new direction. Bc independent and original in your creative approach. Refuse to deal with people who have closed minds.

***Friday, October 26 (Moon in Taurus)*** With the moon and sun in your first house, your feelings and thoughts are aligned. You get recharged for the month ahead, and you're attractive to the public and to the opposite sex.

***Saturday, October 27 (Moon in Taurus to Gemini 8:12 p.m)*** Spiritual values are highlighted. Foster generosity. Relax, enjoy yourself, and continue getting yourself recharged. Your attitude determines everything. Be happy, positive, and upbeat. Expect an invitation from a friend.

***Sunday, October 28 (Moon in Gemini)*** With the moon in your second house of finances and resources, relationships may be affected by money matters. Watch your spending. Any money problems you face will most likely be a minor concern.

***Monday, October 29 (Moon in Gemini to Cancer 8:50 p.m.)*** Contrary to your native tendencies to persist on the same path, you'll feel an urge to be versatile and changeable. You might consider diversifying your interests or projects, promoting new ideas, and exploring whatever makes you curious.

***Tuesday, October 30 (Moon in Cancer)*** With the moon in your third house, you make connections with neighbors and relatives. A short trip might be involved. Revise whatever you're working on, basing your changes on new things that you've recently learned. Don't let the past control your present.

***Wednesday, October 31 (Moon in Cancer)*** You may be embarking on a journey into the unknown, seeking the answer to a mystery. There could be secrets, intrigue, and confidential information involved. Guard any secrets entrusted to you. Maintain emotional balance. Go with the flow. Spirituality is emphasized.

## NOVEMBER 2007

***Thursday, November 1 (Moon in Cancer to Leo 12:48 a.m.)*** Mercury goes direct. That means any confusion in communications will fade away. Misunderstandings are resolved. Forgive and forget. Travel disruptions and delays no longer carry the day. Things mechanical work smoothly.

***Friday, November 2 (Moon in Leo)*** The moon is in your fourth house. Domestic matters take precedence. Stay close to home or retreat to a private place. Tend to details,

such as beautifying your home. Love and nurture those around you. Meditate and find your balance.

***Saturday, November 3 (Moon in Leo to Virgo 8:45 a.m.)*** There could be something mysterious going on around you. You may stick your nose into the unknown. Avoid confusion and conflicts. Gather information, but don't make any absolute decisions until tomorrow. On the mundane side, tend to medical and dental obligations.

***Sunday, November 4—Daylight Saving Time Ends (Moon in Virgo)*** With the moon in your fifth house, you enter a time of high creativity. You can tap deeply into the collective unconscious. In love, you'll experience great emotional depth. You're protective and nurturing toward children.

***Monday, November 5 (Moon in Virgo to Libra 6:47 p.m.)*** Complete a project so you can make room for something new. Visualize the future, set your goals, and get to work. Accept whatever comes your way, but put off starting a new project.

***Tuesday, November 6 (Moon in Libra)*** You may be an arbitrator, balancing the emotions of those around you as you seek harmony and peace in your workplace or at home. The real issue is how well your thoughts and feelings are balanced. Your sensuality makes romance the highlight of your evening. A candlelight dinner with music would be ideal.

***Wednesday, November 7 (Moon in Libra)*** The moon is in your sixth house of daily work and health, which means you may feel somewhat emotionally repressed. Pay attention to your health needs. Help others where you can, but don't act like a martyr.

***Thursday, November 8 (Moon in Libra to Scorpio 7:19 a.m.)*** Venus moves into your sixth house of daily work, health, and service. Your feelings of affection for coworkers are strong. Your emotional ties to a person or group are

also strong, making it easy for you to be of service, especially to those in need.

***Friday, November 9 (Moon in Scorpio)*** The moon is in your seventh house of partnership and marriage. Focus on relationships, either business or personal. If you're looking for a commitment, you're likely to find it, especially if you can remain calm and detached in the face of conflict.

***Saturday, November 10 (Moon in Scorpio to Sagittarius 7:59 p.m.)*** You gain a sense of what freedom is about. Don't confuse it with security. Release old structures; get a new point of view. Experiment. Take a risk. Question authority.

***Sunday, November 11 (Moon in Sagittarius)*** The moon is in your eighth house of shared resources. Your experiences are intense, especially any issues concerning things you share in a partnership or marriage. You may feel restless and want a change. Express your thoughts in writing. There could be dealings with taxes, insurance, an inheritance, and any shared money.

***Monday, November 12 (Moon in Sagittarius)*** With the moon in your eighth house, you may gain benefits, support, or an inheritance through a partner. You may find it challenging to control your emotions. Do your best to stay calm in the face of changing circumstances.

***Tuesday, November 13 (Moon in Sagittarius to Capricorn 8:01 a.m.)*** Things go your way. You may feel a surge of energy. Remain goal-oriented. Be courageous. Expect tangible results, especially in terms of money. A bonus or an unexpected windfall may come your way.

***Wednesday, November 14 (Moon in Capricorn)*** The moon is in your ninth house. You feel a strong urge to get away from the usual routines. While you feel attached to your home and domestic life, you may yearn to establish a

new base in a faraway place. That's the big picture that's coming into view. Make it your goal, and it'll happen.

***Thursday, November 15 (Moon in Capricorn to Aquarius 6:31 p.m.)*** Mars goes retrograde in Cancer until January 29, which means there could be instances of irrational action, introspection, and depression. You may have to rethink and reorient current projects. These conditions won't be nearly as severe for you as for those born under the sign of Cancer.

***Friday, November 16 (Moon in Aquarius)*** With the moon in your tenth house of profession and career, you experience an elevation of prestige. Your life is public. Business dealings are highlighted. You work hard, and as long as you don't stray from the accepted parameters, you accomplish whatever you set out to achieve.

***Saturday, November 17 (Moon in Aquarius)*** Group activities are highlighted. Play your hunches. Use your research skills and then communicate what you've found. Your ideas reach the public. You make an impact, but avoid emotional displays in public.

***Sunday, November 18 (Moon in Aquarius to Pisces 2:15 a.m.)*** You're building foundations for the future. Use your perseverance and push ahead. Control your impulses to wander off. Fulfill your obligations. Be methodical and thorough. It's a day for hard work, which will pay off.

***Monday, November 19 (Moon in Pisces)*** With the moon in your eleventh house, focus on your wishes and dreams. Examine your goals closely; revise them if they no longer express who you are. Friends play an important role. You work well in a group, especially one that involves like-minded people.

***Tuesday, November 20 (Moon in Pisces to Aries 6:25 a.m.)*** It's all about service to others. Be diplomatic;

help others where you can. Be understanding, tolerant, and generous.

***Wednesday, November 21 (Moon in Aries)*** The moon is in your twelfth house, which deals with your hidden strengths and weaknesses. You may feel like keeping whatever you're doing secret, especially if it relates to a new project or new ideas. You may work better in private, but avoid self-deception.

***Thursday, November 22 (Moon in Aries to Taurus 7:19 a.m.)*** Happy Thanksgiving! Play it your way. Be thankful for all that you've received, and know that you have the capability of expanding your base and gaining more recognition for your work. Unexpected money may come your way.

***Friday, November 23 (Moon in Taurus)*** With the moon in your first house, your feelings and thoughts are aligned. You feel physically vital, and you're recharged for the month ahead. You're appealing to the public, and relations with the opposite sex go well.

***Saturday, November 24 (Moon in Taurus to Gemini 6:29 a.m.)*** Uranus goes direct, which brings a burst of new energy into your life. It also opens the door to unusual and idiosyncratic people who help define your individuality. You have a greater sense of freedom; any creative efforts are original.

***Sunday, November 25 (Moon in Gemini)*** The moon is in your second house of finances. Your thoughts turn to your perspective on money. You deal with banks or financial institutions, handling payments and collections. You might get a raise or receive an unexpected check.

***Monday, November 26 (Moon in Gemini to Cancer 6:07 a.m.)*** You may get an invitation from a friend. Take advantage of it. Spread your wings. Ease up on your rou-

tines. Have fun. Your attitude determines your day. Stay upbeat.

***Tuesday, November 27 (Moon in Cancer)*** With the moon in your third house, you might spend time writing in a journal. Your thoughts may be unduly influenced by the past. Expect some contact with neighbors, possibly an invitation to a social gathering.

***Wednesday, November 28 (Moon in Cancer to Leo 8:23 a.m.)*** Expand your knowledge. Take a workshop or seminar. Read, write, and learn. People take note of your writing and communications skills. Experiment. Change your perspective.

***Thursday, November 29 (Moon in Leo)*** The moon is in your fourth house. Communicate with family members. Spend time at home. Work on a journal. Hold off on buying real estate. Your emotions may tint the picture. Wait a few days to review the matter.

***Friday, November 30 (Moon in Leo to Virgo 2:45 p.m.)*** Intrigue lurks in the shadows. Investigate a mystery; gather confidential information. Avoid confusion and conflicts. See things as they are, not how you would like them to be. Don't make any final decisions based on what you've learned.

## DECEMBER 2007

***Saturday, December 1 (Moon in Virgo)*** With Mercury moving into your eighth house, your thoughts turn to getting out of debt. You may need to pay attention to taxes, insurance, or mortgages. Or you could teach a course related to those subjects.

***Sunday, December 2 (Moon in Virgo)*** With the moon in your fifth house of creativity and love, your emotions tend to overpower your intellect. In love, you'll find great

emotional depth in a relationship. Your energy is strong and flows smoothly with little resistance. Be yourself. You'll have great involvement in the creative side of your life.

***Monday, December 3 (Moon in Virgo to Libra 1:02 a.m.)*** Business dealings go well. Be courageous. Focus on a power play. You have a chance to expand your base, gain recognition, and increase income. Make sure that you appear successful, even if you don't feel that way.

***Tuesday, December 4 (Moon in Libra)*** The moon is in your sixth house of daily work, health, and service. You could feel emotionally drained. Visit the gym or run an extra mile as personal health concerns take precedence. Watch your diet. Take time to visit someone who is ill.

***Wednesday, December 5 (Moon in Libra to Scorpio 1:32 p.m.)*** Venus moves into your seventh house, which means smooth sailing in relationships, both personal and professional. It's a good time to sign contracts. Women may play a prominent role.

***Thursday, December 6 (Moon in Scorpio)*** You probably feel energetic and hope to accomplish a great deal. Different areas of your life might be rowing against each other. In relationships, difficulties with the opposite sex may arise. You need to create harmony between your personal and professional lives.

***Friday, December 7 (Moon in Scorpio)*** You can expect intense emotional experiences and high passions. Control issues may arise. Avoid going to extremes. Use your intuition and your stability. Forgive and forget.

***Saturday, December 8 (Moon in Scorpio to Sagittarius 2:12 a.m.)*** Build foundations. You're working hard, but you need to stay focused. Don't let your energies get scattered. Write and rewrite. Be methodical and thorough. You can overcome any obstacles. If you've lost something recently, you're likely to find it.

***Sunday, December 9 (Moon in Sagittarius)*** With the moon in your eighth house, you could attract powerful people. Intense experiences could result from the contact, especially if joint resources are involved. An interest or pursuit of metaphysical matters might play a role.

***Monday, December 10 (Moon in Sagittarius to Capricorn 1:51 p.m.)*** It's about service to others. Do a good deed without any expectations of a return favor. Be generous and tolerant. You make good use of your sense of humor and your willingness to work hard.

***Tuesday, December 11 (Moon in Capricorn)*** With the moon in your ninth house, you explore new ideas that could relate to worldviews, mythology, and philosophy. How can you take your product or ideas to a foreign country?

***Wednesday, December 12 (Moon in Capricorn)*** The moon is in another earth sign, which bolsters your well-grounded self. Your ambition and drive to succeed are highlighted. You may encounter an opportunity related to your profession or work. You may deal with banks and financial institutions.

***Thursday, December 13 (Moon in Capricorn to Aquarius 12:02 a.m.)*** Finish projects, clear your desk, and get ready for a new cycle. Accept what comes your way. Spend some time in reflection; consider how you can expand your base.

***Friday, December 14 (Moon in Aquarius)*** You feel romantic, expressive, and highly idealistic. You may set off on a new project. You may encounter others who don't agree with your ideals. Back off, if necessary. Control your emotions when communicating.

***Saturday, December 15 (Moon in Aquarius to Pisces 8:15 a.m.)*** Cooperation and partnership are highlighted. You might be discussing the division of responsibilities. Understand your partner's point of view. Show your apprecia-

tion. Try to remain cooperative and helpful. Allow things to develop in their own time. Don't make waves.

***Sunday, December 16 (Moon in Pisces)*** With the moon in your eleventh house, friends play an important role. You put more emotion into thoughts about your wishes and dreams. Examine your overall goals. Use your intuition in dealing with a group of people. Pay attention to your dreams.

***Monday, December 17 (Moon in Pisces to Aries 1:53 p.m.)*** By early afternoon, you'll be ready to brainstorm or launch a new project. Your power of persuasion is magnetic, attracting the attention and interest of those around you. That's especially true when you're passionate about whatever you're doing.

***Tuesday, December 18 (Moon in Aries)*** Jupiter moves into your ninth house. You may be headed for a long trip in the near future. You undertake an expansion of your worldview, and you have beneficial dealing with foreign-born people or a foreign country.

***Wednesday, December 19 (Moon in Aries to Taurus 4:38 p.m.)*** Saturn goes retrograde in your fifth house and stays there until May 2, which means you may experience some delays in your creative efforts that may require you to revise your work. In romance, you may rethink a relationship.

***Thursday, December 20 (Moon in Taurus)*** Mercury moves into your ninth house, which means you should experience some rapid communications related to a long journey. Gain new knowledge by taking a seminar or workshop, or undertake independent study.

***Friday, December 21 (Moon in Taurus to Gemini 5:14 p.m.)*** You're in a position to gain power, recognition, and even fame. Open your mind to a new approach that

expands your base and results in new riches coming your way. Be courageous.

***Saturday, December 22 (Moon in Gemini)*** With the moon in your second house, you identify closely with your possessions or values, and you'll feel best when you're at home this evening. Your investments could pay good dividends. Stay adaptable in dealing with banks or financial institutions, or in handling payments and collections.

***Sunday, December 23 (Moon in Gemini to Cancer 5:19 p.m.)*** You're at the top of your cycle. You get a fresh start. Be independent and creative. Get out and meet new people; have new experiences. Don't follow others.

***Monday, December 24 (Moon in Cancer)*** With the moon in Cancer, you'll be happy at home with your family. Tend to your loved ones. Do something special with your spouse and children. Enjoy the holiday!

***Tuesday, December 25 (Moon in Cancer to Leo 6:53 p.m.)*** Merry Christmas! Spiritual values are emphasized along with social activities. You offer affection and love to those around you. The emphasis is on the family unit. Have fun, relax, listen to others, and enjoy good conversation.

***Wednesday, December 26 (Moon in Leo)*** With the moon in your fourth house, you may feel like retreating to a private place and spending time alone. Meditate and go deep within. Recall your dreams from last night. Is there a bad habit that you can change?

***Thursday, December 27 (Moon in Leo to Virgo 11:45 p.m.)*** It's all about freedom of thought and action. You may seek out a change of scenery. Variety is the spice of life. Be versatile and changeable. Let go of old structures; find a new point of view.

***Friday, December 28 (Moon in Virgo)*** Your energies flow smoothly with little resistance. Life seems easier. Your

health is good; you're feeling vital. There's no need for fretting or worrying. Relax. Tend to details. Stick close to home.

***Saturday, December 29 (Moon in Virgo)*** It's a good day for group activities. Personal and professional relationships are harmonious. You get along well with the opposite sex. Your creative energy flows well. You feel close to your family and loved ones. A good day overall!

***Sunday, December 30 (Moon in Virgo to Libra 8:38 a.m.)*** Venus moves into your eighth house, which is good for matters dealing with mortgages, loans, and investments. Others are more than willing to help you. The day's energy is also good for exploring metaphysical matters.

***Monday, December 31 (Moon in Libra)*** Romance is highlighted. You seek harmony and peace. With the moon in your sixth house, which relates to health and repressed feelings, watch how much you drink.

HAPPY NEW YEAR!

## SYDNEY OMARR

Born on August 5, 1926, in Philadelphia, Pennsylvania, Sydney Omarr was the only person ever given full-time duty in the U.S. Army as an astrologer. He is regarded as the most erudite astrologer of our time and the best known, through his syndicated column and his radio and television programs (he was Merv Griffin's "resident astrologer"). Omarr has been called the most "knowledgeable astrologer since Evangeline Adams." His forecasts of Nixon's downfall, the end of World War II in mid-August of 1945, the assassination of John F. Kennedy, Roosevelt's election to a fourth term and his death in office . . . these and many others are on the record and quoted enough to be considered "legendary."

## ABOUT THE SERIES

This is one of a series of twelve Sydney Omarr® Day-by-Day Astrological Guides for the signs of 2007. For questions and comments about the book, e-mail tjmacgregor@booktalk.com.

# 2007

## A BRAND-NEW YEAR—
## A PROMISING NEW START

With expert readings and forecasts, you can chart a course to romance, adventure, good health, or career opportunities while gaining valuable insight into yourself and others. Offering a daily outlook for 18 full months, this fascinating guide shows you:

- The important dates in your life
- What to expect from an astrological reading
- How the stars can help you stay healthy and fit
  And more!

Let this sound advice guide you through a year of heavenly possibilities—for today and for every day of 2007!

**SYDNEY OMARR'S® DAY-BY-DAY ASTROLOGICAL GUIDE FOR**

**ARIES**—March 21–April 19
**TAURUS**—April 20–May 20
**GEMINI**—May 21–June 20
**CANCER**—June 21–July 22
**LEO**—July 23–August 22
**VIRGO**—August 23–September 22
**LIBRA**—September 23–October 22
**SCORPIO**—October 23–November 21
**SAGITTARIUS**—November 22–December 21
**CAPRICORN**—December 22–January 19
**AQUARIUS**—January 20–February 18
**PISCES**—February 19–March 20

**IN 2007**